Second Edition

100

B E S T

Ski Resorts of the World

GERRY WINGENBACH

The
Globe
Pequot
Press

GUILFORD, CONNECTICUT

To buy books in quantity for corporate use
or incentives, call **(800) 962–0973, ext. 4551,**
or e-mail **premiums@GlobePequot.com.**

Text design: Mary Ballachino

ISSN 1556-7923
ISBN 0-7627-3863-4

Manufactured in the United States of America
Second Edition/First Printing

FOR MY DAD, WHO ALWAYS MADE
CANADIAN WINTERS THE BEST SEASON.

Second Edition

100

B E S T

Ski Resorts of the World

a photo essay

Val d'Isère

Tremblant

Crans-Montana

Portillo

Arosa

Val d'Isère

Steamboat Ski Resort

Steamboat Ski Resort

Beaver Creek Resort

Zermatt

Davos

Keystone Resort

CONTENTS

NORTH AMERICA

EUROPE

Austria

France

Germany

Italy

Spain

SOUTH OF THE EQUATOR

The information listed in this guidebook was confirmed at press time but under no circumstances is it guaranteed. We recommend that you call establishments before traveling to obtain current information.

INTRODUCTION

On a perfect blue-sky day in January, my buddy, veteran Chamonix mountain guide Armel Faron, and I rode the spectacular aerial tram that whisks sightseers high above the Chamonix Valley to the Aiguille du Midi, the fortresslike rocky outcrop that stands next to Mont Blanc, the highest mountain in the Alps.

With skis cinched to our rucksacks, we began the roped descent of the steep, snow-plastered arête that leads to the top of the headwall of the Mer de Glace, the largest glacier in the French Alps. From this airy mountain saddle, we embarked on the legendary Vallée Blanche ski route, which drops 9,200 feet and stretches for 15 miles before ending back at Chamonix. It is the longest lift-serviced ski run in the world.

Depending upon snow conditions, it is not difficult skiing. But it is dramatic. The steep granite peaks that rim the valley were the proving grounds for many of the legendary mountaineers of the twentieth century. On the Vallée Blanche, Armel carved his way through fields of crevasses intersected with blue-ice seracs—train-size blocks of ice that can tumble and crush a skier without notice. I followed in his tracks. Halfway down we stopped and sat on the glacier with our skis as backrests and the sun on our faces, enjoying the remarkable panorama along with richly stuffed baguettes and local Côtes du Rhône wine from my rucksack.

I recall this remarkable day for you only because I am frequently asked what is the best ski resort in the world. The answer is, there is no best ski resort in the world. But there are best days in the mountains. That was one of mine.

In the grand scheme of things, skiing and snowboarding matter not one iota. Most people live just fine without them. But

some of us cannot. For those who cannot, the best ski resorts tempt and teeter us on the edge of nirvana. They lift us beyond ourselves to a wondrous world where we completely focus on the here and now. That's the essence of skiing.

Most of us didn't begin skiing by swooping down the big mountain ranges of the world. And fortunately, adventure on skis or snowboards doesn't depend on the size of the mountain. My own downhill pleasures started at a mom-and-pop-run rope tow called Rabbit Hill. The name says it all: It was nothing but a few dips and dos hopping along the river valley on the ranchlands that form the eastern slopes of the Canadian Rockies. After a day of skiing at Rabbit Hill, my friend Jim Hunter—who grew up to dominate the Canadian National Men's Alpine Ski Team—would strap his skis to the roof of his dad's pickup, then step into his bindings and ride a downhill racer's crouch while his dad barreled down the highway heading for home.

It was around that time that I started to dream about bigger mountains.

Since then, I've coached ski racers in Canada, New Zealand, and the United States. I've ridden chairlifts in Chile and followed Austrians down the Swiss Alps. I fell head-over-heels for a fleet-footed Italian mountain girl who guided me around the rocky spires of the famed Dolomites. I traversed the Rocky Mountains from north to south and back again.

Any veteran sportswriter knows that the best stories are in the loser's locker room. The best adventure tales always include disasters. There are no losers or disasters in this book. But there might be controversy. It's unlikely that well-traveled skiers or snowboarders would agree on the one hundred best ski resorts in the world.

The criteria I used for selecting the resorts in this book were simple. They all offer spectacular mountain terrain, reliable snow conditions, and, at the end of the day, comfortable digs with adequate dining and some degree of life beyond the slopes.

Skiers and snowboarders differ in their desires and needs. Everyone brings something unique to the mountains. The friends, spouses, and children we ski with make different demands on a resort. But the best ski resorts in the world have delights and pleasures that appeal to everyone. Yet no two resorts are alike. People often tell me they've been going to one particular resort for years. That's fine. But in my opinion marriage should be monogamous; skiing should not. Variety, as they say, is the spice of life.

Skiing and snowboarding offer unique opportunities to explore some of the world's most dramatic topography. They also offer an excuse to get out and experience winter, which is surely the most remarkable season. Just as important, skiing presents a perfect introduction to the extraordinary people who reside in the mountain regions of the world. It allows us to rub shoulders with them and share a heartfelt pleasure. These personal exchanges alone make traveling to ski in far-off places worthwhile.

The selection of the one hundred best ski resorts that follow was mine alone. If you disagree with them, I'd love to hear from you. The love of skiing is as subjective as love itself. But I promise you that every resort in this book is capable of giving you one of the best days of skiing or snowboarding in your life.

Europe versus North America

With few exceptions, North America and Europe are home to the greatest ski resorts in the world. But there are vast differences between the two continents.

The European Alps offer the biggest mountains and the widest range of skiing.

Many of the resorts, like Chamonix and Zermatt, offer twice the vertical drop of most major Rocky Mountain ski areas (imagine Aspen on top of Vail). In the Alps resorts often link up with other resorts via ski lifts and ski trails, and also shuttles and trains. Most of the skiing is above tree line and offers sweeping panoramas of jaw-dropping scenery, ranging from dramatic glacier-covered peaks to bucolic landscapes dotted with cowsheds. But average annual snowfalls in the Alps are meager compared to the depths recorded in the Rocky Mountains.

In North America, the Rockies usually receive regular big dumps of snow throughout the season. The resorts are world leaders in slope grooming and snowmaking, with many areas offering skiing and snowboarding by Thanksgiving. (In Europe this is more likely to happen in mid-December.) North American skiing generally plays out below the tree line, which offers protection from the elements and enhances visibility in bad-light conditions. The high areas of the Alps often close during inclement weather and high winds.

But comparisons are difficult. As you'll notice in the fact box for each resort, North American resorts report the number of trails, the total acreage, and the average annual snowfalls. In Europe resorts report the total miles of maintained trails, and acreage is seldom calculated because, unlike most resorts in North America, they don't rope off the out-of-bounds areas. In theory there are no boundaries in the Alps. But if you go off-piste, you'd better know what you're doing or travel with a guide, because beyond the main runs, you're on your own. Also, European resorts seldom report average annual snowfalls. Perhaps because it would be meaningless since snowfall varies so greatly from year to year. Or maybe this is because it snows less in the Alps, with some resorts getting only two or three big snowstorms during the ski season.

Europe also uses a different method of rating trails (or, as they say, pistes). In North America runs are posted (from easiest to toughest) by a green circle, blue square, black diamond, and double black diamond. In Europe the trails are marked blue for easiest (green in France), red for intermediate, and black for advanced and expert runs.

Costs for the two continents are fairly comparable, depending on fluctuations between the dollar and the euro. It's easy to argue that from the East Coast of North America, a ski vacation to Europe costs less than a ski trip that involves flying to a Rocky Mountain resort. Low-season winter fares to Europe are competitive with those for flying across the United States. Lift tickets in Europe are about half the price of their North American counterparts; the costs of lodging and dining are about the same on the two continents.

Choosing a Resort

The biggest factor in determining where people ski is usually cost. The first consideration is getting to the resort. Ski areas located close to home obviously involve the lowest transportation costs. But if you've been there and done that, the next option is flying (and sometimes taking the train, especially in Europe).

Once you decide that you're getting airborne, there's no limit to where you can go. It comes back to your budget.

Following are a few considerations in selecting a resort:

- Do your homework (this book and the Internet are good places to start). Narrow your choice to a region that you'd like to visit and where the costs of getting there meet your budget.

- Select a resort that appeals to your interests on and off the slopes. You only ski six hours a day. What will you do the rest of the time? If shopping, fine dining,

and nightlife are important, don't settle for a quiet resort in the middle of nowhere.

- Check that the majority of the terrain matches the abilities of your party. If your group differs in skill levels, is it important that you ride the same lifts, ski down different runs, and meet at the bottom?

- If you are traveling with skiers who don't want to ski every day, or there are non-skiers in the group, find a resort that offers other options, including easy day trips to places of interest.

- If you can't decide between a winter ski vacation or a summer sightseeing holiday, consider combining the two in an early-winter or late-spring ski trip. You'll also avoid the aggravating crowds of high season at both destinations.

- Remember that most resorts are constantly upgrading lifts and occasionally opening new terrain. The place that had shortcomings years ago might have changed for the better.

- Resort Web sites provide real-time snow reports and often on-mountain video.

Cutting Costs

Ski packages offered by specialized travel agencies generally offer huge savings compared to go-it-alone trips. If you're considering a package, look closely at what you're getting. Ideally it will include transportation (air plus ground), accommodations, breakfasts, lift tickets, local taxes, tips, and sometimes equipment rental and ski instruction. Unwrap the package, consider the quality of each item, and give it a monetary value. Then compare your totals to the cost of the package.

If you're traveling independently, here are some money-saving tips:

- Consider staying at a small nonresort village down the road.

- January is often a month of bargains. So are the last few weeks of the season. Avoid peak times like Christmas, February school holidays, and Easter.

- Multiple-day lift tickets, half-day tickets, and preseason ticket purchases can yield considerable savings.

- Is a rental car necessary? There are usually shuttles to and from the airport.

- Tap into the advice doled out by tourist information offices. Most North American resorts have a toll-free number. In Europe, village tourist offices, which are accessible via their Web sites, offer invaluable advice and booking options.

- If you're planning an extended stay in Europe and visiting several resorts throughout the Alps, the Eurail Pass remains one of the best values in travel and eliminates a lot of hassles. Contact them toll-free at (888) 382–7245, or visit their Web site at www.raileurope.com.

Ski School

Bend-the-knees-and-follow-me ski schools have gone the way of long skis. So have the so-called Austrian technique, American technique, and every other type of technique that followed someone's preconceived idea of style rather than function. Every sport embraces biomechanical efficiency. Swimmers are taught to emulate Olympians not because it looks good, but because it's efficient. But for many years, ski schools taught what they considered stylish, even though the top World Cup racers all ski the same way—their form follows function. And their goal is the same as yours. They want to get down the mountain in control by carving round turns, not the skidded turns that ski schools taught for so long.

The fact is, not many skiers take lessons. First-time skiers frequently attend ski school, but only 15 percent return for more classes. Skiers at intermediate and higher levels would rather be caught in an avalanche than in ski school. And worst of all, ski school so often took the fun out of skiing for kids.

But things have changed. Bunny slopes have become playgrounds where kids amuse themselves on skis and learning to ski is merely a by-product of having fun. Modern ski schools also do a much better job with adults. Skiers are encouraged to learn skills by breaking down the activity's components and building on small achievements. Instructors emphasize students' strong points instead of their weaknesses. Success breeds success. Ski schools now teach carved turns using the design properties built into skis. Intermediate and advanced skiers, and even experts, are signing up for clinics that offer intensive coaching plus video feedback. If you haven't been to ski school for a while, you won't recognize the place.

And if you believe you've had a bad lesson, tell the director of the ski school. Every director wants that feedback, and the good ones will make it right.

But more than anything else, the shorter, shaped skis have revolutionized the sport and flattened the learning curve. It's easier to ski than ever before, especially in ungroomed snow.

Clothing and Equipment

Cold is not just a personal experience. Facing the weather head on is something all skiers and snowboarders have in common. Dressing for the weather is the best defense. Some veterans say that there are no cold days, just improperly dressed skiers.

Temperature frequently varies at different elevations. And some chairlifts always seem cold, especially if you've worked up a sweat. The best advice is to dress in layers so you can shed and add clothing at will. Also, the air pockets between layers offer insulating qualities.

The new synthetics, like polypropylene and capilene, worn next to the skin wick moisture away from the body. Turtlenecks, long underwear, and ski socks made from synthetics will all add to your comfort. A soft neck gaiter pulled up over your chin will morph a winter gale into a tropical breeze. Cotton, on the other hand, hangs on to moisture.

Protect your skin from the sun's radiation by using sun protection creams. Protect your eyes with sunglasses or goggles, even on cloudy days.

Most veteran skiers advise buying your own boots. A good fit is essential to both comfort and ski technique. But skis are another matter.

If you ski only one or two weeks a year, it might make sense to rent. Quality rental outlets handle quality skis and, more importantly, the latest-model bindings, which are tested and adjusted for your body type and skiing ability. Bindings that release when they must are your most important piece of equipment.

The best place to rent equipment is at the base of the mountain. The problem with renting miles from the ski area is the lack of slopeside assistance. If you have equipment problems, you might be down for the day. You might even be down for the week if you ignore the pain of ill-fitting boots and ski hard all day long. Bloody blisters are a bummer.

Safety and Health

Some general rules of safety include:

- Don't ski alone.

- Wear a helmet.

- If you're going into the backcountry, seek advice from the ski patrol on current conditions. Everyone in your party should have avalanche transceivers, shovels, and probes and know rescue protocol.

- Have at least a rudimentary knowledge of how to identify potential avalanche

slopes. Be careful on snowy days and during whiteout conditions, when you can't see to assess hazards. If in doubt, stay out.

- Statistically, more accidents happen late in the day when skiers and snowboarders are tired. Know when you've had enough.

- Know how to recognize frostbite: white-tinged skin that's numb to the touch.

- If injured, stay warm and send for the ski patrol.

- Skiers and snowboarders below you have the right-of-way.

- The best snow and the least congestion are often found along the edges of a run.

Altitude sickness is a serious health concern. In the American West and some European resorts it's not uncommon to ski between 9,000 and 11,000 feet. A recent University of Colorado Medical School study reported that 25 percent of all skiers coming to Colorado suffer from some form of acute elevation sickness, which causes breathlessness, headaches, and sleeplessness, keeping some people off the slopes. The symptoms start six to seventy-two hours after arrival; they last until the body adjusts to the diminished supply of oxygen above 6,000 feet.

If you don't handle altitude well, or suffer from cardiovascular or pulmonary diseases, you might want to ski in the East, the lower Canadian Rockies, or the low-elevation resorts of Europe and New Zealand.

More Tips

Consider a nonski day in the middle of a ski week—your body, your companions, and even your kids will enjoy the break. You'll ski better the next day, and usually there are plenty of other things to do. You can stick with a winter theme and enjoy ice skating, sleigh rides, snowshoeing, cross-country skiing, or any of the other off-slope activities offered at resorts.

Saturdays are the turnaround day at destination resorts. Ski-week visitors are going home and new ones arriving. It's often the quietest day on the mountain.

When packing, place your boots and other ski essentials in a carry-on bag to ensure arrival. You can hit the slopes with rental skis if your bags get lost.

Excess luggage is a burden. Remember the old proverb regarding packing: If in doubt, leave it out. If you'll be traveling around Europe, walk around the block with all your baggage before you leave home. If this proves an awesome or impossible task, reassess what you're taking.

NORTH AMERICA

North American ski resorts set the world standard for slope maintenance and on-mountain customer service. At the best resorts, high-speed lifts dominate.

Western ski areas receive the most reliable snowfall of all the world's major resorts. Overnight storms can drop several feet of fluffy powder. Western resorts also generally offer the biggest mountains and the greatest variety of terrain. With few exceptions, trails are below the tree line, which helps visibility on bad-light days and makes for interesting and well-defined runs. (In Europe, where most of the skiing is above the tree line, inclement weather and high winds can close the top half of resorts for days at a time.)

In the East, snowmaking has achieved the status of art, supplanting even Mother Nature. New England resorts offer classic forested trails that follow the contours of the mountains. And Quebec's romantic resorts are reminiscent of Europe, but without the sometimes couldn't-care-less attitude. Québécois cuisine would make any Parisian gourmand proud.

As a group North American resorts generally offer spacious slopeside accommodations. In recent years dining options have improved considerably: Some of the best restaurants in places like Steamboat are now at midmountain, just like in Europe. And while the North American brand of ambience may not be centuries old, it is uniquely American and includes such Wild West treasures as Crested Butte, Telluride, and Stowe.

Keep in mind that in California and New England, many of the resorts are close to urban areas and become jam-packed on weekends. Private vehicles and long drives are the norm at most North American resorts. Still, there's no denying that the routes involve passing through some of the continent's most eye-catching scenery.

And what of the America-versus-Canada question?

Canadian resorts tend to be colder than American resorts (with the exception of maritime Whistler). But they often have better early- and late-season snow. And don't forget that commercial heli-skiing was invented in western Canada; the remote interior ranges of British Columbia offer the best heli-skiing slopes in the world. Canada also is one of the world's best ski bargains for U.S. visitors because of favorable currency exchange rates.

In the end, however, there's really little difference in the operation and facilities found at the best resorts of the United States *and* Canada. And that speaks highly of both nations.

ALYESKA RESORT

Girdwood, Alaska

There's snow and there's scenery. There's also 2,500 vertical feet of skiing that runs the gamut from gentle glades to rolling ridges to steep chutes. The snow falls in shovelfuls, some years topping out at more than 1,100 inches. One April alone, it snowed 255 inches.

The views from the summit include the wildly scenic Chugach Mountains, Turnagain Arm, and Glacier Valley. On the forty-five-minute drive from Anchorage to the resort, you'll see jaw-dropping panoramas over a fjordlike tidal basin where the mountains literally plunge to the sea. From the slopes, an inlet of the Pacific Ocean is visible.

The skiing comes without any of the nasty consequences of altitude sickness. Alyeska's highest lift-serviced elevation stretches above the tree line, even though it tops out at only 3,000 feet. Many Colorado resorts have a base elevation of more than 8,000 feet, making Alyeska comfortable for skiers and boarders who suffer headaches, sleeplessness, and lethargy when skiing big-mountain elevations in the Rockies and the Alps.

Getting around Alyeska is handily done on nine strategically placed lifts. Lift lines are minor on weekends and nonexistent midweek. A sixty-passenger aerial tram zips up the mountain in just five minutes, rising over the forested lower half to the glaciers and open bowls near the summit, all the while yielding a bird's-eye view of the mountain's two faces.

For the most part, Alyeska is a blue-run cruiser's mountain. The tough stuff is on the North Face, its gnarly terrain reaching pitches of 50 degrees and dropping 2,350 vertical feet. Boarders freeride the entire mountain. You'll also find a terrain park and pipes.

Rising above the lifts is the Alyeska Glacier. From there, you can hike to the summit and ride expert-rated Glacier Bowl and Headwall. Intermediates can ski the entire 2,500 vertical feet in one long, continuous run. Beginners are not so fortunate: There's a big area for novices, but it's low down on the mountain.

It isn't as cold as you might expect. Alyeska rises out of Pacific maritime Alaska, where average winter day temperatures are in the twenty-degree range. On the mountain there is often a temperature inversion, making the summit ten degrees warmer.

But it is dark. In midwinter the days are short; the lifts open at 10:30 A.M. and close at 5:30 P.M. On weekends, there is night skiing. By mid-February, however, Alyeska gets more daylight hours than any other North American resort.

The mountain gets heaps of snow. But it also gets Pacific storms that can cause severe whiteouts on the mountain, bringing an early end to a great day of skiing.

Alyeska opened in 1959 when there were fewer than ten families living in the area. Today Girdwood, the town near the base, feels like the small-town America of years ago.

 If you want big mountains at low elevations, Alaska's the place for you. Alyeska's base elevation of 250 feet is the lowest in the world among the best resorts—but it receives a whopping average annual snowfall of 560 inches. The extraordinary views alternate from ocean waters to glacier-draped peaks.

In the 1980s Alaska's only four-diamond-rated hotel, the Westin Alyeska Prince, opened at the base of the aerial tram. The new hotel helped the ski area gain momentum and find a place on the world ski map. But so, too, did a couple of local skiers. Olympic gold medalists Tommy Moe and Debbie Armstrong both learned to ride a fast ski by carving miles and miles on Alyeska.

Several heli-skiing and snowcat operations cater to the extreme faces of the snowbound Chugach Mountains. In addition to skiing, the area offers snowmobiling, ice skating, glacier flight-seeing, and dogsledding. Nearby, ocean glacier cruising runs year-round.

Skiers also should visit nearby Anchorage, where the inhabitants make the best of winter. Plan on visiting in late February during the annual Fur Rendezvous festival, or in early March to partake in the carnival-like atmosphere surrounding the start of the Iditarod dogsled race.

Alyeska Resort
1000 Alberg
Girdwood, Alaska 99587

Phone: (800) 775–6656; (907) 754–1111

Web Site: www.alyeskaresort.com

E-mail: info@alyeskaresort.com

Elevation: Top—2,750 feet; base—250 feet

Vertical Drop: 2,500 feet

Total Area: 1,000 acres

Number of Trails: 68

Longest Run: 2 miles

Terrain: 11% beginner; 52% intermediate; 37% advanced/expert

Average Annual Snowfall: 560 inches

Lifts: 9 total

Snowmaking: 480 acres

Central Reservations: (800) 880–3880

Snow Report: (907) 754–7669

Accommodations: The main hotel is the 307-room Alyeska Prince Hotel with tram and chairlift access. There also are bed-and-breakfast inns and condo rentals available 4 miles away in Girdwood.

Getting There: Alyeska Resort is forty-five minutes south of Anchorage, Alaska.

Keep in Mind: The weather is fickle. Arctic chill is often a lesser problem than maritime fog.

BEST BETS

Beginners: The areas served by Chairs 3 and 7.

Intermediates: Chairs 1 and 4 offer both open-bowl and glade skiing.

Advanced: Follow the High Traverse through the Shadows and pick your line.

Experts: Hike to the summit and ski untracked Glacier Bowl and Headwall.

Lunch: Seven Glacier Restaurant.

Off the Slopes: Sightseeing, any way you can arrange it.

Best Hotel: The Westin Alyeska Prince Hotel.

HEAVENLY SKI RESORT

South Lake Tahoe, California

"All scenery in California requires distance to give it its highest charm," Mark Twain wrote. His words resonate when skiing or snowboarding down the sugarcoated slopes of Heavenly Ski Resort.

This is the only two-state ski resort in America. From the California side, the slopes overlook majestic Lake Tahoe, shimmering like a brilliant blue sapphire nestled in soft folds of white velvet. When you traverse the mountain into Nevada, you gaze out on a Zane Grey landscape of muted browns, greens, and yellows of vast desert reaches.

Heavenly is one of the most scenic ski resorts in America. It's also the largest ski mountain in California, making it a must-ski-and-see destination for snowriders of all abilities. If you need more variety, there are several other all-star ski resorts in the Lake Tahoe region, including Alpine Meadows, Kirkwood, Northstar-at-Tahoe, Sierra-at-Tahoe, and Squaw Valley. All totaled, there are more than a dozen ski resorts within a 40-mile radius of Lake Tahoe's south shore.

Among snowboarders, the Lake Tahoe region is considered by many to be the snowboarding capital of North America. And Heavenly offers the highest elevation, longest vertical drop, and the region's largest snowmaking system. From the heart-stopping steeps of Mott and Killebrew Canyons to the gentle wide-open cruisers of the ski area's Nevada side, Heavenly offers a Pandora's box of exciting terrain for skiers and boarders. There are good terrain parks and halfpipes on both the California and Nevada sides. But it's best known as an intermediate-to-advanced mountain, with wide-open bowls, fantastic tree skiing, and the ever-present sun hanging over everything like a yellow kite.

When it snows, it really snows. Located in the high Sierra Nevada, with a summit elevation of 10,040 feet, Heavenly traps winter storms rolling in from the Pacific and boasts an average annual snowfall of 360 inches.

Vail Resorts bought the ski area in 2002 and has built new lifts, added new runs, and built Heavenly Village, a pedestrian area next to South Lake Tahoe.

It takes several days of exploring to get to know all the secret stashes of the huge, 20-square-mile mountain. In reality, it's more like a grouping of peaks that absorb and disperse skiers. It's also an upside-down mountain, with moderate terrain up top and steeper skiing on the lower flanks. Almost all the mountain is below the tree line.

Picture-postcard scenery, big dumps of snow, and nightlife at Nevada casinos contribute to Heavenly's popularity. This is a huge mountain with seemingly endless terrain under frequently sunny skies.

Heavenly is located directly above the towns of South Lake Tahoe, California, and Stateline, Nevada, on the southern edge of Lake Tahoe. You can start out skiing Heavenly from the Lake Tahoe side, or by driving over to the Nevada side to either the Stagecoach or Boulder bases. Starting from Nevada is a good way to avoid morning crowds.

A high-speed gondola, one of the world's longest, whisks skiers from Stateline's 5,500 lodging rooms and legendary nightlife to a high ridge overlooking Lake Tahoe and Carson Valley, Nevada.

Most of the Nevada side consists of intermediate runs with good access to the entire mountain. For experts, the Mott Canyon chair on the upper Nevada side offers 2,000 vertical feet of double-black-diamond terrain. Spread around the mountain are four base lodges and four on-mountain facilities that offer a full complement of services.

Most visitors stay in the communities that surround Lake Tahoe where there's plenty of off-slope action, including Stateline's high-rise casinos and wall-to-wall neon. The resort is heaven for families and groups who can't agree on what they want. Nonskiers can shop, gamble, and be entertained by headliners in casino hotels. You'll find good value in accommodations and dining, since they are subsidized by gambling. But don't expect the glitz of Las Vegas.

Up on the mountain there's an alternative to the fast-paced skiing and nightlife. Every day USDA Forest Service rangers lead two-hour "Ski with a Ranger" programs that explore the area's natural history from the resort's miles of gentle cruiser runs. There's also an adventure park with cross-country skiing, snowshoeing, and tubing.

What's the downside? Getting around the mountain is complicated because of an awkward lift layout. Carry a trail map. Getting to where you want to ski often requires military-type planning.

Generally, the California side is more suited to beginners. Intermediates find long blue runs on both sides of the mountain. Experts tackle the moguls under the California-side lifts and the steep and often deep stuff on the Nevada side.

Heavenly Ski Resort
P.O. Box 2180
Stateline, Nevada 89449
Phone: (775) 586–7000

Web Site: www.skiheavenly.com

E-mail: info@skiheavenly.com

Elevation: Top—10,067 feet; base—6,540 feet

Vertical Drop: 3,500 feet

Total Area: 4,800 acres

Number of Trails: 86

Longest Run: 5.5 miles

Terrain: 20% beginner; 45% intermediate; 35% advanced/expert

Average Annual Snowfall: 360 inches

Lifts: 30

Snowmaking: 3,300 acres

Central Reservations: (800) 243–2836

Snow Report: (775) 586–7000

Accommodations: Everything from high-rise casinos to slopeside condos to mom-and-pop, flattop motels and aging, wood-frame condominiums.

Getting There: Heavenly is a 3½-hour drive from San Francisco International Airport and a little more than an hour from Reno's airport. There's also a small airport at South Lake Tahoe.

Keep in Mind: Use the trail map to find your way around.

BEST BETS

Beginners: Powderbowl and Waterfall chairlifts take you to several wide, well-groomed boulevards.

Intermediates: Ridge Run trails provide easy access to many great blue runs.

Advanced: Gunbarrel on the California side.

Experts: Mott and Killebrew Canyons offer 1,600 vertical feet of 40-degree chutes.

Lunch: Monument Peak Restaurant at the top of the gondola.

Best Hotel: Christiana Inn slopeside near the California base.

MAMMOTH MOUNTAIN

Mammoth Lakes, California

Hey, dude. This is the place—Laguna Beach on snow. Here you'll find a 6.5-mile-long mountain base exposing groomed swaths and moguled canyons that sparkle under the California sunshine. It's the real thing, offering size, terrain, and heaps of snow.

Mammoth Mountain offers major riding for elite snowboarders and their wannabe followers. Its wide bowls, steeps, and terrain parks are frequently backdrops for the sharply focused cameras of the glossy boarding magazines and "big-air" movies. Snowboarders rule. Mammoth appeals to riders in a big way and has shaped the mountain to suit them, including the day-to-day upkeep of three terrain parks and halfpipes, each catering to a different ability level.

 Mammoth Mountain's massive size and endless terrain make it one of the best ski mountains in the United States. It offers a long, November-through-June season with high annual snowfalls. Snowboarding is huge, and the resort is often a filming venue for the world's top riders.

Mammoth is, well, mammoth. There's enough terrain to lose both yourself and the crowd for days on end. The imaginable and unimaginable ski terrain stretches across eight peaks and includes wide bowls for cruisers, long gentle slopes for novices, and treacherous, double-black steeps for experts.

The mountain is a classically shaped dormant volcano. Its broad shoulders tower over a world of arching mountains in the heart of the Sierra Nevada on the eastern edge of Yosemite National Park. Legendary expert-only runs barrel off the high ridge to wide bowls that are the cone of the volcano. There are also easily accessed backcountry trails tumbling from the 7-mile-long ridge at the top of the Panorama Gondola.

Beginners enjoy long, rolling terrain on the lower cinder cones of the mountain. Intermediates can ski in the bowls, in the trees, or on long, well-groomed blue runs around midmountain.

The sheer girth and 11,000-foot height of Mammoth trap heaps of powder on its broad-sloped shoulders. Pacific storms roll in, dump their loads, and are followed by long periods of sunny days. The ski season begins in early November and some years doesn't end until the Fourth of July.

Mammoth Mountain's success is largely due to one man. Since its beginnings in the 1950s, Dave McCoy has nurtured Mammoth and made it the state's busiest alpine resort. People were always telling him it was too high, too remote, and too stormy for a ski resort. Now what started as a great ski mountain has grown into a full-service resort.

Los Angeles and Orange County are a five- to six-hour drive away through the San Bernardino Mountains and Mojave Desert. A busy Saturday can bring 12,000 skiers. But most days the mountain and the lift system can handle the crowds. There's always new terrain to discover and quiet, off-the-beaten-path trails to pick your way down while enjoying the sunshine. For the most part, intermediate and novice runs lace the lower portions of Mammoth, while expert runs crisscross the upper slopes.

Most visitors stay at Mammoth Lakes, a sprawling, rustic, year-round resort town 4 miles from the main lift base. There's also plenty of action at the base, where the new Village at Mammoth buzzes with activity and a shiny gondola rises into the blue sky. It's another project headed by Intrawest, the Vancouver, Canada–based ski village developer that owns Whistler Mountain and other ski resorts. Mammoth visitors can now enjoy ski-in/ski-out accommodations.

If you want more, there's skiing at nearby June Mountain's wide-open runs for intermediates and novices. June Mountain is thirty minutes away and accepts Mammoth Mountain lift passes.

Other off-slope recreation includes cross-country skiing, ice skating, dogsled rides, horse-drawn sleigh rides, and lift-serviced sledding. There are also plenty of side trips worth taking, including Yosemite National Park and Mono Lake.

Mammoth Mountain Ski Area
P.O. Box 24
Mammoth Lakes, California 93546

Phone: (800) 626–6684; (760) 934–2571

Web Site: www.mammothmountain.com

E-mail: info@mammothmountain.com

Elevation: Top—11,053 feet; base—7,953 feet

Vertical Drop: 3,100 feet

Total Area: 3,500 acres

Number of Trails: 150

Longest Run: 3 miles

Terrain: 30% beginner; 40% intermediate; 20% advanced; 10% expert

Average Annual Snowfall: 384 inches

Lifts: 28

Snowmaking: 474 acres

Central Reservations: (800) 626–6684

Snow Report: (888) 766–9778

Accommodations: Slopeside lodging and plenty of hotels, motels, and condos in the town of Mammoth Lakes, 4 miles from the ski area.

Getting There: Five hours (300 miles) north of Los Angeles via I–5 north to State Route 14 east to U.S. Highway 395 north to State Route 203. Reno is 165 miles.

Keep in Mind: Weekends are busy.

BEST BETS

Beginners: Road Runner.

Intermediates: Quicksilver, Back for More, and Haven't the Foggiest.

Advanced: The Cornice Bowl.

Experts: Hangman's Hollow.

Lunch: Mountainside Grill at the Mammoth Mountain Inn.

Off the Slopes: Sightseeing in Yosemite National Park.

Best Hotel: Mammoth Mountain Inn.

SQUAW VALLEY USA

Olympic Valley, California

Anybody can sing in the shower. But if you really do think you can ski or snowboard anything, the stage is set for you beneath the chairlift on Squaw Valley's KT-22 peak.

Early in the season, when the Sierra Nevada's snowpack is limited on the 2,000 vertical feet of steeps and cliffs, the fall lines in this pristine wilderness are as challenging as inbound skiing gets anywhere. It's no place for the timid.

"We don't tell people where they can or cannot ski," says Squaw owner Alexander Cushing. "They tell us."

On K-22 there are steep pitches that stop short above rocky cliffs where you must traverse from the edge of the abyss and find a new line. You play for more than you can afford to lose. If you fall, you're likely to tumble down a rock face as riders on the chairlift above watch, thinking: *Go ahead, make my day.*

But fear not. Seventy percent of the terrain at Squaw Valley is geared to beginner and intermediate skiers and snowboarders, offering wide-open bowls and carefully groomed runs. All of it is easy to get to.

Squaw has always been committed to providing the newest and best in lift technology. The first chairlift, built in 1949, was the largest double chairlift in the world at the time. Today, with North America's

first funicular railway, a 150-passenger gondola, and numerous six- and four-person high-speed chairlifts, most veteran skiers consider Squaw's lift system the slickest in the country.

Squaw Valley is a skier's and snowboarder's mountain. Its six peaks all have different personalities, offering extraordinary snowriding for every skill level. Much of the skiing is above tree line, and they've graded the lifts green, blue, or black, just like the runs. The terrain resembles the Alps.

It's best known for its role as the site of the 1960 Olympic Winter Games. It was an amazing coup for Cushing. Five years earlier, he convinced the International Olympic Committee to award the games to a town with no mayor and a ski resort with just one chairlift and two rope tows.

Immediately after winning the bid, construction began preparing Squaw Valley for the world's first televised games. Jean Vuarnet from France, the first Olympian to compete on metal skis, won the men's downhill.

From the new Village at Squaw base area, the cable car and funicular carry novices and intermediates to the green and blue runs on the upper mountain. Experts can ride chairlifts straight to the in-your-face chutes. (The resort has been featured in many of the extreme skiing and boarding movies.) Each of Squaw's six peaks has something unique to offer along with a stunningly beautiful view of Lake Tahoe. Snow King dishes out plenty of intermediate terrain and the best tree skiing on the mountain. KT-22 has legendary chutes and extreme skiing. The three peaks called Emigrant, Broken Arrow, and Squaw Peak offer more intermediate terrain.

 Home of the 1960 Winter Olympic Games, Squaw Valley is a great mountain with a vast lift system accessing six distinct peaks that rise beneath an annual snowpack of 450 inches. Between the powder dumps are days and days of sunshine.

At the top of the cable-car lift is the village in the sky called High Camp. Here you'll find restaurants, bars, an Olympic-size ice rink, a bungee-jumping tower, the Olympic Heritage Museum, and an outdoor swimming pool that opens for the season in March. It's also a unique high-altitude beginner's area, with expansive views that are usually the domain of experts.

From High Camp's cobalt-blue skies and breathtaking views, you can take it easy at the beginner's area near High Camp, or head over to the mostly intermediate runs of Snow King Peak, which are popular among snowboarders. Along with wide bowls, groomed cruisers, and steep chutes, there are two terrain parks and two halfpipes. Three-mile-long Mountain Run has lights for night skiing. So does Central Park terrain park.

In 2001 the first phase of the Village at Squaw opened with myriad condos, shops, and restaurants. And there's more to come.

Off-slope recreation includes 25 miles of cross-country terrain, ice skating, sleigh riding, and snowtubing.

Squaw Valley
P.O. Box 2007
Olympic Valley, California 96146

Phone: (800) 403–0206

Web Site: www.squawvalley.com

E-mail: info@squawvalley.com

Elevation: Top—9,050 feet; base—6,200 feet

Vertical Drop: 2,850 feet

Total Area: 4,000 acres

Number of Trails: 177

Longest Run: 3.5 miles

Terrain: 25% beginner; 45% intermediate; 30% advanced/expert

Average Annual Snowfall: 450 inches

Lifts: 33

Snowmaking: 400 acres

Central Reservations: (800) 403–0206

Snow Report: (800) 403–0206

Accommodations: Ski-in/ski-out condos and luxury hotels at the base. Another 40 hotels are within 8 miles.

Getting There: Six miles from the north shore of Lake Tahoe. Reno is the closest major airport (42 miles). Sacramento is 95 miles and San Francisco, 195 miles.

Keep in Mind: Crowds on weekends.

BEST BETS

Beginners: The green runs from High Camp.

Intermediates: Mountain Run and all of Snow Peak.

Advanced: Olympic High follows the route of the 1960 men's downhill.

Experts: Headwall on KT-22.

Lunch: Poolside Cafe at High Camp.

Off the Slopes: There's gaming across the Nevada line.

Best Hotel: The Resort at Squaw Creek.

ASPEN
Aspen, Colorado

Pondering Aspen, the first thing you have to do is separate the town from the ski slopes. Next, separate the town's reputation from the reality.

Most references to Aspen focus on the historic town and the wealth. It is widely regarded as the most chic of Colorado's ski towns—think *South Beach at 8,000 feet.* Its image is replete with high rollers who don't need altitude to get high. But if that's your only impression, you're missing the bigger picture.

The gorgeous town of 6,000 residents sits mountain-locked at the head of the extraordinary Roaring Fork Valley, with a beauty and an energy all its own. Antique street lamps complement stately cottonwood trees. There are plenty of block-long parks enjoyed by the more than 1,000 children who attend local schools.

The surface of Aspen has aged gracefully from its mining-day origins in the 1880s. Strict development codes have preserved historic buildings and homes. Nothing is more than four stories high, and downtown power lines are buried.

You'll see the rich and famous in Aspen who come to see and be seen. But they also come for the great skiing, rugged year-round beauty, and the town's cultural attractions. There is a steady slate of arts events, including the Aspen Music Festival's winter classical series, the Aspen Film Festival Academy Screenings, and performances by the Aspen Ballet. And yes, it is one of the wealthiest communities in America, with median home prices well over $2 million. People who can live and ski anywhere choose Aspen. But despite the glamour, Aspen remains a tightly knit town where the noon whistle blows.

Skiing Aspen means taking your pick of any one of four ski mountains, each with its own resort ambience. Taken together, they offer more than 300 miles of trails, with 315 runs and thirty-nine lifts. A single lift pass and a free shuttle bus let you ski it all.

Forming the backdrop to the town is perfectly shaped Aspen Mountain, which opened to skiers in 1937 and debuted on the world stage in 1950 by hosting the World Alpine Ski Championships. Although it offers only 675 acres of ski terrain, Aspen is known as the biggest little mountain in the world. There are no easy routes down from its 11,212-foot summit. The mountain ripples and folds into itself, and you're reminded that it's the legs and not ski technology that make the skier. There are bumps and steeps, as well as natural terrain features perfect for snowboarders. On the best days—and there are plenty of best days—you get it all with fluffy, talclike powder snow.

 Aspen is America's best-known ski resort, a cherished destination for its romantic blocks of old Victorian houses, twinkly lights over snow-covered streets, and some of the most majestic ski slopes in North America.

The mountain is made of three distinct ridges. To the west is Ruthie's with its dizzying pitches and World Cup downhill racecourse. In the middle is Bell's Ridge, a white world of bumps and glades. And over on Gentleman's Ridge, there's open giant-slalom-type skiing and the steep walls of Walsh's Gulch. Cutting down the heart of the mountain is steep, bobsledlike Spar Gulch.

Snowmass is the giant with more acreage than the other three mountains combined (it has its own entry in this guide). It's the most popular and offers the greatest diversity of skiing and snowboarding terrain. And at the base of the mountain, a new luxury village is taking shape.

If you're looking for easier terrain, as well as solitude and the chance to focus on technique, head for Buttermilk. With its combination of great grooming and perfectly pitched terrain, Buttermilk is one of the world's premier learning mountains. It also boasts some of the world's most exciting terrain-park features for X-minded snowboarders and skiers.

Aspen's other ski area, Aspen Highlands, offers impeccably groomed cruiser slopes along with plenty of steep and challenging terrain. The hiking-accessed 12,383-foot Highlands Bowl is out of this world, with pitches of 40 degrees or more. Recent years have seen a new posh, stone-and-beam village at the base of the mountain anchored by a Ritz-Carlton hotel. Pick your pleasure, Highlands has it all.

For nonskiers, Aspen offers a full quiver of ways to play in the winter. You'll find world-renowned shopping, spas, and fine restaurants. The resort has aged nicely, just like the film stars who put it on the map. It has had a few face-lifts, but it's the unchallenged Grande Dame of American skiing.

Aspen Ski Company
P.O. Box 1248
Aspen, Colorado 81612

Phone: (800) 525–6200

Web Site: www.aspensnowmass.com

Central Reservations: (800) 598–2004

Snow Report: (888) 277–3676

Accommodations: A wide range of hotels, lodges, and condos in Aspen and downvalley.

Getting There: Aspen is 200 miles from Denver International Airport, 5 miles from Aspen Airport.

Keep in Mind: Book early for the holidays, and bring your no-max credit cards.

Aspen Mountain

Elevation: Top—11,212 feet; base—7,945 feet

Vertical Drop: 3,267 feet

Total Area: 675 acres

Number of Trails: 76

Miles of Trails: 64 miles

Longest Run: 3 miles

Terrain: 35% intermediate; 35% advanced; 30% expert

Annual Snowfall: 300 inches

Lifts: 8

Snowmaking: 210 acres

Snowmass (see also pp. 22–24)

Elevation: Top—12,510 feet; base—8,104 feet

Vertical Drop: 4,406 feet

Total Area: 3,100 acres

Number of Trails: 87

Miles of Trails: 137 miles

Longest Run: 5 miles

Terrain: 7% beginner; 55% intermediate; 38% advanced/expert

Annual Snowfall: 300 inches

Lifts: 21

Snowmaking: 280 acres

Buttermilk

Elevation: Top—9,900 feet; base—7,870 feet

Vertical Drop: 2,030 feet

Total Area: 430 acres

Number of Trails: 42

Miles of Trails: 21 miles

Longest Run: 3 miles

Terrain: 35% beginner; 39% intermediate; 26% advanced/expert

Annual Snowfall: 300 inches

Lifts: 9

Snowmaking: 108 acres

Highlands

Elevation: Top—11,675 feet; base—8,040 feet

Vertical Drop: 3,635 feet

Total Area: 790 acres

Number of Trails: 130

Miles of Trails: 65 miles

Longest Run: 3.5 miles

Terrain: 20% beginner; 33% intermediate; 47% advanced/expert

Annual Snowfall: 300 inches

Lifts: 4

Snowmaking: 110 acres

BEST BETS

Beginners: Buttermilk.

Intermediates: Golden Horn and Thunder Bowl on lower Highlands.

Advanced: The glades and bumps on the Face of Bell on Aspen Mountain.

Experts: The steep, deep trails of Walsh's Gulch on Aspen Mountain.

Lunch: Dine well on all four of Aspen's mountains.

Off the Slopes: Cultural offerings, exciting après-ski, and gold-card shopping.

Best Hotel: The Little Nell.

BEAVER CREEK RESORT
Avon, Colorado

After you travel the private access road to chic Beaver Creek Resort, the first lift you're likely to ride is an outdoor escalator. The moving stairway means skiers need not clatter up a dozen or so steps as they move from the elegant stone-and-timber village to the first ski lift.

Beaver Creek is Vail's rich sister. Its elegance is so enticing to the well-heeled that former U.S. president Gerald Ford left his home in upscale Vail for new digs at Beaver Creek. Located 10 miles downvalley from Vail, Beaver Creek received its inheritance money at birth in 1980 and set a standard from day one that only Utah's Deer Valley can match.

The resort is single-minded in its intent to provide outstanding guest service, meticulous slope grooming, and fine dining.

At times it's a bit over the top. Isn't it wise to exercise those muscles before we ski? On the other hand, if you have children and equipment in tow, that moving sidewalk between the main base area and the lift may be one of life's little pleasures. It's these extravagant little things that add up to luxury at Beaver Creek Resort.

The skiing is high end, too. The backbone of Beaver Creek is the Centennial chair and its long, perfectly pitched intermediate runs. Behind the main mountain is another face with steep, thigh-burning runs. The resort is speckled with endless groves of aspens with trails winding through their shadows. But Beaver Creek doesn't make beginners toil on lower-mountain bunny slopes: There's a designated "Beginner Zone" near the summit. Even without the

The country club of ski resorts is run like a five-star hotel. The perfectly pitched and groomed slopes are just one of the amenities. Its compact village bustles with luxury lodgings and some of the finest dining in Colorado. Beaver Creek is one of the most exclusive resorts in America.

elegant village, the mountain alone makes Beaver Creek a destination for skiers.

The world was introduced to Beaver Creek when it staged the World Alpine Ski Championships in 1989. A decade later, a new downhill run called Birds of Prey, designed by former Olympic downhill champion Bernhard Russi, became the talk of the alpine world—and it remains so today. Many skiers label it the best run in Colorado.

Whether you prefer to carve on the racecourses or weave through the trees, Beaver Creek offers a multitude of possibilities, including terrain parks and pipes. If you want more, a shuttle bus runs to nearby Vail, where your Beaver Creek lift ticket is as good as gold.

Ski school participants rave about the quality of instruction. At Beaver Creek, instructors serve as coach, companion, and guide. Any ski coach will tell you that a key ingredient to successful ski teaching is choosing the right terrain. Beaver Creek has specially sculpted slopes for learning to carve on skis and snowboards. A dedicated children's ski and snowboard school gets kids sliding down the mountain like barnbound horses. All trails lead back to the hot chocolate–like warmth of the upscale village, where all you need is a no-limit credit card.

For those who seek winter pleasures beyond chairlifts, Beaver Creek is one of a handful of resorts in North America with a dedicated snowshoe and cross-country ski

park at the top of the mountain rather than at the base. It sports 20 miles of groomed track and rustic trails. The resort offers a different activity each night of the week. The Vilar Center for the Arts, for example, hosts numerous cultural events throughout the season, including ballet and Broadway shows.

The accommodations are fabulous. In the land of the pampered, the suits that run Beaver Creek know that guests ski for about six hours a day, at most. Making the other eighteen hours as perfect as a sun-splashed run down Birds of Prey is the resort's aim.

For example, one of Beaver Creek's top-shelf ski packages comes with a private chef. At the end of a glorious ski day, you ride the lift back up to a private cabin on the mountain, where you're greeted at the door with a glass of champagne, hors d'oeuvres, and cozy slippers. As you toast by the fire, the chef prepares a five-course dinner. In the morning the same chef returns to fix breakfast fit for an Olympian.

Or if that's a bit rich for your blood, you can settle for a luxury ski-in/ski-out hotel room. Either way, it's all very comfortable.

Beaver Creek Resort
P.O. Box 915
Avon, Colorado 81620

Phone: (800) 427–8308

Web Site: www.beavercreek.com

E-mail: bcinfo@vailresorts.com

Elevation: Top—11,440 feet; base—8,100 feet

Vertical Drop: 4,040 feet

Total Area: 3,340 acres

Number of Trails: 146

Longest Run: 2.7 miles (Centennial)

Terrain: 34% beginner; 39% intermediate; 27% advanced/expert

Average Annual Snowfall: 331 inches

Lifts: 16

Snowmaking: 580 acres

Central Reservations: (800) 427–8308

Snow Report: (970) 476–4888

Accommodations: Beaver Creek has luxurious, spacious accommodations, offering more than 33 mostly ski-in/ski-out properties.

Getting There: Vail/Eagle County airport is 25 miles away; Denver International Airport is 120 miles.

Keep in Mind: This is an upscale resort.

BEST BETS

Beginners: Booth Gardens.

Intermediates: Larkspur Bowl.

Advanced: Ptarmigan or the black-diamond section of Raven Ridge.

Experts: Birds of Prey.

Lunch: Allie's Cabin at the top of the Haymeadow beginner area.

Off the Slopes: A lovely skating rink is the centerpiece of the village.

Best Hotel: Park Hyatt Beaver Creek Resort & Spa.

BRECKENRIDGE SKI RESORT
Breckenridge, Colorado

The ski and snowboarding runs spread out across four interconnected mountains, numbered from 7 to 10, in the serendipitous Ten Mile Range of the Rockies. The altitude is exceptionally high, with many ski lifts climbing to well above 11,000 feet along the Continental Divide. If altitude presents physiological problems for you, this is not your mountain. With its base at 9,600 feet, Breckenridge is one of the highest resorts in the country.

Superb above-timberline skiing is Breckenridge's most distinguishing characteristic. But the exposure to the weather gives the resort the biting nickname "Breckenwind." The high altitude and exposure also ensure abundant snowfall and a long ski season. Breckenridge usually offers exceptionally good skiing during early and late winter. Continued emphasis on snowmaking has made more of the mountain skiable in the early season.

Snowboarders have always felt at home at Breckenridge. Back in 1985 it was the first resort in Colorado to allow snowboarders to

use the lifts. There are easily accessed bowls and chutes where boarders often outnumber skiers. The mountain has four terrain parks and four halfpipes. The Freeway terrain garden and SuperPipe at Peak 8 are nationally known among boarders.

But long before the first ski lifts were built in 1961 on Peak 8, Breckenridge was a bustling town. Founded in 1860 at the peak of the gold rush, Breckenridge for a time had the only post office between Denver and Salt Lake City. Today the past survives in the Breckenridge Historic District, which lists more than one hundred buildings on the National Register of Historic Places. It's hard to imagine that this brightly painted Victorian town was listed in a directory of Colorado ghost towns fifty years ago, before the ski lifts were installed. But even in those lean years, it maintained its identity. It still exudes a sense of place lacking in most of the nearby Colorado resorts that rose from construction parking lots.

Back in its mining days, Breckenridge had a reputation for debauchery and decadence.

It still has today. This is a pretty town, but it's very much a party town.

Breckenridge is a sister resort to Beaver Creek, Keystone, and Vail, which are all owned by Vail Resorts, Inc. In the past decade, heaps of money have gone into improving facilities on the mountain. Lift passes are good at all four resorts as well as Arapahoe Basin, just up the road at the summit of Loveland Pass.

 A massive network of twenty-seven lifts sprawls across more than 2,200 acres of fine alpine skiing. Historic Breckenridge is Colorado's oldest continuously occupied mountain town and one of America's best and rowdiest ski towns.

Breckenridge has high-speed, state-of-the-art lifts and vast areas of exceptional terrain. The enormous alpine bowls on Peak 8, and the north faces of Peak 9 and Peaks 7 and 10, add plenty of in-your-face steeps. The resort boasts black diamonds on more than 50 percent of its terrain. The most popular excursion for advanced skiers starts at the summit of Imperial Bowl, which tops Peak 8 and is just shy of 13,000 feet. That's about as high as the top resorts get north of the equator.

But Breckenridge hasn't forgotten its bread-and-butter constituency. The wide-open intermediate and beginner terrain back in the tree line is exceptionally well groomed. Among the resort's more than 2,200 skiable acres are hordes of cruisers, knee-busting bump runs, and endless glades. You can ski here for days and still not discover all the terrain.

In recent years Breckenridge has become one of the busiest ski areas in America. Boarders and skiers ride lifts from four base areas, which helps disperse crowds in the morning. Realizing that new facilities are needed to keep up with demand, resort officials recently expanded base area developments on Peaks 7 and 8.

Veteran local skiers suggest starting the day by taking the Rocky Mountain chairlift to the Peak 8 quad. From the top of Peak 8, a T-bar accesses nearly 800 acres of above-timberline bowl skiing. Other skiers and snowboarders might want to stick with Peak 9's chair and North Bowl for challenging, uncrowded terrain. Bump skiers should head to Peak 8 and laps on Little Johnny and High Anxiety.

If it's blue cruising you desire, Breck serves it up in spades. For beginners, Peak 9 and its user-friendly, six-passenger chairlift delivers gently pitched terrain. If you're up for more of a challenge, check out Centennial and Doublejack on Peak 10.

Beyond skiing, there's snowmobiling, dogsledding, ice skating, museums, a vibrant nightlife, and a good local music scene.

Breckenridge Ski Resort
P.O. Box 1058
Breckenridge, Colorado 80424

Phone: (970) 453–5000

Web Site: www.breckenridge.com

E-mail: breckguest@vailresorts.com

Elevation: Top—12,998 feet; base—9,600 feet

Vertical Drop: 3,398 feet

Total Area: 2,208 acres

Number of Trails: 146

Longest Run: 3.5 miles (Four O'Clock)

Terrain: 15% beginner; 33% intermediate; 52% advanced/expert

Average Annual Snowfall: 300 inches

Lifts: 27

Snowmaking: 516 acres

Central Reservations: (800) 221–1091

Snow Report: (970) 453–6118

Accommodations: Lodging runs the gamut from bed-and-breakfasts to condos, much of it within a 5-minute walk of the lifts.

Getting There: Breckenridge is 98 miles west of Denver International Airport via I–70, exit 203, Highway 9 to Breckenridge. Transportation is available on regularly scheduled shuttles for the airport.

Keep in Mind: The altitude is high, exceeding 9,000 feet at the base.

BEST BETS

Beginners: At least half of Peak 9 is beginner terrain, with strictly enforced slow-skiing zones.

Intermediates: Head to Peak 10 and cruise Centennial and Crystal runs.

Advanced: Peaks 7, 8, and 9 serve up large bowls and steep chutes. (Peak 7 is entirely advanced/expert terrain.)

Experts: The North Face on the back of Peak 9. Try Tom's Baby.

Lunch: Ten Mile Station, at the base of Peak 10.

Best Hotel: Lodge and Spa at Breckenridge.

COPPER MOUNTAIN RESORT

Copper Mountain, Colorado

Located 75 miles west of Denver, Copper Mountain has always been a popular destination for Colorado's Front Range skiers. The resort shares the pleasures of the wildly scenic Ten Mile Range with Keystone and Breckenridge. Vail and Beaver Creek also hover nearby. But the USDA Forest Service, which controls almost all the ski terrain in the West, went so far as to declare Copper Mountain "the most nearly perfect ski mountain in the United States."

Until a few years ago, the mountain was Copper's only asset. Then came a spiffy village to match the peerless mountain.

Colorado gets far more skiers than any other state, and tight competition among Rocky Mountain resorts has pushed the boundaries, leading to high-speed quads, six-person chairlifts, impeccable snow grooming, and gourmet dining. Resort marketing departments overlook no detail that allows them to best a competitor. (Copper Mountain touts the "largest restrooms in ski country.")

Vail, Beaver Creek, Breckenridge, and Keystone, the four major nearby competitors, are all showcase properties of Vail Resorts, Inc., which has deep pockets from selling slopeside real estate.

As a result, Copper Mountain had to evolve or perish. But until a few years ago, the resort had evolved into just a hodgepodge of buildings. Nightlife meant dancing on the bar at Molly B's Rocky Mountain Tavern.

Enter Vancouver-based Intrawest resort developers and an infusion of $500 million.

Huge, ridable bowls are just a part of the enormously varied terrain at Copper Mountain. Beginners, intermediates, and experts all get nicely partitioned terrain suited to their comfort levels. The new village at the base is worthy of the mountain.

Now Copper Mountain locals like to joke that this is the country's best truck-stop-turned-ski-village. The place rocks.

Intrawest applied the same village design principles that made Canada's Whistler and Tremblant resorts popular—carless alleyways showcasing sightlines to the slopes. Today Copper's renaissance base area is worthy of the mountain. The new pedestrian-only village features multilevel buildings anchored by retail shops, restaurants, and top-shelf accommodations. Improvements include Copper Station, a massive day lodge and conference center located in the East Village. Beginner ski and snowboard facilities are in the new Schoolhouse at Union Creek, which has become a magnet for families.

But the mountain remains the star of this show. Lifts climb higher than 12,000 feet. The natural terrain separates skiers and boarders by their ability levels. Beginner trails are on the far western slope, intermediate runs are in the center of the mountain, and expert slopes are on the east side. The back-of-beyond is replete with lift-served bowls that rival Vail's legendary back bowls. And if you like skiing glades, there are plenty at Copper.

In total, twenty-two lifts crisscross 2,450 acres of wildly varying terrain that nicely sorts skiers within their own zones of comfort. A six-passenger chair cuts the base-to-summit ride to a mere nine minutes, hardly enough time to get to know the trail map. Boarders ride state-of-the-art halfpipes and cruise Bouncer Terrain Park, which includes tabletops, spines, and kickers for riders who like their tricks. Long a loyal friend to boarders, Copper hosts the annual Copper Mountain Snowboard Series—the nation's longest-running amateur snowboard competition.

Kids love the Schoolhouse at Union Creek and its child-size decor. Their introduction to the snow is by riding down a giant slide from the second floor. A short distance away, the gentle terrain that defines the west side of Copper Mountain provides a natural, progressive learning environment in an area secluded from advanced skiers and snowboarders. There are designated "Family Ski Zones" in place on beginner and intermediate terrain that separate the rush of fast skiers from families.

Other activities at Copper include ice skating, cross-country skiing, tubing, snowshoeing, and sleigh-ride dinner tours.

Copper Mountain has always had a loyal following of high-energy Colorado snow lovers. It doesn't matter that their ski clothes don't match or that you'll see some ingenious uses for duct tape. The mountain is what matters.

Copper Mountain Resort
209 Ten Mile Circle
P.O. Box 3001
Copper Mountain, Colorado 80443

Phone: (888) 219–2441

Web Site: www.coppercolorado.com

E-mail: info@coppercolorado.com

Elevation: Top—12,313 feet; base—9,712 feet

Vertical Drop: 2,601 feet

Total Area: 2,450 acres

Number of Trails: 125

Longest Run: 2.8 miles

Terrain: 21% beginner; 25% intermediate; 36% advanced; 18% expert

Average Annual Snowfall: 280 inches

Lifts: 22

Snowmaking: 380 acres

Central Reservations: (888) 263–5302

Snow Report: (800) 789–7609

Accommodations: Accommodations vary from five-bedroom mountain homes to hotel rooms, all located just steps from the mountain.

Getting There: Copper Mountain Resort is 75 miles west of Denver and 20 miles east of Vail off I–70 at exit 195.

Keep in Mind: High altitude—exceeding 12,000 feet.

BEST BETS

Beginners: The green runs of the Union Creek. Work your way up the high-speed American Flyer lift and ski Coppertone.

Intermediates: Above tree line, Union Bowl delivers a nice mix of glades and wide-open bowl skiing. For a cruiser, take any of the blue runs under the American Eagle chair.

Advanced: The back bowls—Spaulding, Resolution, and Copper.

Experts: Copper Peak is your place in the sun. Try Cornice Chute via the Storm King surface lift. The first turn is a free fall.

Lunch: Solitude Station at the top of American Eagle lift.

Best Hotel: Cirque.

CRESTED BUTTE MOUNTAIN RESORT
Mount Crested Butte, Colorado

The mountain is always bigger than you.

At some resorts, it's easy for a skier to get lulled into thinking otherwise. It won't happen at Crested Butte. Half the terrain is either single or double black diamond.

Set in the high, extraordinary Elk Mountain Range of west-central Colorado, Crested Butte Mountain Resort dishes out some of the West's woolliest extreme skiing—it's steep, complex, and riddled with cliff bands. It boasts perhaps the most radical in-bounds ski terrain in the country.

A dozen or so years ago, when most Rocky Mountain ski resorts were shaving their mountains and fencing off steeps to provide groomed theme parks so intermediate cruisers could feel like heroes, Crested Butte bet the farm on its steep north faces. The resort invited the world to the first U.S. Extreme Freeskiing Championships. Next came the U.S. Extreme Boarderfest.

The extreme events pushed Crested Butte's extraordinary terrain into the spot-

light, and the mountain gained incomparable respect from those who can both talk the talk and walk the walk.

But bring the kids if you're coming to Crested Butte. There's plenty of mountain for everybody. Club Med even opened its first family-oriented North American ski resort village here a couple of years ago. And Crested Butte resort has been family owned and managed ever since the owners built Colorado's first gondola in 1962.

The mountain dishes up plenty of fine intermediate and beginner skiing on some of the best snow in Colorado. And its off-the-beaten-path location means there's plenty of elbow room. The atmosphere is laid back. The sounds of laughter are as ubiquitous as the sunshine. And the surrounding rocky summits tower between 12,000 and 14,000 feet, spectacular enough to humble X-minded tricksters.

The old town, located 3 miles downvalley from the modern village at the base of the mountain, is as authentic as a pair of

It's known as the "the last great Colorado ski town." And the mountain is about as sweet as they come, too. The place might not have invented extreme skiing, but it did legitimize it by opening lawsuits-be-damned skiing. The first extreme skiing and boarding competitions were held here—yet families love the place.

faded jeans. There are few places like it left in the West. The weather-beaten Victorian false-front buildings lining the town's main street represent one of the largest National Historic Districts in Colorado. Schoolkids should get credit in history class just for walking down the boardwalk.

Today these historic treasures house fine restaurants, galleries, and shops. But it's easy to see through them, back to the 1880s when mule trains slogged down the wide street loaded with supplies for the surrounding gold and silver mines. Back then, the legendary outlaw Butch Cassidy once ran out the back door of a local saloon as the sheriff walked in the front door.

More recently, Crested Butte's sheriff busted the event coordinator for the extreme skiing and boarding competitions because she rode her horse into a saloon.

There are no four-lane interstates, skyscrapers, or traffic lights. The town's speed limit is still 15 miles per hour. And Crested Butte is one of the few places in the country where you can stroll from the post office to a wilderness area that is larger than some countries.

Even the food is Wild West. When you order a steak at the Wooden Nickel restaurant, it's likely to be the best you've ever eaten. It's also likely to be elk. The local hardware store has a bridal registry. You can't reinvent a place like this, no matter how hard some resorts try. They ought to let you ski free and charge a lift-ticket price just to walk the town.

But lording over it all is that big mountain called Crested Butte, a majestic standalone peak rising out of a 9,000-foot-high valley. It's often called the "Matterhorn of the West" because of its distinctive geological cowlick.

Extreme skiers and snowboarders ride the High Lift to the outrageously steep headwall where the pitch hovers around 45 degrees. It's like falling through a cloud. Once they reach tree line, another chairlift opens up the entire north face of the mountain, a double-black-diamond world of chutes and bowls. This is tough, you-better-finish-your-turns country.

There are intermediate trails from the top of the mountain to the base, with plenty of options to push your skill level. Beginners have the entire lower shoulder of the mountain to themselves, offering plenty of long, well-groomed green runs. For boarders, there's a 370-foot halfpipe and a terrain park.

If you'd like to wallow in the spectacular scenery away from the downhill slopes, there are 20 miles of groomed cross-country trails and 100 miles of wilderness trails. There's also snowshoeing, ice skating, and sledding. Dogsled tours and horse-drawn sleigh rides operate in the valley.

Crested Butte Mountain Resort
12 Snowmass Road
P.O. Box A
Mount Crested Butte, Colorado 81225

Phone: (800) 810–7669

Web Site: www.crestedbutteresort.com

E-mail: info@cbmr.com

Elevation: Top—12,162 feet; base—9,375 feet

Vertical Drop: 2,775 feet

Total Area: 1,073 acres

Number of Trails: 85

Longest Run: 2.6 miles

Terrain: 15% beginner; 44% intermediate; 10% advanced; 31% expert

Average Annual Snowfall: 240 inches

Lifts: 15

Snowmaking: 300 acres

Central Reservations: (800) 544–8448

Snow Report: (888) 442–8883

Accommodations: There are plenty of condos slopeside in the village at the base of the mountain. There's also a Club Med dedicated to families. A handful of lodges and bed-and-breakfasts are located 3 miles from the base in the historic town.

Getting There: Crested Butte is 230 miles southwest of Denver, 30 miles north of Gunnison, and 90 miles northeast of Montrose. Direct jet service from Denver and Dallas to the Gunnison and Montrose airports.

Keep in Mind: Don't expect great shopping or glitzy nightlife. This is the real West.

BEST BETS

Beginners: Any of the green runs off the Keystone lift.

Intermediates: Ruby Chief off the Paradise lift.

Advanced: Ruby Road to International, Crystal, or Twister off the Paradise lift.

Experts: Headwall, the North Face, Phoenix and Spellbound Bowls.

Lunch: Bubba's Restaurant at Paradise Warming House.

Best Hotel: The Grand Lodge Crested Butte.

KEYSTONE RESORT
Keystone, Colorado

Keystone is a place to bring your family. Or your best girl or guy if they're not into telling ski stories about conquering big mountains in a single leap.

This is a no-nonsense resort. And it's popular, too. In recent years, Keystone has ranked among the top resorts based on the number of skier visits. The recognition is due partly to the variety of exceptional terrain on its three mountains, and partly to the off-mountain fun. No wonder families love it.

And if you haven't skied here for a few years, well, you won't recognize the place.

The neighborhoods of Keystone—and they do call them neighborhoods—evolved with the arrival of ski vacationers. There is no real town. Keystone is a resort community, a kind of Disneyland in the snow. Local history doesn't go back much beyond the 1970s.

In the past few years, a delightful pedestrian-only village has evolved at the original Mountain House base area. Another posh-looking stone-and-timber village has revitalized the River Run base area.

Whether it's watching the Tuesday-night torchlight parade wind down Keystone Mountain, participating in cooking classes offered by the Alpine Institute, or hanging at the teen center, Keystone pitches activities at everybody. Lodging guests of the resort have free access to dozens of amusements, including skating, yoga classes, and more. If you need to party hard, head to nearby Breckenridge or Frisco.

Keystone goes beyond the norm in offering extensive kids' activities. Multiple on-mountain adventure areas feature forts, snow caves, and tunnels. There's even a private ski class called "Mom, Dad and Me," which should separate the merely good-looking instructors from the good-looking instructors who can actually teach. In fact, the Professional Ski Instructors of America ought to make teaching Mom, Dad and Me the final exam for their highest level of certification. You go, Mom.

But fun extras aside, the terrain alone makes Keystone a worthwhile destination. Three mountains, back-to-back-to-back, are loaded with 116 trails served by twenty lifts. The resort offers more than 3,000 acres of tree skiing, bowls, and groomed cruising runs, along with two beginner areas and a new sixty-six-acre terrain park with a cool fifty-one rails and slides. If you can't find some of your favorite skiing and boarding at Keystone, it's not available in the Rockies.

And what's here is impeccably cared for. The nightly slope grooming on beginner and intermediate runs compares with Deer Valley and Beaver Creek, the industry leaders. There's even night skiing until 9:00 P.M. on seventeen runs.

Keystone is nestled in the White River National Forest in the heart of Summit County, home to some of Colorado's best skiing. The sun shines about 300 days of the year, and the average high in winter hovers around thirty degrees during the day. And they don't call it Summit County for nothing. The skiing plays out between 9,000 feet and 12,000 feet. Some skiers have problems adjusting to the altitude.

The resort has a loyal and growing following of skiers who want ambience and value in top-shelf ski country. There's a wealth of good accommodations, many of them ski-in/ski-out condominiums. The premium property is the Keystone Lodge, a member of Preferred Hotels & Resorts Worldwide and an AAA four-diamond establishment. A free, resortwide shuttle cruises the seven neighborhoods that stretch along the river valley floor, eliminating the need for a car. There's even a shuttle from Keystone to Breckenridge, Beaver Creek, and Vail, where multiday Keystone lift tickets are interchangeable.

 Families love Keystone for its tidy neighborhoods, big-mountain skiing, and consistently good snow and weather. X-games wannabes find exciting adventure parks and terrain features to scare their mothers. There also are plenty of long cruising runs and off-the-slope activities.

Most of Keystone's beginner runs topple down to the resort from the front of Keystone Mountain. The doyen of green runs is 3-mile-long Schoolmarm, one of the longest beginner trails in Colorado. The back side of Keystone Mountain offers steep tree skiing and boarding. The terrain then folds back on itself and rises to North Peak, which offers fields of bumps and steeps. The Outback, Keystone's third mountain, delivers 800 acres of glades and bowls, with no beginner's way out. You're now about 6 miles away from the base areas, with views of nothing but blue skies and white-topped mountains.

Advanced skiers should head out early, taking the River Run gondola and then the Outpost gondola to uncrowded trails, wide-open bowls, and powder in the trees.

For ski-hard powder hounds, Keystone delivers back-of-beyond bowls via snowcat.

Keystone Resort
21996 U.S. Highway 6
P.O. Box 38
Keystone, Colorado 80435

Phone: (877) 625–1556

Web Site: www.keystoneresort.com

E-mail: keystoneinfo@vailresorts.com

Elevation: Top—11,640 feet; base—9,300 feet

Vertical Drop: 3,126 feet

Total Area: 2,722 acres

Number of Trails: 116

Longest Run: 3 miles

Terrain: 12% beginner; 34% intermediate; 54% advanced/expert

Average Annual Snowfall: 230 inches

Lifts: 20

Snowmaking: 650 acres

Central Reservations: (800) 427–8308

Snow Report: (907) 496–4111

Accommodations: Keystone has more than 1,600 choices for lodging, ranging from cozy bed-and-breakfast rooms to luxurious private homes.

Getting There: Keystone Resort is located 90 minutes west of Denver International Airport. Take I–70 west through the Eisenhower Tunnel to Dillon, exit 205. Continue 6 miles east on U.S. Highway 6.

Keep in Mind: The altitude is between 9,000 and 12,000 feet.

BEST BETS

Beginners: Schoolmarm, the longest green run in Colorado.

Intermediates: Frenchman, Starfire, and Flying Dutchman.

Advanced: Last Hoot on the front side of Keystone Mountain.

Experts: The Windows area on the back side of Keystone Mountain.

Lunch: The Alpenglow Stube, perched at 11,444 feet, touts itself as the highest gourmet restaurant in America.

Best Hotel: The Keystone Lodge.

SNOWMASS RESORT
Snowmass, Colorado

There are the other three Aspen-area ski mountains—and then there's Snowmass. You have to ski it to believe it. Snowmass has both the longest vertical drop and the highest lift-serviced terrain in the United States.

The mountain stretches into thin air at 12,510 feet. It's bigger than the combined acreage of its three sisters, Aspen Mountain, Buttermilk, and Aspen Highlands. And more people who come to Aspen ski Snowmass than the combined number of skiers on the other three mountains. Snowmass handles them with deceptive ease.

Carved out of the Elk Mountain Range 10 miles from downtown Aspen, Snowmass's stock-in-trade is blue-chip intermediate skiing with long, wide, and immaculately groomed trails. This is the place for snowriders to carve turns and soar like Olympians. But there's also plenty of in-your-face ski terrain, including enough curl-your-toes steeps to excite the best skiers in the world. The mountain averages more than 300 inches of snow every winter.

"Snowmass offers some of the best backcountry skiing in Colorado," says Chris Davenport, Aspen native and former world extreme skiing champion. "And most of it is lift accessible."

Can beginners ski this mountain complex? You bet your wedge turn they can. Green runs are plentiful. But if you get bored, ride the free shuttle to nearby Buttermilk, the best beginner mountain in the country. Shuttles also run to Aspen Mountain and Aspen Highlands. And a Snowmass lift ticket is good at all four mountains owned by the Aspen Ski Company.

Families love Snowmass. The self-contained resort is recognized as one of the top-rated family resorts in North America. The accommodations are slopeside; 90 percent are ski-in/ski-out. Just walk out the door, put on your equipment, and go.

Every week, the resort quarterbacks a wide range of events aimed at family fun, including snow games, scavenger hunts for the young, and chaperoned nights for teens. Hey dude, care for some mountain tubing and pizza? The tightly packed village at the base of the mountain is not likely to lead many children astray. You'll even find licensed ski-in/ski-out child care facilities.

Snowmass is teenager friendly and snowboarder friendly to the max. A special terrain map steers riders away from flat spots and points out terrain parks and perfect-for-boarding trails. A midmountain amusement park features snow castles, the towering halfpipe of Trenchtown, self-timed racecourses, and a picnic center. Monday through Friday, intermediate skiers of all ages are welcome to schuss with a naturalist from the Aspen Center for Environmental Studies and explore the natural wonders of the mountain.

Early in the morning, before the lifts open to the general public, skiers can sign up to join a mountain professional for a first run in light powder or on newly groomed corduroy.

Nonskier activities include snowshoeing, guided snowmobile trips, and horse-drawn carriages. And historic and au courant Aspen is just a twenty-minute shuttle ride away.

But more than anything, Snowmass is known for the vastness of its extraordinary ski terrain. There's something for everyone, sprawled across a staggering variety of slopes that stretch along an elongated ridge of peaks and valleys. Well-placed lifts make it easy to move around the mountain. One run you are meandering through stands of aspens; the next, you're high above the trees on wide-open bowls.

Amazingly, it's never crowded on this mighty mountain. There are few hard-core skiers waiting for the lifts to open. Nobody's racing for first tracks in the powder. It takes several days of long, hard skiing to fully get to know Snowmass's six mountain sections. All but two of them funnel into the base area, making it easy for individuals to ski at their comfort level and still meet their group at the bottom. You don't have to dance with the one who brought you to Snowmass, but you can always ride the chair together.

The resort built its reputation on the stellar cruiser runs off the Big Burn lift, where long, wide, snowy boulevards are broken only by occasional stands of evergreens. If it's cold and windy, slide over to Sam's Knob area, where the elevation is lower and the trails are less exposed to the elements. The Campground lift has some of the longest advanced-intermediate trails on

This is as big as a single ski resort gets in North America. It's also the most popular mountain among Aspen's quartet of heavenly summits. You'll find plenty of everything, even lift-accessed backcountry, but the emphasis is on feel-good, ski-well intermediate cruising.

the mountain. The Elk Camp lift is flush with some of the easiest intermediate runs on the mountain.

The best green runs are Assay Hill and Fanny Hill. Both are located near the village and have their own chairlifts.

Expert skiers head for the High Alpine area and its endless variations on powder and stone in the double blacks of Hanging Valley. There you'll find wide-open bowls and tree skiing.

A surface platter lift, which is less exposed to wind and cold than a chairlift, drops skiers on a high-above-tree-line alpine ridge called the Cirque. If you yearn for backcountry, Davenport, the extreme skier extraordinaire, suggests you make the fifteen-minute climb to the top of the Himalayan-like ridge of Mount Baldy, where a 2,000-vertical-foot powder bowl beckons.

Here you'll find beauty and freedom of the hills that's usually reserved for mountaineers. Don't let fear hold you back. Confidence goes a long way on skis. When you think about skiing in the hot days of July, this is what you'll remember.

Snowmass
Aspen Skiing Company
P.O. Box 1248
Aspen, Colorado 81615

Phone: (800) 525–6200
Web Site: aspensnowmass.com

E-mail: info@aspensnowmass.com

Elevation: Top—12,510 feet; base—8,104 feet

Vertical Drop: 4,406 feet

Total Area: 3,100 acres

Number of Trails: 87

Longest Run: 5 miles

Terrain: 7% beginner; 55% intermediate; 38% advanced/expert

Average Annual Snowfall: 300 inches

Lifts: 21

Snowmaking: 180 acres

Central Reservations: (800) 598–2004

Snow Report: (888) 277–3676

Accommodations: A wide range of slopeside accommodations in Snowmass Village and nearby Aspen.

Getting There: Snowmass is 200 miles from Denver International Airport and 5 miles from Aspen Airport.

BEST BETS

Beginners: Assay Hill and Fanny Hill.

Intermediates: The blue runs in the Elk Camp area.

Advanced: The High Alpine area.

Experts: The Hanging Valley Wall.

Lunch: Gwyn's High Alpine Restaurant.

Best Hotel: Silvertree Hotel.

STEAMBOAT SKI RESORT
Steamboat Springs, Colorado

Why do cowboy hats bend at the side? So you can fit four people in a pickup and eight skiers in Steamboat's gondola.

The rugged, timbered slopes of Steamboat Ski Resort tower above the sagebrush and grassy meadows of northwest Colorado cattle country, a place where mamas let their babies grow up to be cowboys.

But they also teach them to ski. No town in North America has raised as many Olympians as tiny Steamboat Springs— fifty-four at last count. Not surprisingly, Steamboat is known far and wide as "Ski Town, USA." No one is challenging the moniker. The locals like to boast that Steamboat Springs is the "official supplier to the U.S. Ski Team," and they're not talking milk or beef.

Ever since the winter of 1912 when a young Norwegian immigrant named Carl Howelsen dazzled local ranchers with his jumping and cross-country skills, skiing has been a way of life. The first lift was installed in 1938. Today, Howelsen Hill rises behind the town's main street, and schoolkids along with local racers and jumpers continue to train there.

But the real skiing takes place ten minutes away at Steamboat Ski Resort, a modern ski-in/ski-out village nestled at the foot of Mount Werner. The mountain takes its name from Buddy Werner, the Olympic skier from Steamboat Springs who was the first American racer to seriously challenge the Europeans before his death in a Swiss avalanche in 1964. The broad-faced mountain is topped by four lift-serviced summits that exceed 10,000 feet.

There's plenty of breathless freeriding for boarders, as well as a terrain park.

Most of Steamboat's 3,000 skiable acres cater to intermediate skiers who want long runs on well-groomed slopes. But Steamboat also lays claim to some of the best tree skiing in the West, with skiable glades of aspen, fir, and pine accessible from Pioneer Ridge, Sunshine, and Storm Peak. When it snows, powder hounds are in heaven, painting the mountain with parabolic ruts in snow so dry and light that the resort has trademarked the name Champagne Powder to describe it. Steep chutes studded with moguls challenge the fearless and technically sound.

One of the pleasures of skiing Mount Werner is its 360-degree exposure to the sun. You can follow the rays from first turn to last run. And lift lines are rare. There are few day skiers due to the resort's distance from urban centers. Destination skiers hardly tax the uphill lift capacity, especially with the presence of strategically placed high-speed quad chairlifts.

 No ski town epitomizes the American West like Steamboat Springs. And not just in landscape: People in this part of Colorado respect the area's ranching roots. That white cowboy hat you always see Olympian Billy Kidd wearing on his home mountain says something about a way of life. Steamboat might be the best family resort in the West.

Families flock to Steamboat. The ski terrain offers beginner, intermediate, and expert runs on all four mountain faces, allowing skiers of mixed abilities to ride the lift together and ski within their individual comfort levels before meeting at the

BILLY KIDD

The best-known skier at Steamboat Ski Resort is Olympic silver medalist and world champion Billy Kidd. His official title is director of skiing, but even Billy admits, "It's just a fancy title for hanging around." Forever dressed in a ski suit and cowboy hat, you can spot him a mile away.

Billy, how many Stetsons do you have?

"Well, I got a few," he says. "You got to have a black hat for formal events."

Most days you can catch Billy (only because Billy is hanging around waiting for you) at 1:00 P.M. at the top of the gondola, where an electric sign announces whether he's skiing that day. From his midmountain soapbox, the affable champion doles out free ski pointers along with anecdotes about Steamboat. Then he leads his newfound friends down intermediate Heavenly Daze. He'll show and tell you how the best skiers carve turns. He'll make you smile. He'll pose with you for a picture. And when it's over, it will dawn on you that you just partook in an extraordinary ski lesson from a true champion.

Go, Billy, go!

bottom. Village accommodations are mostly slopeside condos whose kitchens have probably cooked more pizzas than your local Pizza Hut. Village nightlife is relatively tame, which keeps the kids out of trouble.

If you're looking for elegant digs, check out the nicely located Steamboat Resort Grand Hotel or the nearby Sheraton.

Steamboat's friendly Western ambience appeals to families. The lift operator who greets you in the morning is likely to be an old rancher wearing a Stetson and a smile, joking with the youngsters as he earns a little pocket money before the hard labor of calving season.

Many of the village guests never ride the free shuttle to the old town of Steamboat Springs. It's their loss. The town is a turn-of-the-twentieth-century Western jewel, offering good restaurants, rowdy bars, and nearby natural hot springs in which to soak those tired ski muscles. There also are inexpensive accommodations, ranging from motels to rooms in private homes.

Steamboat Ski & Resort Corporation
Steamboat Springs, Colorado 80487

Phone: (970) 879–6111

Web Site: www.steamboat.com

E-mail: info@steamboat.com

Elevation: Top—10,568 feet; base—6,900 feet

Vertical Drop: 3,668 feet

Total Area: 2,939 acres

Number of Trails: 142

Longest Run: 3 miles

Terrain: 13% beginner; 56% intermediate; 31% advanced/expert

Average Annual Snowfall: 339 inches

Lifts: 20

Snowmaking: 438 acres

Central Reservations: (877) 237–2628

Snow Report: (970) 879–7300

Accommodations: Plenty of slopeside lodges, condos, and fine hotels in the village at the base, and more hotels, lodges, and bed-and-breakfast inns at Steamboat Springs.

Getting There: Denver International Airport

is a 3-hour drive, 157 miles from the resort. Several U.S. carriers fly into Yampa Valley regional airport in Hayden, 22 miles from the resort.

Keep in Mind: Hard to get to other than direct flight.

BEST BETS

Beginners: Four lifts serve the lowest and gentlest terrain on the mountain. Work your way up to Boulevard off the Christie II and III lifts.

Intermediates: Upper Storm Peak and its bowl-like areas.

Advanced: One O'Clock, Two O'Clock, and Three O'Clock on the flank of Sunshine Peak.

Experts: The upper reaches of Mount Werner to Chutes 1, 2, 3, or the Ridge and Crowtrack.

Lunch: Enjoy the Scandinavian flavor of Ragnar's.

Best Hotel: Steamboat Resort Grand Hotel.

TELLURIDE SKI AREA
Telluride, Colorado

The magnificent folds of southwest Colorado's San Juan Mountains deliver plenty of challenging expert skiing. Two trails, the Plunge and Spiral Stairs, rank as the steepest in the state. Both tumble 3,000 vertical feet into the gingerbread Victorian setting of the century-old mining town at the foot of the mountain.

Born-again Telluride is tucked into a brilliant box canyon beneath the San Juan's breathtaking summits. It may be America's most scenic ski area.

Founded in 1888, the place has evolved from a Ute Indian hunting ground to a booming mine town to a ghost-town-turned-ski-resort. The surrounding Rocky Mountains contain the highest concentration of 14,000-foot peaks in the United States. The town is authentic Old West. Butch Cassidy supposedly robbed his first bank in Telluride, and boxer Jack Dempsey once washed dishes here.

Historic Telluride, with its Victorian homes and clapboard storefronts, is 12 blocks long and 5 blocks deep, with a year-round population of 2,200. And although

the town is compact, the slopes are uncongested. Sixteen lifts feed eighty-four trails. With virtually no day-skier traffic, because the resort is far from urban centers (the closest traffic light is 45 miles away), there are usually no lift lines.

The skiing is nicely partitioned into three alpine regions offering varying degrees of challenge. The mountain face that backdrops the old town is where experts choose a line and carve tight, high-speed slalom turns. The midmountain area dishes out most of the intermediate terrain. Beginners get a mountain to themselves and some of the longest green runs in Colorado. Snowboarders get it all, plus a thirteen-acre terrain park.

Off the slopes, cross-country skiers enjoy 19 miles of groomed tracks.

And what about snowfall? One longtime cowboy wrangler who has watched the goings and comings of Telluride says, "I used to tell people they wouldn't like it here in the winter, the snow's too deep."

For most visitors, the first and most enduring impression of Telluride is the friendliness of the town's people. There is a sense of community here that is uncommon in many resort towns. Perhaps the only western comparison is Steamboat Springs. And like Steamboat, Telluride is booming and has changed dramatically over the last decade.

 Telluride is a jewel—both the mountain and the town. From lodging to dining to grooming, everything is top-shelf luxury served with cowboy hospitality. One of Colorado's most challenging ski mountains also has plenty of beginner terrain.

A newer ski village and housing development nearby has become a playground for the rich and famous. Tom Cruise and Keith Carradine have homes at Telluride. Ralph Lauren and Dennis Weaver saddle up at nearby ranches. And the resort boasts fifty-five ski-in/ski-out restaurants.

But even with the changes, the old town, which is listed on the National Register of Historic Places, just may be America's best ski town. The 1887 San Miguel County Courthouse dominates Colorado Avenue, the town's main street. The rest of the commercial area is a 4-block-long collection of woolly saloons, fine restaurants, and real estate offices.

A popular watering hole is Leimgruber's Bierstube, which claims to be the largest U.S. importer of Munich's favorite beer, a draft called Paulaner. After skiing, Leimgruber's sports a rowdy scene in which patrons spill out onto the veranda, no matter what the temperature. But later in the evening, the place features fine dining by candlelight.

In the 1980s a major development called Mountain Village sprouted 6 miles from town at the base of the other side of the ski mountain; it was incorporated in

1995. The pedestrian-friendly colonnade is laced with luxurious ski-in/ski-out accommodations, eclectic eateries, and upscale shops. Palatial homes perch alongside ice-free heated roads that fan out along the mountain's lower slopes.

The atmosphere is nothing like the old town. Still, it does appeal to families who enjoy the comfort of slopeside condo living with novice areas just a skate and a pole push away. The new village is connected to Telluride by road, gondola, and the ski area's network of lifts and trails.

But the past doesn't seem so long ago in Telluride, where ski lifts were slow in coming. Old-time residents tell tales of early days when locals parked a 1927 Nash at the bottom of the hill, took off a tire, and connected a rope between the wheel and a pulley on a tree to create a rope tow.

Lift construction had a couple of sporadic starts in the 1950s and 1960s, but it wasn't until 1972 that Telluride took off. Back then the surrounding mines were closing, and Telluride's population dwindled to a mere 500. The town was drying up. A gabled Victorian home could be had for back taxes, and the counterculture types bought in.

Telluride is a special place, where the pursuit of outdoor recreation in the extraordinary mountain setting is as single-minded as a chain saw and as uniquely American as rodeo and Jimi Hendrix.

Telluride Mountain Resort
565 Mountain Village Boulevard
P.O. Box 11155
Telluride, Colorado 81435

Phone: (866) 287–5015

Web Site: www.tellurideskiresort.com

E-mail: skitelluride@telski.com

Elevation: Top—12,255 feet; base—8,725 feet

Vertical Drop: 3,500 feet

Total Area: 1,700 acres

Number of Trails: 84

Longest Run: 4.6 miles (Galloping Goose)

Terrain: 24% beginner; 38% intermediate; 38% advanced/expert

Average Annual Snowfall: 309 inches

Lifts: 16

Snowmaking: 204 acres

Central Reservations: (888) 827–8050

Snow Report: (970) 728–7425

Accommodations: The old town offers small hotels, lodges, and bed-and-breakfast inns. The Mountain Village has a full range of properties, ranging from basic condos, to luxury homes, to fine hotels.

Getting There: Several airlines offer regularly scheduled service into Telluride Regional Airport. By car, it's 7 hours from Denver International Airport.

Keep in Mind: It is well off the beaten track.

BEST BETS

Beginners: Double Cabin.

Intermediates: See Forever.

Advanced: The Plunge.

Experts: Dynamo chute.

Lunch: Giuseppe's mountaintop restaurant.

Best Hotel: Hotel Telluride.

VAIL
Vail, Colorado

For many skiers and snowboarders, Vail is King of the Mountains. It's the largest single ski mountain in North America. And if you add up the far-reaching slopes, the boundless Colorado snowfall, and the European-like village, what you get is a Vail that is all things to all skiers. And even non-skiers.

 America's largest single-mountain ski area also offers more high-speed lifts than any other resort in the country. The front side of the mountain is made for blue cruisers. The flip-side is where you find the unmanicured and legendary back bowls. At the end of the day, your legs will ache but your soul will soar.

For expert riders, Vail means backwoods bowls stuffed with light, dry powder. For carvers and cruisers, Vail is seemingly endless manicured boulevards through a Rocky Mountain wonderland. For non-skiers, Vail is a fairy tale–like village cluttered with interesting shops and dining to die for.

Set in the White River National Forest, a 2.3-million-acre haven straddling the Continental Divide, Vail is checkered with the largest network of high-speed lifts in the United States.

There's much to love on Vail's 5,000-plus acres of extraordinary ski and snowboard terrain, which stretches for 7 miles along the Gore Valley. You could slice the mountain in half, and each slice would be one of the top ten ski resorts in North America. It's that gargantuan. If it were a restaurant, it would be all-you-can-eat.

Much of Vail's ski fame has risen from the bowls on the mountain's back side, a white treeless world in a region of humpbacked mountains sprinkled with aspen, spruce, and lodgepole pine. Don't expect views of towering rockbound crags like the ones you'll see at other Rocky Mountain resorts. You go back there for the great ungroomed skiing. There's heaps of it. The Back Bowls stretch 6 miles east to west, the biggest swath of lift-served terrain in North America. And in the evening, when you sit by a roaring fire and reflect on your day in the Back Bowls, you realize their contribution is not to size but to the free spirit in skiers.

You'll also find adventurous terrain in untamed Blue Sky Basin. Its 645 acres of powder are accessed by three high-speed quad chairlifts. The slopes face north and stay largely ungroomed because every run weaves through trees.

But for the most part, Vail's terrain consists of intermediate cruising. Miles and miles of it. Skiers of varying abilities all fly down the perfectly groomed slopes heading for lunches in the European-style pedestrian village.

Off the slopes, you name your game and you'll probably find it. Après-ski dining abounds. And the place rivals Aspen and Whistler for nightlife.

Four mountain centers—Golden Peak, Vail Village, Lionshead, and Cascade Mountain—are strung alongside I-70 to make up Vail's base area. A shuttle bus connects them.

If you want more of the outdoors, the resort's Adventure Ridge area, located atop Eagle's Nest, has outdoor activities for all ages. Try tubing, sledding, snowmobiling, and ski-biking during the day or in the evening.

Of course, skiing and snowboarding still reign at Vail. The size alone ensures that there's something for every skier and snowboarder. Green runs are accessible from every lift on the front side of the mountain. For intermediates, perhaps no resort in America offers so much variety with as much or as little challenge as needed.

Snowboarders love Vail, and the resort has worked hard to earn that affection. It has graded flat spots and created boarder-friendly zones with terrain parks and halfpipes. One park has lights for night riding. Generally, the west side of the mountain is for beginners. Intermediates should ride the front side and leave the back bowls for the experts.

If you're a glutton for pleasure and you still need more, Vail lift tickets are good at Beaver Creek and the nearby sister resorts of Breckenridge and Keystone in Summit County.

Vail
P.O. Box 7
Vail, Colorado 81658

Phone: (970) 845–2500

Web Site: www.vail.com

E-mail: vailinfo@vailresorts.com

Elevation: Top—11,570 feet; base—8,120 feet

Vertical Drop: 3,450 feet

Total Area: 5,289 acres

Number of Trails: 193

Longest Run: 4 miles (Riva)

Terrain: 18% beginner; 29% intermediate; 53% advanced/expert

Average Annual Snowfall: 346 inches

Lifts: 34

Snowmaking: 390 acres

Central Reservations: (800) 427–8308

Snow Report: (800) 404–3535

Accommodations: Luxury to budget, Vail Valley has more than 41,000 beds.

Getting There: Vail is 120 miles west of Denver International Airport along I–70.

Several major U.S. carriers serve Vail/Eagle County airport, 35 miles west of Vail.

Keep in Mind: Vail is expensive.

BEST BETS

Beginners: Gopher Hill lift in the Golden Peak area.

Intermediates: Christmas run.

Advanced: Riva Ridge. Also Race Track and Hunky Dory off the Wildwood Express. For adventure skiing, head to Blue Sky Basin.

Experts: Nonstop laps on the Back Bowls.

Lunch: Cucina Rustica in the village.

Best Hotel: Sonnenalp Resort at Vail.

WINTER PARK RESORT
Winter Park, Colorado

Depending upon how you feel about Salt Lake City, Denver is either the greatest or the second greatest ski city in America. Just west of Denver, the earth tilts violently upward to form the Front Range of the Rockies. The mountain ranges that rise here are the highest in the lower forty-eight states, with fifty-four peaks over 14,000 feet.

Within ninety minutes to five hours of Denver are a wealth of top-tier resorts that draw big-mountain skiers from across the country and around the world. The names read like a Who's Who of American ski areas—Aspen, Breckenridge, Telluride, Vail.

So where do the ski-mad citizens of Denver schuss and ride and soak up the extraordinary scenery?

Winter Park is the clear favorite. The sign at the entrance to the resort reads COLORADO'S FAVORITE. It's no lame boast. This remarkable ski area offers heaps of

snow, far-ranging terrain, and easy access from Denver. It's the oldest continually operated resort in the state. And it's one of the largest.

From Denver, a scenic highway winds through snow-crusted pinnacles, climbs up Berthoud Pass, and crosses the Continental Divide before descending into the town of Winter Park, population 600, give or take a coyote or two.

 Hundreds of thousands of skiers and snowboarders fly into Denver bound for Colorado's big-name resorts like Aspen and Vail. Many visitors don't know that nearby Winter Park Resort has some of the state's toughest runs and some of the best learning hills, all wrapped up in a family resort.

The ski trails sprawl along see-forever vistas hovering around 11,000 feet on the Continental Divide. Twenty-four chairlifts serve up 134 trails and every powder stash and hidden glade in between. But the extraordinary views alone will take your breath away. Who could imagine that rock and snow would take such liberties?

The Continental Divide, which embraces the resort on two sides, is a snow magnet, trapping storms from all directions; most years more than 30 feet gets dumped on Winter Park. The other Who's Who of Colorado resorts would trade their golf courses and best drinking establishments for that much powder.

Each mountain at Winter Park has a distinct personality. Winter Park, the beginner and intermediate cruisers' mountain, is the original part of the resort that opened in 1939. Thousands have learned to ski here.

Next door facing you like a dare is Mary Jane, named for a turn-of-the-twentieth-century woman of negotiable virtue who courted railway workers. It dishes out some of the best fall-line bump skiing in the West. The average pitch is a throat-gurgling 37 degrees, and the moguls look like snow-grooming machines that got bogged down and snowed in. Nobody ever got hauled off Mary Jane on a toboggan in a catatonic state from understimulation.

Other skiing pleasures include the heart-pounding steeps and joint-chattering chutes of Vasquez Cirque, and the near-perfect glades off Parsenn Bowl. All totaled, there's more than enough skiing to outrun your cell phone and plenty to write home about. A whopping 57 percent of the runs at Winter Park are labeled EXPERT.

But for all its appeal as an expert playground, the resort is an ideal family mountain. Remember, most of Denver learned to ski here. The ski school accepts children as young as three, and beginners can ski from the top of Winter Park on green trails.

Off-slope activities in the surrounding Arapaho National Forest include cross-country skiing, dog-sledding, snowmobiling, tubing, and soaking in natural hot springs.

A unique feature of Winter Park is the option to arrive at the resort's base via train. Amtrak's California Zephyr serves Winter Park daily with westbound and eastbound service. On weekends, a special ski train departs Denver's Union Station, snakes through the Moffat Tunnel beneath the Continental Divide, and drops skiers at the base of the mountain two hours later. It's a scene out of the Swiss Alps.

In the last few years, base facilities have

NO MOUNTAIN TOO HIGH

"Imagine never walking, never running, never even feeling the crisp mountain air rush past your face," says Hal O'Leary, the founder of Winter Park's acclaimed National Sports Center for the Disabled (NSCD). He's a man who knows the difference between a life of giving and a life of getting.

"Imagine being told you can't do certain things," says O'Leary.

The NSCD opened in 1970 with twenty-three amputee children and an infectious can-do attitude. From there, it has evolved into the mother of all disabled ski and sports programs, providing lessons for more than 3,000 annual participants in a wide variety of mountain sports. Backed by an innovative equipment lab, its outstanding instructors welcome children and adults with almost any physical or developmental disability.

Their slogan says much about their aspirations: No Mountain Too High.

been upgraded by Intrawest, the world's leading ski resort developer. But if you're old enough to remember when ski lodges smelled like wet wool and peanut butter, the base area at Winter Park will warm you with nostalgia. The emphasis here is on good, hard skiing, which doesn't always come with frills. Stick a little duct tape on that ski outfit and you're set.

Winter Park Resort
150 Alpenglow Way
P.O. Box 36
Winter Park, Colorado 80482

Phone: (970) 726–5514; Denver direct (303) 892–0961

Web Site: www.skiwinterpark.com

E-mail: wpinfo@mail.skiwinterpark.com

Elevation: Top—12,060 feet; base—9,000 feet

Vertical Drop: 3,060 feet

Total Area: 2,770 acres

Number of Trails: 134

Longest Run: 4.5 miles

Terrain: 9% beginner; 34% intermediate; 57% advanced/expert

Average Annual Snowfall: 351 inches

Lifts: 24

Central Reservations: (800) 729–5813

Accommodations: A handful of hotels and condominiums are located slopeside. Several large motels and condominium complexes are located 2 miles away in the towns of Winter Park and Fraser.

Getting There: Winter Park is 67 miles northwest of Denver, 85 miles from Denver International Airport. Amtrak offers daily service, and special ski trains run from Denver on weekends.

Keep in Mind: Crowds on weekends.

BEST BETS

Beginners: The fenced 25-acre beginner area called Discovery.

Intermediates: The blue runs off Winter Park's Eskimo chairlift and Mary Jane's Parsenn Bowl.

Advanced: The front side of Mary Jane.

Experts: The black-diamond runs off the Challenger chairlift.

Lunch: The Lodge at Sunspot.

Best Hotel: Iron Horse Resort.

SUN VALLEY RESORT
Sun Valley, Idaho

"Among the many attractive spots I have visited, this combines more delightful features than any place I have seen in the United States, Switzerland, or Austria for a winter sports resort."

This endorsement from Count Felix Schaffgotsch, an Austrian aristocrat and alpine expert, was just what the Union Pacific Railroad wanted. Company chairman

W. Averell Harriman had enlisted Schaffgotsch to ride every western rail line and spur in search of the perfect spot for a winter resort that could rival the great ski centers of St. Moritz and Gstaad. In 1936 construction of the first major destination ski resort in North America was under way. By the following winter, a 220-room lodge, complete with a heated outdoor swimming pool, was open. And the world's first chair-lift rose out of the blue-skied valley.

The celebrity photos of movie stars that line the halls of Sun Valley Lodge give testament to the glamour of past guests, who included Clark Gable, Judy Garland, and Gary Cooper. In Suite 206 Ernest Hemingway wrote much of *For Whom the Bell Tolls*. In 1941 ice queen Sonja Henie twirled her way around the classic, filmed-on-location *Sun Valley Serenade*. And in 1948 local girl Gretchen Fraser became America's first Olympic gold medalist in a winter sport.

Today this southern Idaho resort remains surrounded by the 756,000-acre Sawtooth Wilderness, with forty peaks above 10,000 feet and miles of clear, blue alpine streams. Sun Valley still maintains its blue-blood, country-club reputation. Skiers no longer arrive by rail; major airports and freeways are hours away. Its isolation, history, and rural charm continue to draw celebrities—Clint Eastwood, Arnold Schwarzenegger, and Bruce Willis are among the many who have homes here.

The resort has two lift-serviced mountains. The diminutive Dollar Mountain offers ideal runs for beginners and a base lodge designed for kids. Bald Mountain (known as Baldy) is a perfectly pitched behemoth that is often called the best single ski mountain in America. Both are within yodeling distance of Sun Valley Resort, a small, self-contained village just a pristine mile from the real cowboy saloons in the town of Ketchum.

If you were to build a mountain from the ground up for the sole purpose of skiing, Baldy would serve as the perfect blueprint. Long runs, uninterrupted by flats or run-outs, are its trademark. The three-peak massif is veined with seventy-five runs and eighteen strategically placed lifts. The vertical drop of 3,400 feet combines long intermediate trails with steep bowls. The base elevation is a mere 6,000 feet, making breathing easy. The snow is dry and plentiful,

 Before Aspen, Alta, and Vail, Sun Valley was the ultimate, and the original, American winter destination. Built by railroad baron W. Averell Harriman, Sun Valley became an instant legend when the resort constructed the world's first chairlift in 1936 and invited Hollywood for a ride. Not only did Ernest Hemingway come to write and fish and hunt here, but he also brought his family and moved in.

with a desert-montane climate keeping the air crisp and clear. The Wood River Valley is striking in its beauty.

Dollar Mountain, with four lifts and 628 vertical feet, is a separate teaching mountain. There's also a halfpipe for boarders on Dollar. Children can enjoy a special learning center for ages three and up. Nearby is a Nordic center with more than 25 miles of groomed cross-country trails.

In recent years Sun Valley has upgraded all aspects of the resort, restoring it to state-of-the-art luxury. Baldy now has seven high-speed lifts, new runs, and a huge computer-controlled snowmaking system. Three recently built spectacular log, stone, and glass facilities—Warm Springs, Seattle Ridge, and River Run Lodges—are reminiscent of the great national park lodges in the West. Sun Valley Lodge and Sun Valley Inn have refurbished rooms as well.

In the old days Ketchum provided a bit of low life to complement the polished elegance of Sun Valley Lodge. Today the old mining town houses many après-ski establishments with Western character. One of the more popular places to dine is Trail Creek Cabin, a rustic restaurant in the woods reached by horse-drawn sleigh.

Other Sun Valley activities include sleigh rides, ice skating, and strolling around the galleries and shops.

Sun Valley Ski Resort
Sun Valley, Idaho 83353

Phone: (800) 635–4150

Web Site: www.sunvalley.com

E-mail: ski@sunvalley.com

Elevation: Top—9,150 feet; base—5,750 feet

Vertical Drop: 3,400 feet

Total Area: 2,054 acres

Number of Trails: 75

Longest Run: 3 miles

Terrain: 36% beginner; 42% intermediate; 22% advanced/expert

Average Annual Snowfall: 200 inches

Lifts: 19

Snowmaking: 645 acres

Central Reservations: (800) 322–3432

Snow Report: (800) 635–4150

Accommodations: The Lodge, Inn, and cottages of Sun Valley Resort, plus lodges, condos, and motels found in Ketchum and the base of Dollar Mountain.

Getting There: Commuter airlines fly to Hailey, Idaho, 10 minutes from Sun Valley. Major airports are located in Boise and Twin Falls, with ground transportation to the ski area.

Keep in Mind: Sun Valley doesn't get the quantity of powder that other Rocky Mountain resorts receive.

BEST BETS

Beginners: Dollar Mountain.

Intermediates: Warm Springs.

Advanced: Easter Bowl.

Experts: Limelight and Exhibition.

Lunch: Sunday brunch at Sun Valley Lodge.

Off the Slopes: Explore the surrounding Wood River Valley.

Best Hotel: Sun Valley Lodge.

SUGARLOAF/USA
Carrabassett Valley, Maine

Maine's loftiest ski mountain is located in the middle of nowhere, near the western edge of the state and close to the border where New Hampshire and Vermont run head-on into the Canadian province of Quebec.

Sugarloaf is a place that goes to great heights to reinforce the East's reputation for expansive terrain and challenging runs. It even offers lift-serviced skiing above the tree line, which is unheard of east of the Rocky Mountains.

Only its isolation keeps it from being better known. The resort is a four-and-a-half-hour drive from Boston, an hour longer than the drive to busy Sunday River. Many who make the trek up Route 27 to Sugarloaf do so because others don't. They like the solitude far from the often madding eastern ski crowds. They take pleasure in skiing and snowboarding uncrowded slopes with few lift lines (except on weekends). And many report some other intangible pleasure in just being here. And who can blame them? The runs offer something for everyone, traversing a huge, rolling massif carved by glaciers that slid over Canada's

It's a lone bandit of a mountain, bald and big, piercing the Maine sky at 4,237 feet. From the summit, the view takes in parts of Maine, Vermont, New Hampshire, and Canada. Its colossal size provides ample room for its 129 runs, which are steep at the top, less so at the bottom, and immaculately groomed.

Laurentian Mountains before reaching the Maine landscape.

This is where famed U.S. Ski Team members Bode Miller and Kirsten Clark learned to ski.

Beginner terrain dominates the lower flanks of Sugarloaf Mountain. But there's also a 3.5-mile-long green trail enticing beginners to ski from the summit. The east side of the mountain is where experts head for intimidating black-diamond terrain and the exposed, soul-soaring snowfields of the upper mountain. Sugarloaf also has one of the largest halfpipes in the country and sweet terrain parks buzzing with table jumps and rails.

The midmountain area of Sugarloaf is for cruisers who enjoy carpetlike snow groomed to within an inch of its life. But all the terrain is fair game. The resort has a border-to-border policy allowing you to ski anywhere you want on its 1,400 acres. There are as many hidden stashes of nifty lines through glades as there are named runs. And the locals are happy to show you around the neighborhood. They'll play mouse to your cat; expect to get tossed all over the snow-plastered mountain.

It's mostly fall-line snowriding at Sugarloaf. And it's mighty enough to have hosted World Cup downhills and a litany of junior races that regularly test the guts and desire of young racers with Olympic dreams. They boast that the way to the U.S. Ski Team is

through Sugarloaf. The mountain's racing club predated the lifts.

At the mountain's base is Sugarloaf Village, a self-contained community housing dozens of quirky shops, rowdy bars, and eclectic restaurants. There are no nationally advertised cheeseburgers here. Hotels, condos, and homes are sprinkled through the woods below the village. Most of the staff are good-natured Mainers who have never learned to pronounce the letter *r,* which is why they drive "ca's." Isolation breeds familiarity among skiers, and people "from away" are made to feel like part of the scene. Locals realize that visitors have traveled long to reach this snowy back-of-beyond and figure everyone may as well enjoy one another and have a good time. In January, Sugarloaf celebrates the White World Week, a winter carnival that has warmed the coldest month for more than thirty years.

The father of Sugarloaf was aptly named Amos Winter. He was from nearby Kingfield and taught his neighbors to ski and then recruited them to cut trails. When Sugarloaf opened in the 1950s, he became the area's fun-loving manager whose on- and off-mountain antics grew in legend after his death.

Other winter activities at Sugarloaf include cross-country skiing, dogsledding, snowshoeing, toboggan runs, and ice skating.

Sugarloaf/USA
5092 Access Road
Carrabassett Valley, Maine 04947

Phone: (207) 237–2000

Web Site: www.sugarloaf.com

E-mail: info@sugarloaf.com

Elevation: Top—4,237 feet; base—1,417 feet

Vertical Drop: 2,820 feet

Total Area: 1,400 acres

Number of Trails: 129

Longest Run: 3.5 miles (Tote Road)

Terrain: 26% beginner; 31% intermediate; 27% advanced; 16% expert

Average Annual Snowfall: 240 inches

Lifts: 15

Snowmaking: 490 acres

Central Reservations: (800) 843–5623

Snow Report: (207) 237–6808

Accommodations: More than 900 ski-in/ski-out condos at the base.

Getting There: Located off Route 27 between Kingfield and Eustis, Maine, Sugarloaf is a 2-hour drive from Bangor; it's 3 hours from Portland. Both cities have airports.

Keep in Mind: Midwinter can be cold.

BEST BETS

Beginners: Boardwalk.

Intermediates: Tote Road.

Advanced: Narrow Gauge.

Experts: White Nitro, reportedly the steepest run in New England.

Lunch: Double Diamond in the Mountain Village.

Off the Slopes: Explore the town of Kingfield, 15 miles south of Sugarloaf, and dine at One Staley Avenue for a taste of Maine.

Best Hotel: Sugarloaf Grand Summit Hotel.

SUNDAY RIVER SKI RESORT
Bethel, Maine

There's a dandy, deceptively long glade called Blind Ambition at Sunday River. If it's true that a name reflects the essence of a place, then the owners of this western Maine resort might consider renaming the entire ski area Blind Ambition. Few resorts have been so determined, and so successful, in making a dramatic ski mountain out of a moose hill.

Sunday River sits in the heart of the Mahoosuc Mountains on the edge of the White Mountain National Forest, near the New Hampshire border. It was a creaky, popular little day area for years. But in the 1980s the owners set their sights on making it a destination resort. They purchased a battery of snow guns and a flotilla of grooming machines to balance the unevenness of Mother Nature. Before long, skiers were soaring down Sunday River's slopes when other New England resorts were praying for snow. Local visionaries started calling the place "Some Day Bigger."

Next, Sunday River got serious about trail building. One peak at a time, one peak after another, they expanded the ski terrain, added high-speed lifts, and ensured it all with belching snow guns. They built it, and the skiers came, particularly the Boston crowd.

At last count, 128 named runs, and many unnamed favorites, tumble and wind their way down eight interconnected peaks spanning 3 miles from White Cap Mountain in the east to Jordan Bowl on the resort's western perimeter. Each summit has plenty of hidden downhill delights and dilemmas. Moving across the range of lifts feels like an adventure. It's a fun place to ski and snowboard.

The recently upgraded base facilities are almost as sprawling as the ski terrain. There are three base lodges and a broad selection of slopeside condominiums. The main hub is South Ridge directly below North Peak. From the summit of North Peak are stunning views of Mount Washington, New England's highest peak, as well as other mountains of the Presidential Range.

The bulk of the area's lodging consists of hundreds of ski-in/ski-out condo and hotel rooms located at the White Cap and Locke Mountain base areas. On the far west side of the resort, 5 miles from South Ridge and served by its own high-speed quad, is the Jordan Grand Resort and Conference Center, the resort's premier hotel. Its plush amenities include a health club, heated outdoor pool, and the usual array of shops.

The slopes entice skiers and boarders of all abilities. Straight down North Peak are some of the resort's choice green trails, gently rambling down to the South Ridge complex. Some of the best advanced terrain is off Barker and Locke Mountains, the heart of the original ski area before the infusion of money and subsequent growth. The slopes offer classic, wrap-around-the-mountain New England–style runs. White Cap peak also has its share of intimidating terrain, including the double-black glades of Chutzpah and Hard Ball. White Heat has a lengthy, steep pitch so wide that the resort maintains Volkswagen-size moguls on one side and groomed gravylike snow on the other. You can bail in or bail out.

You can't ski the resort's vertical drop of 2,340 feet on a continuous run, but each of the eight peaks offers about half that much drop. The speedy lifts encourage you to ski until you drop. The terrain is surprisingly varied; trails are wide and mainly follow the fall line. Rolls and contours provide air-catching rollers. Also here are terrain parks, halfpipes, and fourteen begging-to-be-skied glades squeezed between the cruisers. It takes a full day to explore the resort and get to know its secrets.

Unlike Sunday River, nearby Bethel is a town frozen in time and saved from the sprawl of prosperity. Just fifteen minutes from the slopes, it is as New England as the broad Maine accents of the town's inhabitants. Extravagant inns and fine restaurants are sheltered in handsome brick buildings. It's a gem of a ski town and worth exploring.

Sunday River Ski Resort
P.O. Box 450
Bethel, Maine 04217

Phone: (800) 543–2754

Web Site: www.sundayriver.com

E-mail: snowtalk@sundayriver.com

Elevation: Top—3,140 feet; base—800 feet

Vertical Drop: 2,340 feet

Total Area: 663 acres

Number of Trails: 128

Longest Run: 3.5 miles

Trails: 25% beginner; 35% intermediate; 23% advanced; 17% expert

Average Annual Snowfall: 155 inches

Lifts: 18

A massive snowmaking system, one of the longest seasons in the Northeast, and superfast quads are just some of the components that attract droves of skiers to this large resort. Forty-eight miles of trails on eight interconnected mountains offer endless variety. Skiers also enjoy the turn-of-the-twentieth-century New England charms of the nearby town of Bethel.

Snowmaking: 600 acres

Central Reservations: (800) 442–5826

Snow Report: (207) 824–5200

Accommodations: Plenty of ski-in/ski-out accommodations at Sunday River's base. Bethel has plenty of fine New England inns.

Getting There: Located 6 miles north of Bethel, Maine, off Route 2 in the town of Newry. The resort is 75 miles from Portland and 180 miles from Boston.

Keep in Mind: It can be cold midwinter.

BEST BETS

Beginners: Lollapalooza.

Intermediates: Barker Mountain.

Advanced: Agony.

Experts: The trees of Oz; the wide steeps of White Heat; or the Spruce Cliffs area.

Lunch: Legends in the Summit Hotel.

Off the Slopes: Explore the turn-of-the-twentieth-century charms of Bethel.

Best Hotel: The Jordan Grand Hotel at the base of Sunday River; the Bethel Inn and Country Club in town.

BIG MOUNTAIN RESORT
Whitefish, Montana

With a name like Big Mountain, it had better have big terrain. Especially in Montana, which, unlike Texas, is a place of understatement. Don't worry. They've got some mighty slopes up there, and the name suits the place just fine.

Three thousand acres of extraordinary mountain terrain are riddled with cruisers and glades and nature-built elevator shafts. The scenery is postcard perfect, a vast panorama sweeping from Glacier National Park to Canada to Idaho. The town of Whitefish, ten minutes away and hard on the eastern edge of the million-acre national park, is colorful and authentic. The stomping ground and supply depot for the region's hardworking ranchers and farmers, the town moves to its own rhythm. (Small-stakes poker games are legal in some of the bars.) It's as unpretentious as a worn-out Stetson.

Big Mountain's terrain is as varied as the local Wal-Mart. Mom, Dad, the kids, and Olympic downhillers can all enjoy the slopes. Even some of the local ranchers ski. Here's a little tip from one of them: Ski with the pockets of your jeans turned inside out so they don't fill up with snow.

The mountain tops out at a mere 7,000 feet, so you're not likely to feel weak from altitude. (The base sits at 4,500 feet, which is lower than the city of Denver.) Most of the runs face the sunny south, but all four sides of the mountain are skiable. Crowds are virtually nonexistent. It's not unusual to have entire runs to yourself, and stashes of powder remain several days after a storm.

Experts get 550-acre Hellroaring Basin and its intimidating terrain to themselves. Intermediates find their comfort level on the wide giant slalom slopes of the north side, where there's also steep slaloming down tight stands of trees. The front of the mountain offers something for everybody. Beginners might want to stick with Chair 3. Russ's Street is a green run from the summit, but there are a couple of intermediate

Big Mountain remained little known for years, but in middle age it swelled up with an infusion of cash and stretched to the point where skiers could no longer ignore it. Now this northern Montana resort has a play-as-nature-drops-it reputation for some of the best long cruisers and glade skiing in the Rockies.

pitches to negotiate. Chair 6 has an outstanding learning slope and is a free lift for never-ever skiers. Boarders rave about the entire mountain, and many serious competitors have made Big Mountain their home. There's a well-groomed halfpipe, which has lights for night action, as do some of the runs.

Skiing on Big Mountain goes back more than fifty years. Winters are long and hard in the northern Rockies. It must have been cabin fever and the sight of all that snow that nagged a local schoolteacher named Lloyd "Mully" Muldown to build homemade skis back in 1934. He had his eye on some nice-looking terrain high up on the flanks of what he called "the big mountain." Soon he had a real ski club with a warming hut and a rope tow. By 1947, after the success of Sun Valley in neighboring Idaho, which debuted the world's first chairlift in 1936, Big Mountain built a T-bar and lodge.

But the downside is the weather. It can be awfully cold along this stretch of the northern Rockies. (It's only 35 miles to the Canadian border, where they boast about nine months of hockey and three months of bad ice.) The sky can be gray for days on end, and temperature inversions bring blinding fog. It's also rather isolated. But of course, those are some of the reasons why there's plenty of elbow room on the slopes and good value at the base. Another big plus is 300 inches of annual snowfall. The

best month to ski is March. Big Mountain is incomparable on a sunny spring afternoon; the snow remains crisp, and there's a bit of a nip in the clear air.

Other nearby activities include cross-country skiing in Glacier National Park, snowmobile tours, horse-drawn sleigh rides, and snowcat skiing. The resort also offers mechanized sleds and snow cycles on its slopes.

The base area has completed a multiyear renovation, bringing the resort into the twenty-first century. The Glacier Village project includes residential and lodging units, as well as the usual gamut of shops and restaurants.

And why not? There's more than enough room on Big Mountain.

Big Mountain Resort
P.O. Box 1400
Whitefish, Montana 59937

Phone: (406) 862–2900

Web Site: www.bigmtn.com

E-mail: bigmtn@bigmtn.com

Elevation: Top—7,000 feet; base—4,500 feet

Vertical Drop: 2,500 feet

Total Area: 3,000 acres

Number of Trails: 91

Longest Run: 3.3 miles (Hell Fire)

Terrain: 20% beginner; 50% intermediate; 30% advanced/expert

Average Annual Snowfall: 300 inches

Lifts: 11

Snowmaking: 100 acres

Central Reservations: (800) 858–4152

Snow Report: (406) 862–7669

Accommodations: Slopeside lodges are located at the base. There's a wide range of hotels, lodges, and motels around Whitefish.

Getting There: The resort is 8 miles from Whitefish, Montana, and 19 miles from Glacier International Airport in Kalispell. Amtrak's Empire Builder running between Seattle and Chicago also serves the area.

Keep in Mind: Arctic weather can move in.

BEST BETS

Beginners: Interstate, Home Again, Russ's Street.

Intermediates: Toni Matt and the Big Ravine.

Advanced: Grey Wolf and Hell Fire.

Experts: Haskill Slide and Picture Chutes in Hellroaring Basin.

Lunch: Mogul's Bar & Grill.

Off the Slopes: Spend time in Whitefish, one of the West's great ski towns. Glacier National Park is just up the road.

Best Hotel: The slopeside Kandahar Lodge.

BIG SKY RESORT
Big Sky, Montana

"Just as important as working the good life is finding a place to enjoy it." With these words, former newscaster Chet Huntley in 1970 conceived of the idea of a ski and summer resort in southern Montana. Since his death in 1973, they serve as the epitaph to the monument that is Big Sky.

Big Sky is one of the most scenic and least-crowded resorts in the country. Located 50 miles south of Bozeman, the mountain resort is surrounded by three million acres of pristine wilderness. The base area nestles in Gallatin Canyon beneath a towering Matterhorn-like peak called Lone Pine. The sight is overwhelming.

A fifteen-passenger tram hauls adventurous snowriders to the extraordinary Lone Pine summit at 11,166 feet, high beyond the last meager stand of piñon pine. The snow-blanketed panorama extends from the Bitterroot Mountains to the west to the Tetons to the south. On Lone Pine rock-ribbed flanks expose steep faces that somehow manage to hold snow, daring the best skiers to carve their way down as if the snow were a river. For the timid, Andesite Mountain is stocked with wide-open cruising runs. The snow is silky like bone-dry talcum

powder. All totaled, 150 distinct runs are served by seventeen lifts that deliver some of the finest skiing in the Rocky Mountains.

For boarders, Ambush trail has a 320-foot-long halfpipe with its own rope tow. You'll also find big jumps lower down the trail. The Andesite terrain park has tabletops, rails, jumps, spines, and rollers. There are natural pipes around the skirt of Lone Pine and a gentler terrain park on the Crazy Horse trail.

The flavor of the Wild West is evident throughout Big Sky, even in the names of the slopes. Buffalo Jump is an expert chute recalling the way Indians and early settlers gathered meat by herding the animals off a convenient cliff.

The Lone Peak tram leads to some tough stuff, but otherwise Big Sky is a grand family ski area with enough variety to keep everyone smiling on the mountain. Changes, improvements, and expansion are ongoing at the resort. The base area is a stone-and-beam compact community called Mountain Village, dominated by two hotels, the 198-room Huntley Lodge and the Summit, with 212 rooms and eight penthouses. Condominiums and vacation homes spill across the hillsides, all within walking distance of the lifts. The village's mall is jam-packed with restaurants, saloons, and shops.

Six miles by road below Mountain Village is Meadow Village, a not-so-compact community with private homes, condominiums, and fine restaurants.

Alpine skiing is not the only sport at Big Sky. A 3-mile run down a gentle trail called the "Sewer" leads to the Lone Mountain Ranch, a year-round guest ranch that ranks among the top ten cross-country resorts in America. There you can ski on 45 miles of groomed trails, or spend a few days in native lodgepole pine cabins enjoying exquisite home cooking and conversation with the owners and their hospitable staff. Virgin mountain meadows on the ranch provide a haven for wildlife. More than likely elk, moose, deer, and bighorn sheep will outnumber skiers.

As if Big Sky weren't enough of a draw, it's only twenty minutes to spectacular Yellowstone National Park, where wildlife and geysers complement the ever-sparkling white of a Montana winter. Lone Mountain Ranch offers cross-country skiing day trips into the wilds of the park.

Nightlife at Big Sky is tame. Skiers who come for the mountain and its dramatic setting don't mind.

Big Sky? Big everything! **Three monster mountains with 85 miles of trails drop 4,000-plus vertical feet. It** all gets plastered by 35 feet of annual snowfall. Mix that snow with wild terrain and fast lift lines and the result is bigger than the components. The quaint alpine village at the base gets bigger every year.

Big Sky Resort
P.O. Box 160001
1 Lone Mountain Trail
Big Sky, Montana 59716

Phone: (800) 548–4486

Web Site: www.bigskyresort.com

E-mail: info@bigskyresort.com

Elevation: Top—11,150 feet; base—6,800 feet

Vertical Drop: 4,350 feet

Total Area: 3,600 acres

Number of Trails: 150

Longest Run: 6 miles

Terrain: 17% beginner; 25% intermediate; 37% advanced; 21% expert

Average Annual Snowfall: 400 inches

Lifts: 17

Snowmaking: 400 acres

Central Reservations: (800) 548–4486

Snow Report: (406) 995–5900

Accommodations: You'll find a wide variety of slopeside accommodations at Mountain Village and 6 miles away at Meadow Village.

Getting There: Big Sky is an hour's drive from Bozeman's airport.

Keep in Mind: It can be cold in midwinter.

BEST BETS

Beginners: Mr. K and Pacifier.

Intermediates: Crazy Horse.

Advanced: The Big Couloir.

Experts: Vertical Reality and its 50-plus degrees.

Lunch: Huntley Lodge Dining Room.

Off the Slopes: Yellowstone National Park.

Best Hotel: The ski-in/ski-out Huntley Lodge.

LOON MOUNTAIN RESORT

Lincoln, New Hampshire

Its proximity to Boston—just two hours away—makes Loon Mountain popular on weekends. Snowboarders love the mountain for its edginess, with natural hits and carving terrain that won't fizzle out halfway down the 2,100-foot vertical. Skiers love the hero snow and wide-open ballroom skiing. Three-quarters of the mountain is blue cruising, New England–style twisting trails.

Experts should head up to North Peak for black-diamond bump runs. Depending upon snow conditions, there also are some steep glades in the White Mountain National Forest. High on the mountain, the runs are narrow and twisted, and you'd better complete your turns. Lower down, the trails widen and the pitch is perfect for swooping giant slalom turns, on one plank or two. On bump runs, grooming crews frequently cut only half the trail, leaving both bumps and corduroy snow. Expert and beginner runs are nicely separated on the mountain. For the most part, though, the trails challenge but don't intimidate. Loon has state-of-the-art terrain parks cared for by a creative grooming staff that keeps moving obstacles around. You'll find ever-changing hits, rails, and banks, along with a scare-your-mother halfpipe. One of the most popular on-mountain attractions is a nearby warming hut where boarders hang out and listen to music.

Located in central New Hampshire's White Mountains near the quaint New England towns of Lincoln and North Woodstock, Loon is a stunningly scenic ski area with all the amenities. It opened in 1966, about the same time as Waterville Valley, 25 miles away. Today the resorts share an owner, and skiers receive an interchangeable lift ticket.

Loon Mountain's staff does an outstanding job of snow grooming and crushing black ice into bits that resemble a broken windshield and yield to a ski edge. They also do an adequate job of snowmaking given the valley's water restrictions. Lifts are mostly state-of-the-art, but the base area can have long lines on weekends. (The resort touts 16,000 beds.) A gondola makes getting up the mountain comfortable on cold days. To control flow, the resort restricts the number of day tickets sold. (You can book in advance by calling ahead.)

There are two base areas that nicely separate skiers into ability levels before going up the mountain. Beginners should head to the Governor Adams base area, which accesses the easiest terrain; experts should use the Octagon base area. A small steam train travels between the two day lodges. Families with kids in tow love it. Another attraction for kids is a snowtubing park off the Little Sister chairlift. The ski school has a solid reputation.

Other nearby activities include horseback riding along the Pemigewasset River, snow biking, ice skating, and snowshoeing. There are 20 miles of cross-country trails at the resort. Popular with families is the Wildlife Theater, with performances in a barn that include mountain lions, an owl, and a cow. The Paul Bunyan Room in the Octagon Lodge is Loon's most popular watering hole.

Nearby in North Woodstock, the Woodstock Inn is a cozy, romantic New England lodge and dining room. The Sunny Day Diner in Lincoln is a classic diner with great food.

If you care to explore more of bucolic New Hampshire, the lovely and challenging ski area of Cannon Mountain is nearby. They don't come any more classic than this.

Accessibility, ideal intermediate terrain, and a pretty resort town make Loon Mountain a popular ski resort. The skiing delivers forgiving pitches on fabulously groomed, carpet-like runs. The village offers a mountain of slopeside lodgings and fine restaurants.

It was one of the first ski areas in New England, and the learning curve was steep in those days. At the area's base is the New England Ski Museum, with an interesting collection of relics from the sport's earliest days in the East.

**Loon Mountain Resort
R.R. #1, Box 41
Kancamagus Highway
Lincoln, New Hampshire 03251**

Phone: (603) 745–8111

Web Site: www.loonmtn.com

E-mail: info@loonmtn.com

Elevation: Top—3,050 feet; base—950 feet

Vertical Drop: 2,100 feet

Total Area: 275 acres

Number of Trails: 45

Longest Run: 2.5 miles

Terrain: 16% beginner; 64% intermediate; 20% advanced/expert

Average Annual Snowfall: 121 inches

Lifts: 10

Snowmaking: 260 acres

Central Reservations: (800) 229–5666

Snow Report: (603) 745–8241

Accommodations: Plenty of hotel and condo options in both the Village at Loon and nearby Lincoln.

Getting There: Boston is 2 hours away; Montreal 3 hours; and New York City 5½ hours.

Keep in Mind: Crowded on weekends.

BEST BETS

Beginners: Upper and Lower Bear Claw.

Intermediates: Flying Fox.

Advanced: Angel Street.

Experts: Triple Trouble.

Lunch: Summit Lodge.

Off the Slopes: Explore the nearby villages of Lincoln and Woodstock.

Best Hotel: Mountain Club at Loon; Woodstock Inn at Woodstock.

WATERVILLE VALLEY RESORT

Waterville Valley, New Hampshire

At Waterville Valley, families rule. Located deep in the heart of New Hampshire's 770,000-acre White Mountain National Forest, in a string of 4,000-foot peaks, Waterville offers plenty of civilized skiing and snowboarding. Trails drop off from both sides of a broad ridge rising 2,000 vertical feet above the ski area's base. The terrain has some variety, but mostly it's easy going on blue boulevards.

Waterville's terrain is varied enough to appeal to families with mixed skill levels. Experts find genuine double-black moguls and steep-and-sometimes-deep one-skier narrow trails. Beginners wind their way down from the summit on velvety corduroy slopes. Lower on the mountain there's a beginners-only area called Lower Meadows with its own lift serving wide, gentle terrain. Off-slope activities are centered in the village.

The resort attracts families by giving price breaks on children's lift tickets and other perks that range from free ski clinics, to snow toys such as snow bikes, to access to a community recreation center that resembles a first-rate health club. The emphasis is on value and fun. Its single large base area favors families by helping to keep them together. Even the lifts are kid friendly. One of the two quad lifts at the base is decorated like a cartoon dog with a whirling beanie.

The resort recognizes age differences on slope and off. Kids' Fun Zone offers pint-size games and challenges, including tubing, snow blades, and snow biking. There's even a children's scale halfpipe.

You'll find lots of action on the slopes for boarders, too. Along with great fall lines that maintain their pitch from top to bottom, there's a gutsy terrain park called Exhibition with its own lift that accesses a timed bordercross course, a halfpipe, and obstacles including jumps and rails. The center of the action is a yurt warm-up shelter pitched at the base of the halfpipe. It's a popular hangout for teenagers.

Don't get too cozy, though: The mountain offers enough steeps and moguls for experts.

 Long and wide tree-lined cruising runs are the staple of New Hampshire's best-known resort. Waterville Valley was the vision of Tom Corcoran, a veteran of the U.S. Ski Team who in 1965 purchased land near a few old ski trails on Mount Tecumseh in the White Mountains. Since then it has hosted numerous World Cup races and built a reputation for catering to families.

Waterville Valley was incorporated as a town in 1829. In the 1930s the Civilian Conservation Corps helped the local ski club cut runs on the mountain. But in 1965 a local skier named Tom Corcoran, who finished fourth in the giant slalom at the 1960 Winter Olympic Games, bought 425 acres in the valley and began building a ski resort. Waterville sits in a pretty New England box canyon that has hosted ten World Cup races in the last quarter century.

The village of Waterville Valley is about a mile and a half from the slopes at a lower elevation than the ski area base. A free shuttle bus runs between the two. The ski area is on national forestland, so on-mountain facilities are limited to day concessions. They include two on-mountain restaurants.

The village is quite compact, with shops, bars, and restaurants cozily crammed around a pedestrian-only village square. A variety of modern lodges and condos fan out from there. Many of the condos are large enough to accommodate family groups. Like many newly created resort villages, however, the place has a manufactured feel to it. It's impossible to replicate historic ski towns like Aspen or Crested Butte.

Lift tickets are interchangeable with nearby Loon Mountain and Cranmore resorts. Guests also can use the town's athletic club, which has an Olympic-size pool, indoor tennis, and cardiovascular and weight-training equipment. The valley also has 45 miles of groomed cross-country trails, indoor ice skating, sledding, swimming, indoor tennis, snowshoeing, and sleigh rides.

Waterville Valley Resort
1 Ski Area Road
P.O. Box 540
Waterville Valley, New Hampshire 03215

Phone: (800) 468–2553

Web Site: www.waterville.com

E-mail: info@waterville.com

Elevation: Top—4,004 feet; base—1,984 feet

Vertical Drop: 2,020 feet

Total Area: 255 acres

Number of Trails: 52

Longest Run: 3 miles

Terrain: 20% beginner; 60% intermediate; 20% advanced/expert

Average Annual Snowfall: 125 inches

Lifts: 12

Snowmaking: 255 acres

Central Reservations: (800) 468–2553

Snow Report: (800) 468–2553

Accommodations: More than 120 hotel rooms and 1,100 condos in the village.

Getting There: Waterville Valley is 70 miles from Manchester's airport. Boston is 130 miles, and New York 325 miles.

Keep in Mind: Crowded on weekends. Not a lot of expert terrain.

BEST BETS

Beginners: Lower Meadows.

Intermediates: Express.

Advanced: Sel's Choice.

Experts: Ciao, Gema, and True Grit.

Lunch: Schwendi Hutte at the summit.

Off the Slopes: Elegant dining at the William Tell on Route 49.

Best Hotel: The Valley Inn.

TAOS SKI VALLEY

Taos Ski Valley, New Mexico

Even now, more than a decade since his death, Taos Ski Valley founder Ernie Blake's spirit rules this remote and extraordinary mountain. In life he lorded over every aspect of the resort. After his ashes were scattered on the ski area by New Mexico National Guard jets, it snowed 93 inches in three days.

For Ernie (everyone called him Ernie), the joy of skiing was wrapped up in adventure and challenge. A demanding mountain and a pair of skis was a way to flush more out of life.

"I thought American skiers were developing so fast that they'd want some challenging terrain," he said, late in his life. "In part, that was an error, because they really wanted flats where they could look like heroes."

Most skiers didn't grow into the area's fabled wall of steep, elevator-shaft chutes, so over the years Taos adapted the mountain. Almost 50 percent of the terrain is beginner and intermediate, smooth as a baby's bottom. There's a green run down from the top of every lift. The mix of terrain features bowls, bumps, and glades. But pictures of free-falling skiers are the trademarks of Taos, a one-of-a-kind resort in a one-of-a-kind corner of America. The resort sports a Southwestern patina on a European-style village.

Nestled high in the southern Rockies of New Mexico, Taos is a uniquely American ski resort. The intimate village setting blends Southwestern flair and European-style ambience. On the mountain, the skiing is extraordinary. Tradition rules and snowboards are outlawed.

Taos is nestled in a cirque of high, snow-burdened peaks in northern New Mexico at the southern end of the Rocky Mountains. From the summit, it looks the way things were when the world was young. It's a place for those who prefer skiing to resort sprawl. It's also for skiing purists: Snowboards are outlawed.

The mountain towers a mile above the brilliant New Mexico desert and the 800-year-old pueblo of the Taos Indians, the oldest continually occupied apartment complex in America. The Indians claim that their homes have been here for an eternity and cannot be measured in years. The same is true for the mountains.

The contrasting local cultures—Native American, Hispanic, and Anglo—have always thought of the mountains differently. It is said by some Indians that the snowcapped peaks are the breasts of the god who created them. But the Spanish padres rejected that belief and 400 years ago renamed the mountains the Sangre de Cristo—the Blood of Christ—because of brilliant sunsets that painted the summits red.

Then, in the mid-1950s, Ernie built the first ski lift. Now skiers slide between the breasts of the mountain god down the slopes of the Sangre de Cristo. It must amuse the inhabitants of the old pueblo, who despite the comings and goings of others have kept their culture intact.

Ernie discovered the ski terrain around Taos Ski Valley by flying his Cessna low over the southern Rockies looking for snow in the month of June. He wanted to build a ski area where the dry New Mexico powder came in heaps and stayed. Wheeler Peak, the highest mountain in New Mexico, is close by. The skiing starts at 9,200 feet and rises in a turquoise sky to 12,451 feet. If you want to ski from the summit, you hike the last 600 vertical feet. Ernie wouldn't have it any other way.

At first glance, the resort appears small and old-fashioned. And steep. At the base of the mountain, Ernie erected a sign prompted by the sight of Al's Run, the resort's signature slope visible from the parking lot and responsible for more than a few U-turns. It reads: DON'T PANIC! YOU'RE LOOKING AT ONLY $\frac{1}{30}$TH OF TAOS SKI VALLEY. WE HAVE MANY EASY RUNS TOO!

Many who drive the long, winding canyon road up to the base come for a traditional Taos ski week. They enjoy the winter New Mexico sun, the good food, and a warm village bed at the end of the day. Year after year, it never seems to change. People return to the same intimate lodges, the same instructors and bartenders.

Apparently they also learn to ski. Taos has one of the most highly rated ski schools in the country. Ernie once quipped that it was possible to learn to ski at Taos without lessons, but the survival rate was low.

Today the ski school thrives under the leadership of Jean Meyer, a former French junior racing champion. "Most ski schools try to make it easier," Meyer says. "We try to make it an adventure."

Skiing is the love of his life, and he is French, so, of course, he must say more about his love. "We don't follow the pattern of the Professional Ski Instructors of America," he continues. "We are much more sensual in our teaching. The joy is in the flight, the defying of gravity. We use the skis to be creative."

The ski valley also offers the most tempting array of nonski activities this side of the Atlantic. But don't expect the glitz of Aspen or the boom boxes of Whistler. For the most part, the nightlife is as intimate as the skiing.

"People say there's no nightlife at Taos," says Chris Stagg, a former mayor of Taos Ski Valley. "There's plenty of it. It's just that everybody's in bed by 9:30 after skiing the mountain all day."

Diversions include the town of Taos, 20 miles down on the mesa amid the purple sagebrush and other high-desert flora. There you can tour the Taos Indian pueblo, explorer Kit Carson's bullet-riddled home, and exquisite galleries and museums rich with Southwest art.

Taos has always had both an avant-garde and a refuge quality about it. "People live in Taos because nobody would understand them anywhere else," Stagg says.

It's a paradox not lost in New Mexico. The entire state is incongruous. English writer D. H. Lawrence, who for many years lived on a nearby ranch and observed the mix of cultures, wrote that New Mexico was like "comic opera played with solemn intensity."

The state's license plates carry the slogan "Land of Enchantment." And therein lies much of the pleasure in traveling to Taos Ski Valley.

Taos Ski Valley
P.O. Box 90
Taos Ski Valley, New Mexico 87525

Phone: (866) 968–7386

Web Site: www.skitaos.org

E-mail: tsv@skitaos.org

Elevation: Top—11,819 feet; base—9,207 feet

Vertical Drop: 2,612 feet

Total Area: 1,294 acres

Number of Trails: 110

Longest Run: 5.25 miles

Terrain: 20% beginner; 24% intermediate; 45% advanced; 11% expert

Average Annual Snowfall: 305 inches

Lifts: 12

Snowmaking: 648 acres

Central Reservations: (800) 776–1111

Snow Report: (866) 968–7386

Accommodations: There are several Euro-style lodges in the village. The town of Taos has a full range of accommodations, including hotels, motels, and bed-and-breakfast inns.

Getting There: The nearest major airport is Albuquerque, 148 miles. Rio Grande Air offers daily commuter service between Albuquerque and Taos.

Keep in Mind: Snowboards are not permitted.

Beginners: Rubezahl, a 2-mile scenic tour down to the base.

Intermediates: Shalako at the top of Kachina chair.

Advanced: Hike to the top of Kachina Peak.

Experts: The elevator shafts along the high traverse west of Lift 2. Al's Run at the end of the day.

Lunch: The deck of the St. Bernard Lodge.

Best Hotel: St. Bernard Lodge.

WHITEFACE MOUNTAIN
Lake Placid, New York

Lake Placid is a time capsule, frozen in place by Olympic reminders and tradition. In 2004 America's first winter resort, the Lake Placid Club, celebrated its one-hundredth winter season.

Olympic rings still adorn almost everything, vestiges from when the resort hosted the Winter Olympics in 1932 and 1980.

Whiteface is competition tough—a grueling mother of a mountain slashed with steep, 3,000-foot vertical fall lines. Its location in pristine Adirondack State Park—bigger than Grand Canyon and Yellowstone National Parks combined—deters development. Preservation keeps it untrammeled. There's a base lodge and a midmountain lodge. That's it. Off-slope activity is centered 9 miles away at Lake Placid.

At first view, Whiteface Mountain appears daunting. Ski runs labor into the sky on a massive mountain-and-shoulder combination that reaches 4,867 feet, exposed to winter on all four sides. The lower Little Whiteface climbs to 3,676 feet. Whiteface Summit offers variety and

steepness. It's the site of the relentlessly steep men's and women's downhill runs. Skyward, the women's downhill, is a toe-curling 34 degrees, the steepest continuous pitch on the mountain. It's a take-no-prisoners area where the mountain's edgy personality and imposing geography keep ski edges biting. Particularly on icy patches that are blacker than a mountain man's sense of humor.

There are scant intermediate runs from the summit, but the few that do exist are enthralling classics, spirited examples of New England's game face. Generally, experts

Located near Lake Placid's jaw-dropping winter setting, Whiteface Mountain boasts Olympic slopes and the highest ski vertical in the East. There are no slopeside accommodations; everyone overnights in lovely Lake Placid, New York, 9 miles away, which has its own Olympic-size diversions.

own the top of the mountain; beginners rule the lower half. Between Danny's Bridge and the base lodge, there's a terrain park with tabletops and rhythm and rail sections. A competition-sanctioned halfpipe rounds out the package.

Over on Little Whiteface, skiers tackle double-black diamond terrain—some of it one-skier-at-a-time narrow—and get rewarded with a heated-cabin gondola and views across Lake Champlain to Vermont.

Whiteface Mountain Ski Center stands alone, towering above a vast valley of forest and frozen lakes, exposed to the elements. Wind is common, and the resulting chill factor makes skiing a frigid experience. Spring is the best time to visit the mountain.

In vibrant Lake Placid, Olympic tradition is everywhere. But it is particularly evident at the exuberant Olympic venues. Many of them are in almost daily use, frequented by hordes of swifter-higher-stronger hopefuls. The town is as picturesque as small-town America gets. Broad sidewalks border historic facades showcasing shops and restaurants. The town's frozen Mirror Lake provides the perfect centerpiece for unlimited winter sports.

Other Olympic activities at Lake Placid include bobsledding behind an experienced driver, cross-country skiing, and skating at the arena and speed-skating oval. Don't miss the views from the twenty-six-story-high observation area atop the 120-meter ski jump, or the 1932 and 1980 Olympic Winter Museum. Activities at non-Olympic events include a toboggan chute that runs out onto the lake, plus snowshoeing and dogsledding.

With more than 300 miles of trails, the Lake Placid area is particularly attractive to cross-country skiers. The most popular trails are on Mount Van Hoevenberg, site of the Nordic and biathlon races during the 1980 Olympics. The complex offers ten groomed loops showcasing expert, intermediate, and novice trails.

Whiteface Mountain Ski Center
New York Route 86
Wilmington, New York 12997

Phone: (800) 462–6236

Web Site: www.whiteface.com

E-mail: ski@whiteface.net

Elevation: Top—4,386 feet; base—1,220 feet

Vertical Drop: 3,166 feet

Total Area: 220 acres

Number of Trails: 75

Longest Run: 2 miles

Terrain: 20% beginner; 36% intermediate; 44% advanced/expert

Average Annual Snowfall: 168 inches

Lifts: 11

Snowmaking: 200 acres

Central Reservations: (800) 447–5224

Snow Report: (800) 462–6236

Accommodations: A wide range of accommodations at Lake Placid.

Getting There: Adirondack Airport in Saranac Lake is 16 miles away.

Keep in Mind: It can be cold and windy.

BEST BETS

Beginners: New Boreen.

Intermediates: Draper's Drop on Little Whiteface.

Advanced: Men's and women's Olympic downhill runs.

Experts: The Slides.

Lunch: Boule's Bistro in Mid-Station Lodge.

Off the Slopes: View ski jumpers and bobsledders at Mount Van Hoevenberg; skate at the Olympic center in Lake Placid; or tour the High Peaks region of Adirondack Park.

Best Hotel: Lake Placid Lodge.

MOUNT BACHELOR
Bend, Oregon

Picture an upside-down sugar cone with a huge mound of vanilla ice cream. It looks like a volcano, a perfectly pitched 360-degree ski hill. Now, in your mind's eye make it unbelievably big. Imagine a mound more than half a mile high covering more than 3,600 acres. Dream up some ski lifts—modern, superexpress quads that serve every region of the sloping terrain. Throw in a few surface lifts and some triple and double chairlifts. Every winter, add 350 inches of fluffy snow.

The picture you've painted in your mind is Mount Bachelor, central Oregon's masterpiece of a ski resort.

 It is something to see on a clear day, with its bleached-white cone piercing a Wedgwood-blue sky. Mount Bachelor is a prince of a mountain: a giant snowbound volcano of Oregon's Cascade Range draped with ski runs and checkered with high-speed lifts.

Rising above the ponderosa pines of central Oregon's high-desert country near the idyllic town of Bend, Mount Bachelor is a drop-dead gorgeous, dormant volcano begging to be skied. They call it Bachelor because it stands alone, although it's geographically part of the Cascade mountain range. Its location on the eastern, leeward side of the range usually results in drier and lighter snow than other resorts in the Pacific Northwest.

Mount Bachelor is a vertical world ruled by clouds and wind. Some say there aren't enough clear days. Winter's annual 30-foot dump rides in on fierce Pacific storms—the same weather that pounds the Oregon coast with rain for much of the winter. Extreme winds and whiteouts make the top of Bachelor's cone untouchable, sometimes for days at a time. But no place in the country can match the Pacific Northwest on a sunny, see-forever day. When the clouds lift to expose bottomless, untracked powder beneath a dome of washed-blue sky, it appears as if the pearly gates of heaven have opened. Every skier should know this epiphany. The crisp air is scrubbed clean, and some visionaries report seeing Mount Shasta 180 miles south in California.

Bachelor's slopes are mostly top-to-bottom cruisers favoring intermediate and advanced skiers and boarders. It doesn't take an expert to ski down from the summit, although there are plenty of black- and double-black-diamond routes. Intermediates rack up thousands of feet of vertical riding the Outback Express lift. The resort takes snow grooming seriously, and the velvety plush carpets that result are made for flying. If the light is bad, the lower tree-lined slopes offer plenty of terrain.

Expert skiers and riders find heaps of challenging terrain and deep snow in an open-bowl area called Northwest Territory. But on sunny days, go directly to the top on the Summit Express.

Beginners don't exactly have the run of the mountain. They should avoid the Summit and Outback lifts. The other ten lifts are theirs to share, however, with enough wide, easy green runs to give kids a figure skater's smile. Rank beginners have their own lift, a high-speed, detachable quad named Sunshine Accelerator, which the lifties slow to a snail's pace for loading.

Snowboarders feast on the seventy-one runs and 360-degree exposure. For tricksters, the resort has an Olympic-caliber half-pipe that served as the qualifying site for selection of the 2002 Olympic U.S. Snowboarding Team. Superpipes, big air, plus rails, tabletops, and fun boxes are yours to achieve at Mount Bachelor's terrain parks.

And Bachelor hasn't forgotten cross-country skiers. At the mountain's base are twelve loops covering 40 miles of scenic trails. The resort lies in the Deschutes National Forest, and the USDA Forest Service offers a series of interpretive programs, including snowshoe nature walks, stargazing, and geological tours of the dormant volcano.

There's a cozy day lodge at the base, but no accommodations. Perhaps that's a good thing because it pulls skiers into the vibrant community of Bend, a perennial selection on those "best places to live" lists. The town offers sophisticated lodging, dining, and shopping. Closer to the mountain—15 miles from the base and 18 miles from Bend—is the upscale resort community of Sunriver. The lodging closest to the mountain is the Inn of the Seventh Mountain.

Mount Bachelor's essential components are heaps of snow, miles of varied skiing, state-of-the-art lifts, and a fine nearby community. But it all starts with that breathtaking 40,000-year-old volcano. You've got to ski it to believe it.

Mount Bachelor
P.O. Box 1031
Bend, Oregon 97709

Phone: (800) 829–2442

Web Site: www.mtbachelor.com

E-mail: info@mtbachelor.com

Elevation: Top—9,065 feet; base—5,700 feet

Vertical Drop: 3,365 feet

Total Area: 3,683 acres

Number of Trails: 71

Longest Run: 1.5 miles

Terrain: 15% beginner; 25% intermediate; 35% advanced; 25% expert

Average Annual Snowfall: 350 inches

Lifts: 12

Snowmaking: None

Central Reservations: (800) 829–2442

Snow Report: (541) 382–7888

Accommodations: Bend offers a wide range of accommodations.

Getting There: The nearest airport is Robert Fields in Redmond/Bend, Oregon.

Keep in Mind: Potential for wet Pacific Northwest weather.

BEST BETS

Beginners: Leeway, Skyliner, and Marshmallow.

Intermediates: Ed's Garden, Kangaroo, and Downunder off the Outback Express lift.

Advanced: Spark's Lake off the Northwest Territories quad.

Experts: The Pinnacles off the Summit Express. Or try Devil's Backbone off the Northwest Express chair.

Lunch: Skiers Palate Restaurant.

Off the Slopes: Explore the town of Bend.

Best Hotel: Inn of the Seventh Mountain.

ALTA SKI AREA

Alta, Utah

In the history of American skiing, Alta Ski Area is a blazing star. It is hallowed ground to skiers in the same way the Alamo is sacred to Texans. If someone tried to dramatically change the resort, the elder folks of skiing, some who even remember when Alta opened in 1938, wouldn't stand for it. And they would no more allow snowboards on their boundless turf than Texans would wrap their buckskinned image of Davy Crockett in Gore-Tex.

Snowboarders, consider yourselves stiff-armed and head next door to Snowbird, where you are welcome.

The kissing-cousin resorts of Alta and Snowbird occupy storied Little Cottonwood Canyon, a pristine wilderness that was deemed too precious for the Salt Lake City Olympic developers. The two resorts share some of the lightest, deepest lift-serviced snow in the world. Most winters, about 500 inches of it falls; some winters, a lot more.

The source of the legendary eiderdown-like snowfall is moisture-packed clouds from the Pacific Ocean pushed west by winter winds. En route, the deserts bake out most of the water droplets. When the clouds ram the 11,000-foot summits of Little Cottonwood Canyon, the remaining moisture rapidly cools and condenses. The result is huge flakes of snow falling like white popcorn.

Along with the quantity and quality of snow, Alta diehards love the classic, no-frills atmosphere. There are no heated sidewalks. No escalators whisking you to the lifts. The resort even limits the number of skiers on the mountain during busy holiday periods. There's surprisingly little commercialism. At the base are five rustic ski lodges. But the grooming and snowmaking are state-of-the-art, and the lifts rise to

more than 10,000 feet. A new high-speed, bottom-to-top quad has replaced the old Collins and Germania lifts.

Like Steamboat resort in Colorado, Alta looms large in the history of American skiing. The legendary runs are mostly steep and deep, although the mountain stats reveal a fairly even split among beginner, intermediate, and expert terrain on forty named runs. The regulars at Alta chase hundreds of paths down while creatively using the crests and valleys and trees of the mountain.

The skier's code at Alta is to ski it if you see it. It's easy to discover your own secret stashes of powder in Alta's rollicking 2,200 acres. This mountain is about powder, and the trees and sheltered gullies of the area hold it long after a storm.

There's skiing on both the front and back sides of the mountain and two base stations. Beginners find safe haven near the Albion base. Above the Wildcat base, the lift serves intermediate and advanced terrain, including narrow trails, bumps, and glades. The new Collins lift gets you to West Rustler and the steep fluff of Eagle's Nest and High Rustler. Experts also find powder bowls stretching to the back-of-beyond off the Sugarloaf chair. Much of the expert skiing requires a traverse or hike, which helps keep the crowds away.

The pièce de résistance is Alf's High Rustler, named for Alf Engen, a legendary Norwegian skier and one of the founding fathers of Alta. Getting there means traversing an exposed ridge, but the reward is a breathtakingly steep, powder-filled run that ends at the Sitzmark bar at Alta Lodge.

Founded in the late 1800s, Alta was a prosperous silver-mining town riding the ups and downs of world markets until the

There's no snowboarding. Not at this American classic so rich in history and soul. With it's mid-twentieth-century ambience and dramatic setting in Utah's Little Cottonwood Canyon, Alta yields the quintessential ski experience and has one of the most loyal clienteles in the world.

Great Depression. After mining dried up, locals discovered a new mother lode on the powdery slopes. In 1938 they cranked up their own 15-cent chairlift rides and imported the Engen brothers to teach locals to ski down. Alta instructors still work for the Alf Engen Ski School. His son is now the resort's director of skiing.

The collection of five lodges tucked into safe zones between avalanche paths at the base carries you back in time. For the most part, they preserve the old traditions with large communal lobbies and family-style dining. They have a European ambience and include breakfast and dinner in their rates.

Lift-ticket prices are stuck in the 1990s. The regulars know they've got a great place, and they want to preserve it. The focus is all about the challenging mountain and extraordinary snow.

At Alta, you're part of a great family of skiers. Wallow in it.

Alta Ski Area
P.O. Box 8007
Alta, Utah 84092-8007
Phone: (801) 359–1078
Web Site: www.alta.com

E-mail: info@alta.com

Elevation: Top—10,550 feet; base—8,530 feet

Vertical Drop: 2,020 feet

Total Area: 2,200 acres

Number of Trails: 40

Longest Run: 2 miles

Terrain: 25% beginner; 40% intermediate; 35% advanced/expert

Average Annual Snowfall: 500 inches

Lifts: 11

Snowmaking: 50 acres

Central Reservations: (888) 782–9258

Snow Report: (801) 572–3939

Accommodations: You'll find a handful of lodges, condos, and dorms at the base.

Getting There: Alta is located in Little Cottonwood Canyon, 45 minutes southeast of Salt Lake City.

Keep in Mind: No snowboarding. Alta offers great powder skiing on steep slopes.

BEST BETS

Beginners: Crooked Mile or Sunnyside runs on Peruvian Ridge's lower flanks.

Intermediates: Aggie's Alley from the top of the Wildcat lift.

Advanced: Powder bowls under the Sugarloaf chair.

Experts: Alf's High Rustler.

Lunch: Alta Lodge Dining Room.

Off the Slopes: Explore and dine in Salt Lake City.

Best Hotel: The Rustler.

THE CANYONS
Park City, Utah

If Utah were in Europe, the three Park City ski resorts of Deer Valley, Park City Mountain Resort, and The Canyons would be interconnected via lifts and trails. But in North America the three ski areas are fierce competitors. Which makes each one better. And that's probably about the best thing you can say about the go-it-alone attitude of American ski resorts.

The Canyons has more terrain than the other two Park City areas. The resort's lift arsenal of high-speed quads and an eight-passenger gondola whisks snow-riders up eight distinct peaks with 3,300-plus skiable acres of remarkable diversity. You'll find acres of natural terrain parks, tree-lined steeps, and off-piste bowls and glades. There's even a handful of narrow, winding trails, reminiscent of New England skiing.

Once a little-known refuge for frugal skiers with muddy boots (they didn't pave the parking lot until the summer of 2001), The Canyons now boasts the most lift-served skiable terrain in Utah and ranks among the top five in the country. Its expansion plans are aiming for the title of America's largest resort.

Since 1997, when the mega resort owner American Skiing Company purchased what was then called Wolf Mountain (prior to that it was known as Park City West), The Canyons has been all about expansion. Beneath old names and rattle-trap lifts, the new owners found a sprawling mountain offering far-reaching terrain and challenges. With a new name, owner, and attitude, the resort quietly underwent a major renovation while everyone else in Utah focused on readying for the 2002 Olympic Winter Games. The result: a new village at the base anchored by a luxury

hotel and other slopeside accommodations, as well as a growing collection of shops, bars, and restaurants.

The Canyons may look small from the base, but ride the gondola and the area unfolds. Experts find plenty of steep terrain, especially on the north-facing runs off the Ninety-Nine-90 lift (the top elevation is 9,990 feet). Take almost any trail you wish and it plunges you down through the trees on a double-black-diamond roller coaster. Intermediate and advanced skiers enjoy the uncrowded, snow-clogged Pines area off the north side of the Saddleback Express lift. There's a glut of groomed blue runs distributed throughout the resort. Beginners can get high on the mountain by taking the Flight of the Canyons gondola to an exclusive green area near Red Pine Lodge. There also are green runs at the mountain's base.

Snowboarders get it all. The Canyons is rated top-shelf among boarders who find extreme joy in its rolling, natural terrain features, including multiple tabletops, rails, and banked hits. There are even five natural halfpipes. And the terrain park accessed by Red Hawk lift on the front face of the resort

With eight peaks full of bowls and steeps and winding trails, Utah's largest resort (and one of the five largest in the country) is all about terrain. The Canyons has undergone a massive face-lift since American Skiing Company bought the resort in 1997. Together with its tony neighbors, Deer Valley and Park City Mountain Resort, it has made Park City arguably the best little ski town in the country.

is always being tweaked. Freeriders choose from the open bowls of Silverado, tight glades of Escapade Woods, and buffed cruisers of Snow Canyon.

One innovation at the resort is a people mover called The Canyons Cabriolet, an open-air gondola that takes skiers from the parking area to the base village.

The ski school adheres to the American Skiing Company's Perfect Turn method, which builds on a skier's strengths. No tough love here. But the best instruction on the mountain comes from Holly Flanders, two-time Olympian and three-time World Cup champion, who directs acclaimed women's ski workshops.

The Canyons also shares Deer Valley and Park City Mountain Resort's best-known treasure: The colorful ski town of Park City is just five minutes away. Also nearby is the Utah Olympic Park, where you can slide down the track with a bobsled driver, ride a luge, or even take a crack at Nordic jumping. Other resort activities include snowmobiling, snowshoeing, sleigh rides, and hot-air balloon rides. The Canyons offers a fully licensed day-care center for toddlers eighteen months or older.

So what you have is an emerging giant of a resort with a huge playground of ridges and bowls and gullies and trees and, yes, canyons.

The Canyons
4000 The Canyons Resort Drive
Park City, Utah 84098

Phone: (435) 649–5400; (888) 226–9667

Web Site: www.thecanyons.com

E-mail: info@thecanyons.com

Elevation: Top—9,990 feet; base—6,800 feet

Vertical Drop: 3,190 feet

Total Area: 3,500 acres

Number of Trails: 140

Longest Run: 3 miles

Terrain: 14% beginner; 44% intermediate; 42% advanced/expert

Average Annual Snowfall: 355 inches

Lifts: 16

Snowmaking: 160 acres

Central Reservations: (888) 226–9667

Snow Report: (888) 226–9667

Accommodations: Luxury condos and a 4-star hotel at the base, with plenty of other choices in nearby Park City.

Getting There: The Canyons is 4 miles west of the town of Park City and less than an hour from Salt Lake City International Airport.

BEST BETS

Beginners: Exclusive beginner area near Red Pine Lodge.

Intermediates: Boa winds all the way down.

Advanced: The dense glades of Canis Lupis.

Experts: Steep chutes off the Ninety-Nine-90 Express.

Lunch: Lookout Cabin, at the top of the Lookout lift.

Off the Slopes: Main Street, Park City.

Best Hotel: The Grand Summit Resort Hotel.

DEER VALLEY RESORT

Park City, Utah

There was a time when die-hard Utah skiers called it Bambi Basin. They said it was graded as smooth as the Bonneville Salt Flats so the jewelry wouldn't fly off the wealthy. The trash talk played right into the hands of Deer Valley Resort, which is run like a luxury hotel.

When the resort opened in 1981, the ski bums who gave the sport a shot of growth hormone in the 1970s were becoming as out of fashion as the Prince of Wales. America's best ski areas didn't want athletes. They wanted skiers with money. And Deer Valley was no different. So they turned to Stein Eriksen, one of skiing's best-known golden boys, to bring in the rich and wealthy.

In return the Norwegian ski god, the very embodiment of skiing elegance, became director of skiing and namesake of the mountainside Stein Eriksen Lodge, arguably the best boutique hotel at a North American ski resort. In the Alpine Europe tradition, Deer Valley has a charming, Bogner-clad sportsman/hotelier zipping around the mountain in his legs-glued-together skiing style.

But it takes more than a 1952 Olympic gold and silver medalist to build an elite resort. Deer Valley had the deep pockets and clear vision of owner Edgar Stern, the grandson of a onetime chairman of Sears and Roebuck. Stern bought his own sugar-dusted piece of the Wasatch Mountains and carefully plucked the evergreens.

From day one, the resort carved a niche with the wealthy. It shamelessly pampered skiers and set the gold standard for luxury lodging, attentive guest service, on-mountain dining, and the silk carpet–like offerings from a flotilla of snow-grooming machines. And because it's privately owned land, unlike the USDA Forest Service land leased to most western ski areas, upscale condominiums and private residences dot the mountain.

Deer Valley's elegant lifestyle and big-mountain terrain ensnare you. Like the old line, "I've been rich and I've been poor, and rich is better," skiers discovered it was wonderful to be pampered. There are valets to help you carry your skis, and luxurious ski-in/ski-out accommodations. And you do see plenty of rich snowplowing Texans, their grins as broad as their Stetsons. But don't underestimate the quality of the skiing.

The skiing is played out on four different mountains. Bald Eagle Mountain offers plenty of novice and intermediate runs; Flagstaff Mountain is mostly intermediate; Bald Mountain is a cross of intermediate and expert terrain; and Empire Canyon offers steep chutes, powder-choked bowls, and glades of intermediate skiing. The secret to the tough stuff is an expert-only trail map that will lead you to hidden elevator shafts in the trees of Ontario Bowl, Sunset Glade, and the Black Forest.

Deer Valley is nouveau skiing at its best. Park City's upscale, country club–like neighbor even limits the number of daily skiers. The lifts can handle more, but Deer Valley frets that on a cold day, when everybody is inside lingering over lunch, it might crowd the crowds in the resort's award-worthy restaurants.

Deer Valley's indulgence in fine mountain restaurants has propelled dining here into an experience parallel with skiing. Other western resorts have followed with their own brands of high cuisine.

Over the years, as Deer Valley continued to raise the bar for skier amenities, it also refined its ski terrain. The resort constantly expands terrain and upgrades lifts. The classic fall lines are manicured like big

Sorry, dude. No snowboard-ing! Not at Park City's plush, five-star neighbor. Deer Valley is for the well heeled. It sets the gold standard for luxurious lodging, on-mountain dining, and velvety corduroy runs. You can ski the 2002 Winter Olympic Games slalom hill and mogul run and view the aerial jumping hill.

white sand traps. Each of Deer Valley's four mountains is served by high-speed lifts to let you rack up miles of vertical. And you'll feel like an Olympian doing it. Intermediates soar. Experts find plenty of steep pitches, far more than rumor suggests. A full one-third of all the runs are rated advanced/expert.

Most of the skiing is below tree line. Skiers frequently stick to the dreamlike groomed runs so that even days after a snowfall, you'll find untracked skiing in deserted glades of aspens and firs.

A mile above the Snow Park Lodge base area on Bald Eagle Mountain is Silver Lake Village, a self-contained development with a small shopping concourse and a cluster of upscale accommodations, including Stein Eriksen Lodge and the Goldener Hirsh, an elegant knockoff of the original in Salzburg, Austria.

If it's gnarly nightlife you're after, Park City's Main Street is just a mile away via a free shuttle.

Deer Valley Resort
P.O. Box 3149
Park City, Utah 84060
Phone: (435) 649–1000

Web Site: www.deervalley.com

E-mail: info@deervalley.com

Elevation: Top—9,570 feet; base—6,570 feet

Vertical Drop: 3,000 feet

Total Area: 1,750 acres

Number of Trails: 90

Longest Run: 2 miles

Terrain: 15% beginner; 50% intermediate; 35% advanced/expert

Average Annual Snowfall: 300 inches

Lifts: 21

Snowmaking: 500 acres

Central Reservations: (800) 558–3337

Snow Report: (435) 649–2000

Accommodations: There are hotels and condos at the base, as well as a wide selection of lodgings in Park City.

Getting There: The resort is tucked above Park City, less than an hour from Salt Lake City.

Keep in Mind: Snowboards are not permitted.

BEST BETS

Beginners: Success on Bald Eagle Mountain.

Intermediates: Stein's Way.

Advanced: Bald Mountain offers the most advanced terrain.

Experts: Mayflower chutes.

Lunch: Mariposa in the midmountain Silver Lake Lodge.

Off the Slopes: Main Street, Park City.

Best Hotel: Stein Eriksen Lodge at Deer Valley Resort.

PARK CITY MOUNTAIN RESORT
Park City, Utah

Park City Mountain Resort was the venue for both the men's and women's giant slalom races, and the snowboarding events at the 2002 Winter Olympic Games. What a perfect match for Park City's terrain. A few miles down the road, Utah Olympic Park was the site for the bobsled, luge, and ski-jumping competitions. And it's all only forty-five minutes from downtown Salt Lake City.

Park City, the hometown of the U.S. Ski Team, is one of the ultimate intermediate cruiser's mountains. Sure, there are plenty of gentle novice trails and more than a few steep sections to test your confidence, but for the most part the sprawling corduroy slopes are suited for skiers and boarders who like to stand like an athlete and enjoy the ride, coming down the mountain in powerful gulps and with incredible authority. Most of the runs slide off rounded mountain ridges and are separated by stands of forest.

Two high-speed, six-passenger chairlifts, one above the other, whisk skiers from the Resort Center to Summit House. From there, two lifts reach even higher up the mountain to the mostly black-diamond terrain found along a 3-mile ridge with four powder-chocked bowls, crowned by rocky, chute-filled Juniper Peak. The terrain increases significantly if you're willing to traverse and hike. But avoid all areas posted CLOSED in the avalanche-prone Wasatch Mountains.

More than anything else, however, Park City's fourteen lifts serve up great white rivers of groomed intermediate terrain. Most of the mountain's blue and green runs lie between midmountain and the base area. Beginners have a dedicated learning area near the base lodge and plenty of progressively steeper pitches to strive for, gradually working their way up to Summit House and the 3.5-mile-long easy way down.

Strolling the beautifully restored and developed old mining town of Park City is the major off-slope activity for visitors skiing Park City and the nearby resorts of Deer Valley and The Canyons. Except for one week in January, the town is Aspen without the fur coats, but the major attractions are similar—shops, restaurants, and bars along historic Main Street. The weeklong exception in January is during Robert Redford's Sundance Film Festival, when Park City plays host to Hollywood. Independent filmmakers, studio executives, and agents arrive with full entourages.

THE UTAH INTERCONNECT

An excellent intermediate-level backcountry guided tour from Park City to Snowbird is offered four days a week. The route connects six of the major ski resorts in Utah's Wasatch Mountains. After a warm-up run at Deer Valley, the two guides cross over to Park City Mountain Resort and down the back side of Jupiter Peak, skiing down a lovely wooded valley to the Solitude Mountain Resort. From there, you'll enjoy a nice powder run to Brighton Ski Resort. After a few runs in the Solitude-Brighton area and a hearty lunch, the tour heads over the top of Solitude and makes a thirty-minute traverse and hike up the aptly named Highway to Heaven. Now it's downhill to Alta Ski Area, up the lifts, and over to Snowbird Ski and Summer Resort. Five ski areas in one day.

The 2002 Olympics sparked a development boom of condominiums, restaurants, and shops. But to the town's credit, the newcomers blend into the mining-era charm.

In its original heyday Park City was one of America's largest silver-mining towns, boasting twenty-three millionaires by the late 1880s. During the 1930s and 1940s, when the price of silver dropped, it almost became a ghost town. Up on the ski slopes, a few old wooden mine buildings remain, and the resort offers tours of these relics, providing a nice sense of the history. Children love the tours. There also are signs describing the sites if you want to organize your own family treasure hunt.

Park City's terrain parks offer more than fifty rails, fun boxes, and jumps, attracting many of the best tricksters in the world. If you'd rather just ski hard, you can hook up with a posse of ripping skiers and boarders on free daily tours of the mountain's black-diamond areas.

Park City Mountain Resort
P.O. Box 39
Park City, Utah 84060

Phone: (800) 678–9915

Web Site: www.parkcitymountain.com

E-mail: info@parkcitymountain.com

Elevation: Top—10,000 feet; base—6,900 feet

Vertical Drop: 3,100 feet

Total Area: 3,300 acres

Number of Trails: 100

Longest Run: 3.5 miles

Terrain: 18% beginner; 44% intermediate; 38% advanced/expert

Average Annual Snowfall: 350 inches

Lifts: 14

Snowmaking: 500 acres

Central Reservations: (800) 222–7275

Snow Report: (800) 222–7275

Accommodations: Slopeside condos, hotels, and bed-and-breakfasts in town.

Getting There: It's 45 minutes from Salt Lake City.

Keep in Mind: Book early for holiday accommodations.

BEST BETS

Beginners: The 3.5-mile Home Run from Summit House.

Intermediates: Ski the King Kong chair.

Advanced: McConkey's chair.

Experts: Jupiter Bowl.

Lunch: Summit House Restaurant.

Off the Slopes: Main Street in Park City.

Best Hotel: Lodge at Mountain Village.

 This authentic turn-of-the-twentieth-century town at the base of a far-reaching mountain has more nightlife than all other Utah ski resorts combined. The breadth and diversity found on and off the slopes make it a popular destination for families. Plus, it has slopes fit for Olympians.

SNOWBIRD SKI AND SUMMER RESORT

Snowbird, Utah

Even before it opened in December 1971, Snowbird had acquired a reputation for challenging slopes and outstanding powder, thanks to Alta Ski Area, its Little Cottonwood Canyon neighbor. Serious skiers had been flocking to Alta for more than thirty years, riding the canyon's heaven-sent powder and elevator-shaft terrain. You'd have to have been snow-blind driving to Alta if you didn't notice the future Snowbird's 11,000-foot Hidden Peak with its outrageous fall lines.

It certainly caught the eye of entrepreneur and mountain lover Dick Bass. The onetime climber of Mount Everest constructed a 125-passenger aerial tram to climb Hidden Peak's 3,000 vertical feet in eight minutes. He anchored it with an upscale, ten-story lodge and named the place Snowbird. The rest, as they say, is history.

The vastness of Snowbird's smorgasbord of terrain, with its golden summits and black, ribbed-rock cliffs, is reminiscent of the Swiss Alps. The resort ranks high on the list of the most challenging lift-serviced mountains in the world. It is a monument to the joys and struggles and freedom of skiing and boarding. From the top of the tram, it's just you, the mountain, and the pull of gravity.

Snowbird's diverse and humbling terrain is a mélange of snow-stuffed bowls, chutes, couloirs, and cirques.

But Snowbird's reputation as a black-diamond mountain has been softened in the last few years by back-side expansion into the intermediate terrain of Mineral Basin. Its high-speed quad chairlift has one of the steepest ascents in North America,

but the terrain suits intermediate skiers and freeriders who enjoy deep snow and wide-open, cruise-anywhere terrain. Its southern exposure on the lee side of the mountain even takes the nip out of winter air. On days of powder chop, you can kill all 1,400 vertical feet in three big giant-slalom turns.

The back-side expansion also connects Snowbird to the storied Alta resort. A common lift ticket is available. The result is the third largest ski acreage in the country and one of the biggest concentrations of expert terrain. It's not a merger but a meeting of giants.

On Snowbird's front side, riding the tram offers an up-close view of some of the longest and steepest black-diamond runs in the country. It's local sport to try to beat the tram back down. First, you drop into one of the ultrasteep chutes cascading off the Upper Cirque. Then, about a third of the way down the mountain, you choose your line from a handful of steep, tree-lined runs that drop all the way to the mountain's base. That's more than 3,000 vertical feet, which the tram covers in eight minutes. At Snowbird, it's easy to rack up more vertical than is possible on a hard day of heli-skiing.

 Challenging terrain and 500 inches of annual snowfall are why serious skiers come to Snowbird. The resort backs up Utah's claim to "the greatest snow on earth." Plus, there is no major ski resort in the world as easily accessed from an international airport. Fly in and ski or snowboard the afternoon away.

It's also possible to find easier ways down. To the left of the tram going up, where Snowbird's boundary butts against Alta Ski Area, the skiing and boarding are a little easier on the blue bowl of Peruvian Gulch. But be warned: Snowbird has raised the bar for what is commonly pegged a blue run. Most would be labeled black at any other resort. This is particularly so on the right side of the mountain, where blue-black runs follow the Little Cloud lift. The best bet for true intermediates is the high-speed Gadzoom quad, which stretches from the base to two-thirds of the way up the mountain. You can buy a less expensive chair-only lift ticket and avoid the tram altogether.

Beginners find only about half a dozen runs suited to their skills, which cluster low down on the Gad Valley side. Snowbird is a serious skier's and boarder's mountain, and there's no way to pretend your way around it.

Snowbird also serves up multiple terrain parks and a massive superpipe.

But there are alternatives to skiing. The Cliff Lodge at the mountain's base offers plenty of creature comforts, including one of the best spas in ski country. There's also ice skating, snowshoeing, and a family tubing hill. Lodge guests soak up the scenery in an open-air rooftop swimming pool, whirlpool, and sundeck.

Still, the emphasis is on good, hard skiing with deep powder, rugged terrain, and spectacular scenery.

Snowbird Ski and Summer Resort
P.O. Box 929000
Snowbird, Utah 84092

Phone: (801) 933–2222

Web Site: www.snowbird.com

E-mail: info@snowbird.com

Elevation: Top—11,000 feet; base—7,760 feet

Vertical Drop: 3,240 feet

Total Area: 2,500 acres

Number of Trails: 85

Longest Run: 3.5 miles

Terrain: 27% beginner; 38% intermediate; 35% advanced/expert

Average Annual Snowfall: 500 inches

Lifts: 11

Snowmaking: 200 acres

Central Reservations: (800) 232–9542

Snow Report: (801) 933–2100

Accommodations: Lodging at the base is limited to one hotel and three condominium buildings. Salt Lake City is 45 minutes away.

Getting There: Snowbird is 29 miles from Salt Lake City International Airport.

Keep in Mind: Very little beginner terrain and limited nightlife.

BEST BETS

Beginners: Lupine Loop in Mineral Basin and Big Emma from the Mid-Gad station.

Intermediates: Chip's Run, the only real top-to-bottom blue run off the tram.

Advanced: Silver Fox on the front side or any line you choose in Mineral Basin.

Experts: Upper Great Scott or Gad Chutes and North Face.

Lunch: Lodge Bistro.

Off the Slopes: Salt Lake City.

Best Hotel: The Cliff Lodge.

SOLITUDE MOUNTAIN RESORT
Solitude, Utah

Big Cottonwood Canyon with its two ski areas, Brighton and Solitude, has long been a favorite destination for Salt Lake City day skiers. It remains so today, even though Solitude Mountain Resort drastically changed the neighborhood. Over the past few years, the owners have built an elegant European-style village at the base of the magnificent, snow-covered mountain, making it a worthy destination resort. But lift lines are still rare, and the value for dollar spent remains high.

Only a forty-five-minute drive from downtown Salt Lake, Solitude is tucked into the magnificent folds of Big Cottonwood Canyon in the Wasatch Range of Utah's Rocky Mountains. Winter storms dump 500 inches of snow: That's more than 41 feet of Utah powder on a mountain that has won awards for its trail and lift system. The 2002 Winter Olympics wanted the giant slalom run on Solitude, but environmental concerns kept events from being held in Big Cottonwood Canyon.

Solitude offers skiers and boarders spacious bowls, uncrowded trails, tight glades, and steep chutes. And you can ski all 2,000 vertical feet from top to bottom nonstop. You'll also find 400 acres of backcountry-type terrain in Honeycomb Canyon on the area's back side, where a cat track winds you back to the lifts. The track is quite flat, but doable on a snowboard. With no immediate lift back to the top of Honeycomb, the snow stays fresh for days.

Solitude's front side is a wide face swathed by a variety of runs that include everything from bumps to buffed, wide boulevards straight down the fall line. Farther up the mountain, challenging terrain takes over, with cliffs, tight glades, and steep, rock-lined chutes. And if you want to get into Utah's backcountry powder, the resort offers Back Tracks, a guided backcountry tour for groups of up to ten advanced skiers and snowboarders.

Grooming is taken as seriously as at larger resorts. State-of-the-art machinery ensures that 50 percent of the mountain is groomed nightly on a rotating basis, including the steep terrain.

A new base lodge and a high-speed quad servicing the Moonbeam area opened for the 2005 to 2006 ski season.

Families appreciate the value, lack of crowds, and finely groomed trails. Kids ages four to twelve can enroll in the Moonbeam Ski and Snowboard Academy, offering all-day programs that include lunch. You can even ride a city bus from Salt Lake to the chairlift.

Solitude offers a European-style, ski-in/ski-out village. It remains small and intimate with a luxury hotel and 250 condominium units providing 560 beds and about thirty retail spaces.

The resort is home to Utah's oldest cross-country ski center, with more than 12 miles of spectacular scenery. One popular adventure that has become a Solitude tradition is a guided cross-country ski or snowshoe walk under the stars to a secluded five-course gourmet dinner at the Yurt, a Mongolian-style hut perched in the mountain wilderness.

Farther up Big Cottonwood Canyon, where the valley spreads out to a mile in width, you'll find Brighton Ski Resort, another big mountain with a loyal local following. But unlike Solitude, Brighton has made no attempt to keep up with the Deer Valleys and Snowbirds of Utah. Across a mountain range from Big Cottonwood Canyon are the three ski resorts hunkered

"Solitude." The name fits. You won't be struggling with crowds at this terrain-packed hideaway tucked high in Utah's Big Cottonwood Canyon. This is a small resort but a big mountain, with enough annual snowfall to make most of the best ski resorts in the world envious.

around Park City—Deer Valley, Park City Mountain Resort, and The Canyons. In the opposite direction is Little Cottonwood Canyon and the resorts of Alta and Snowbird. From high up the slopes of Solitude, you can see the top of Jupiter Peak at Park City Mountain Resort and a glimpse of the tram at Snowbird. You're in the midst of the best skiing in the state of Utah.

And beneath you are uncrowded, spacious runs on great snow. Together with the magnificent views, they are the essence of the Solitude experience.

**Solitude Mountain Resort
1200 Big Cottonwood Canyon
Solitude, Utah 84121**

Phone: (801) 534–1400

Web Site: www.skisolitude.com

E-mail: info@skisolitude.com

Elevation: Top—10,035 feet; base—7,988 feet

Vertical Drop: 2,047 feet

Total Area: 1,200 acres

Number of Trails: 63

Longest Run: 3.5 miles

Terrain: 20% beginner; 50% intermediate; 30% advanced/expert

Average Annual Snowfall: 500 inches

Lifts: 8

Snowmaking: 120 acres

Central Reservations: (800) 748–4754

Snow Report: (801) 536–5777

Accommodations: A slopeside European-style village with a luxury hotel and condos.

Getting There: Solitude is in Big Cottonwood Canyon, 28 miles from Salt Lake City.

Keep in Mind: Very little nightlife in the canyon.

BEST BETS

Beginners: Moonbeam II chair.

Intermediates: The Powderhorn and Eagle Express lifts.

Advanced: Honeycomb Canyon on Solitude's back side.

Experts: The tight glades and steep rock-lined chutes off the Powderhorn lift.

Lunch: St. Bernard's at the Inn at Solitude.

Off the Slopes: You're just 28 miles from Salt Lake City.

Best Hotel: The Inn at Solitude.

JAY PEAK RESORT

Jay, Vermont

Jay Peak attracts snow in quantities that are common on the Continental Divide, not New England. It also touts some of the East's most difficult terrain. Other Vermont resort owners would swear off Ben & Jerry's ice cream for Jay's extraordinary snowfalls and steep mountain faces.

The resort is located on the northernmost high peaks of the Green Mountains. Its isolation near the Canadian border results in far fewer skiers than the other big New England resorts that are farther south and closer to the East Coast's major population centers.

For the most part, the trails at Jay Peak challenge experts and adventurous intermediates, particularly in the woods, where the resort has mapped a network of twenty-four glades for skiers and boarders to slalom through.

In the late 1980s the resort hired Sel Hannah, one of the East's legendary mountain designers, to shape access routes into the trees and do some environmentally sensitive pruning because advanced skiers were repeatedly abandoning the groomed boulevards and heading into the glades. The project continued into the 1990s, and Jay soon touted the best

Vermont's only cable car climbs to 3,861 feet, offering views that encompass four states and a stretch of Canada. But Jay Peak is best known for its bounty of annual snowfall. Locals credit the big dumps to "the Jay Cloud," and the resort claims more annual snowfall than any other ski area in New England or eastern Canada.

glade skiing in the East. In recent years they've opened up with even more tree skiing. But powder hounds and lovers of springtime corn snow continue to push the boundaries, looking for more stashes of untracked lines on steep faces deeper into the woods.

Eventually, Jay Peak gave up on trying to hold adventurous skiers and boarders back with ski-boundary ropes and signs. The trail map now states: "Woods are not open, closed or marked." You can interpret that any way you like. But if you choose to ski out of bounds, you'd better know what you're doing and ride with trusty companions. Nobody is looking out for you.

Back in the resort's patrolled areas, intermediate skiers and boarders find buttery smooth slopes down classic New England fall lines that follow the rolls and ridges of the mountain. Beginners are the only ones who get shortchanged at Jay. There are few green runs, except for short pitches served mostly by T-bars.

In all, there are seventy-six well-maintained trails. The vast majority are ideally pitched for carvers. There's also a progression of several good bump runs where you can build on your confidence. And with an annual snowfall of 350 inches, you can expect a lot of powder days. You'll find terrain parks and pipes, too.

The skiing and riding at Jay are high energy, but the nightlife is low watt. For most visitors, a Jacuzzi and a few bottles of high-octane Canadian beer are as wild as it gets. The base area is a cluster of nondescript condos anchored by the aging Hotel Jay. A new upscale village continues to evolve, and things are starting to heat up beneath the snowbound mountain. Soon you won't recognize the place.

The nearest real town is Montgomery, a rural hideaway tucked into the shadow of Jay Peak's south side, twenty minutes away. But it's no metropolis. This is the most rural area of Vermont. Nonetheless, Montgomery does have several good restaurants and inns, including the Black Lantern Inn, a restored 1803 stagecoach stop listed on the National Historic Register.

Off-slope activities include ice skating, snowmobile rides, snowshoeing, and sleigh rides.

Jay Peak was established by a local chapter of the Kiwanis Club in 1957 with the aim of jump-starting the local economy. They surveyed the region's strongest assets and kept coming up with mountains and snow. At the same time, Vermont's southern ski resorts were starting to attract outsiders, so community leaders decided a ski area on Jay Peak was a natural. They were right.

Jay Peak might be hard to get to, but so are most great places.

Jay Peak Resort
4850 Vermont Route 242
Jay, Vermont 05859

Phone: (800) 451–4449

Web Site: www.jaypeakresort.com

E-mail: info@jaypeakresort.com

Elevation: Top—3,861 feet; base—1,815 feet

Vertical Drop: 2,153 feet

Total Area: 385 acres

Number of Trails: 76

Longest Run: 3 miles (Ullr's Dream)

Terrain: 20% beginner; 40% intermediate; 40% advanced/expert

Average Annual Snowfall: 350 inches

Lifts: 8

Snowmaking: 300 acres

Central Reservations: (800) 451–4449

Snow Report: (802) 988–9601

Accommodations: Slopeside accommodations at the base, including a full-service hotel and several clusters of condos.

Getting There: Located on Route 242. New York is 6½ hours away; Boston, 3½ hours. The closest airports are Burlington, Vermont, and Montreal, Quebec, both 1½ hours away.

Keep in Mind: There is little nightlife.

BEST BETS

Beginners: Interstate.

Intermediates: Ullr's Dream.

Advanced: Can-Am Super Trail.

Experts: River Quai and Green Beret.

Lunch: Hotel Jay.

Off the Slopes: Cross the border to Mansonville, Quebec, and dine at La Vieille Buche Restaurant.

Best Hotel: At Jay Peak, the Hotel Jay. In Montgomery Village, the Black Lantern Inn.

KILLINGTON RESORT

Killington, Vermont

With thirty-three chairlifts—two of them are heated express gondolas and one is 2.5 miles long—Killington Resort boasts the largest lift network in the East. All that lift power is necessary to cover Killington's vast ski terrain, which is spread over an interconnected range of sugar-dusted mountains and offers a solid mix of runs and near-perfect snowmaking and grooming.

Killington is a megaresort showcasing the heart of Vermont's beautiful Green Mountains. The mix of mountain-to-mountain terrain and 90 miles of runs twisting down with drunken abandon keeps everyone happy for days on end. There are gentle trails, boulevard-like cruisers, in-your-face steeps, and kamikaze shots through tight stands of trees. The seven mountains—Rams Head, Snowdon Mountain, Killington Peak, Skye Peak, Bear Mountain, Sunrise Mountain, plus unconnected Pico Mountain—extend 11 miles border to border and face all points of the compass. There are six base areas and six high-speed quads bound for their respective summits. With a 3,000-foot vertical drop, the area resembles many western resorts. Especially the endlessly scenic 6-mile-long Juggernaut trail off Killington Peak.

Killington Peak is Vermont's second highest and offers the state's highest lift-served skiing.

Because of its gargantuan size, it's easy to get lost and miss some of the best skiing at the "Beast of the East." First-timers might want to join one of the free meet-the-mountain tours for a quick orientation. Each mountain has its own strengths. Bear Mountain, for example, has outlandishly steep terrain. Especially infamous is a mogul run called Outer Limits.

Beginner trails gently swoop down from all seven mogul-shaped mountains, so novice skiers and snowboarders get to enjoy the same sweeping vistas and the thrill of banking like bobsledders from the summits. Killington touts family skiing with innovations such as Rams Head, an entire mountain and base area dedicated to the needs of families who want to ski together.

Intermediate runs are boundless at Killington, and they're either manicured or moguled to perfection. Snow-making is an art here. Skiers are on the slopes when the surrounding farmland is dry as a bone. About 60 miles of skiable runs can be opened solely on the power of belching snow guns and the largest grooming fleet in the East. As a result, the ski season often runs from mid-October to June.

Killington has five terrain parks, four at the main area and one at adjacent Pico Mountain. The 430-foot-long halfpipe and its towering 17-foot walls snake down Highline trail.

With its proximity to major eastern cities, Killington has a well-founded reputation for the proficiency of its ski and snowboard school. Part of this school's success with beginners is due to a dedicated area called Snowshed that is set aside as learning terrain. It has its own lifts, including a high-speed quad and a surface lift. Like all areas owned by American Skiing Resorts, Killington's instructors adhere to Perfect Turn, a teaching method that focuses on students' strengths rather than emphasizing their errors.

The après-ski scene is lively. Although Killington lacks a town center, the main entrance to the resort, Access Road, is a 7-mile-long gauntlet of bars and clubs and shops. This strip is one of the liveliest in ski country, and nationally known bands often

Central Vermont's Killington Resort defines eastern skiing, both in the variety and the vastness of its terrain. With 200 manicured trails zigzagging over seven mountains, and one of the longest seasons anywhere, Killington Resort is known as the "Beast of the East."

energize it. Two of the dance halls offering live music—the Pickle Barrel and the Wobbly Barn Steakhouse—are Killington institutions.

Back on the mountain, Killington has the feel of a resort coming to grips with its own maturity. It offers child care, teen programs, and family-friendly lodging. Nonski activities include snowtubing, snowshoeing, sleigh rides, ice skating, and dogsledding.

But more than anything, Killington Resort is about vast ski and snowboarding terrain—seven mountains' worth. Add the beauty of Vermont's Green Mountains, and this is a must-ski and -snowboard destination.

Killington Resort
4763 Killington Road
Killington, Vermont 05751

Phone: (800) 734–9435

Web Site: www.killington.com

E-mail: info@killington.com

Elevation: Top—4,241 feet; base—1,165 feet

Vertical Drop: 3,050 feet

Total Area: 1,209 acres

Number of Trails: 200

Longest Run: 10 miles

Terrain: 26% beginner; 36% intermediate; 38% advanced/expert

Average Annual Snowfall: 250 inches

Lifts: 33

Snowmaking: 770 acres

Central Reservations: (800) 621–6867

Snow Report: (800) 734–9435

Accommodations: Hundreds of choices among condos, lodges, chalets, and bed-and-breakfast inns close to the mountain.

Getting There: Killington is 5 hours from New York City. The resort's entrance is 11 miles from Rutland. Amtrak's Ethan Allen Express departs New York's Penn Station daily. Gateway airports in Burlington and Rutland.

Keep in Mind: They can get 15,000 skiers on a Saturday.

BEST BETS

Beginners: Juggernaut, the 6-mile ramble off Killington Peak.

Intermediates: Chute, underneath the Snowdon quad.

Advanced: Catwalk on Killington Peak.

Experts: Outer Limits on Bear Mountain.

Lunch: The Summit, Vermont's highest restaurant, atop Killington Peak.

Off the Slopes: There's plenty of nightlife in the Killington area.

Best Hotel: The Killington Grand at the base of the mountain.

MOUNT SNOW

West Dover, Vermont

Mount Snow burst on the New England ski scene in 1954 with seven trails, two chairlifts that went halfway up the mountain, and two rope tows. It wasn't the Alps. Then a heated outdoor pool was added. It still wasn't the Alps. But it was a little like Sun Valley. How could skiers from Boston and New York City resist?

At Mount Snow, the slopes tumble from a humpbacked mountain, falling in sectors according to degree of difficulty. Main Mountain is just what it says. It rises directly from the base area with heavenly intermediate runs twisting down classic trails rimmed by forest. North Face is also what you'd expect from its name. It's the steepest part of Mount Snow. On the opposite, sunny side is a sweet thing named Carinthia, which offers easy blues. So does its neighbor, Sunbrook.

Some beginners, and especially first-timers, will find easier going 2.5 miles away on the twin peaks of Haystack Mountain, although it is only open on weekends and holidays. The terrain is ideally pitched and there are fewer crowds. One area there, Witches Peak, has some steep runs.

The snow is always reliable thanks to blizzardlike snowmaking capabilities and golf-green grooming. The nearby rural communities are postcards, literally. The area has outstanding ski terrain and spectacular scenery—the qualities that make Vermont the best ski state in the East. And that's the problem.

The crowds can be horrendous on weekends and holidays. The resort attracts more than half a million skiers and boarders a year. Despite the hoards, however, it is both a well-run family resort and a great party resort. And remarkably, the nearby communities remain intact.

The mountain's vertical drop is a respectable 1,700 feet. Snowmaking covers the main slopes. Most of the runs are wide, fall-line let-'em-run trails. Mount Snow also is a terrific learning mountain. You can gradually raise the bar as you become more comfortable on increasingly difficult terrain. But there are plenty of trails that take no prisoners, too. And it wouldn't be eastern skiing without the occasional patch of boilerplate.

 Family friendly and close to major population centers makes for all play and no work at this popular resort. Mount Snow is a classic southern Vermont ski area with forest-rimmed fall lines made for carving. For eastern skiers, Mount Snow is a rite of passage. For snowboarders, it offers some of the best terrain parks in the East.

Snowboarding is big at Mount Snow. In 1992 the resort lured riders with the East's first terrain park. Today the resort claims the top-ranked terrain parks in the East. The largest park, Un Blanco Gulch, covers more than eight acres with boxes, rails, tables, hips, and more. But for some, its most appealing feature is its location in full view of the Canyon Express Quad chairlift.

A smaller park called Grommet offers scaled-down attractions for riders under twelve years of age.

American Skiing Company bought Mount Snow in 1996 and gave it a makeover. They added high-speed lifts, upgraded snowmaking capacity, and beefed up the trails and terrain parks. They also built one of their signature Grand Resort hotels, much like those at Steamboat in Colorado and The Canyons in Utah. (American Skiing Company's other resorts include Killington, Sugarbush, Jay Peak, Sunday River, Sugarloaf/USA, Heavenly, and Attitash Bear Peak.)

Snowboarders and skiers carve, skid, and fall on 145 runs that cover 48 miles spread across 771 acres.

Other than the Grand Resort Hotel and a cluster of condos, there's no village at the base. The nearest towns are West Dover and Wilmington on Route 100. They boast fine country inns, regional cuisine, and Vermont charm that flows as thick as the maple syrup.

Several nearby cross-country centers offer more than 60 miles of trails. Snowshoeing, sleigh rides, dogsledding, and spa treatments also are available in the valley.

Mount Snow Resort
12 Pisah Road
West Dover, Vermont 05356

Phone: (800) 245–7669

Web Site: www.mountsnow.com

E-mail: info@mountsnow.com

Elevation: Top—3,600 feet; base—1,900 feet

Vertical Drop: 1,700 feet

Total Area: 771 acres

Number of Trails: 145

Longest Run: 2.5 miles

Terrain: 16% beginner; 62% intermediate; 20% advanced; 2% expert

Average Annual Snowfall: 166 inches

Lifts: 23

Snowmaking: 360 acres

Central Reservations: (800) 498–0479

Snow Report: (802) 464–2151

Accommodations: Condos and lodges near the base, anchored by the ski in/ski-out Grand Summit Hotel. Several good bed-and-breakfast inns in West Dover and Wilmington.

Getting There: New York City is 4 hours away; Boston is 2½ hours. The nearest regional airport is Keene, New Hampshire.

Keep in Mind: Huge weekend crowds.

BEST BETS

Beginners: Deer Run.

Intermediates: Snowdance.

Advanced: Beartrap on Sunbrook.

Experts: Rip Cord on North Face.

Lunch: Harriman's at the Grand Summit.

Off the Slopes: The classic towns of West Dover and Wilmington.

Best Hotel: Grand Summit Resort Hotel.

STOWE MOUNTAIN RESORT

Stowe, Vermont

It's the very definition of quaint—a small, 200-year-old New England village with what might be the tallest steeple in Vermont, backed by the state's highest peak. And up the mountain road is one of the oldest and most distinguished ski resorts in the East.

Stowe Mountain Resort has some of the finest fall-line skiing west of the Rockies. It also has the original steeps that made Stowe such a daring place to ski when it opened more than sixty years ago. The resort's blue-blood lineage and vintage New England flavor give it a quality that is special, even for New England. But for skiers and snowboarders, its core appeal stems from the terrain.

Stowe is a skier's mountain with lots of variety. Its backcountry location means a whopping annual snowfall of 333 inches. And if nature fails, state-of-the-art snowmaking and grooming can turn blue ice to velvet overnight.

A quick, eight-passenger gondola whisks skiers high up on the shoulder of Mount Mansfield, Vermont's highest peak. The views stretch to Lake Champlain, the Adirondacks, the White Mountains, the Green Mountains, and Mont Royal in Quebec. Beneath you, 2,360 vertical feet of mostly fall-line skiing tumbles down awesome faces cut by ski runs and snow-clutching chutes. There also are

long, twisting blue cruisers and wraparound green runs. In total, Stowe delivers 39 miles of skiing and snowboarding on forty-eight trails sprawling across two mountains. Mansfield is big and challenging. The other mountain, the more diminutive and family-friendly Spruce Peak, touts broad sunny slopes for beginners and intermediates, as well as some of the best learning hills in the East.

Snowboarders find plenty of action on all kinds of natural terrain features. The consistent top-to-bottom pitch ranges from meandering meadows to hair-raising drops through tight forests. There are three terrain parks, plus a huge halfpipe.

Stowe challenges the best in anybody, especially those who ride its infamous elevator shaft–like Front Four, a quartet of supersteep slopes on the mountain's front face. These fabled double black diamonds—Goat, National, Liftline, and Starr—are renowned for their steep, craggy, and unforgiving skiing. They represent Stowe's signature terrain and remain historic, must-ski runs for experts.

Yet for all its heart-stopping steeps, Stowe has almost 60 percent intermediate terrain consisting of true, blue cruisers. And there are no run-outs, no boring traverses, no two-chair commutes to the summit. It's also possible to ski over to the nearby resort of Smugglers' Notch, even though the road between them is closed in winter.

Stowe might be North America's most historic ski town. It was here that American skiing undertook its century-long evolution from necessity to downhill pleasure. It's a vibrant community where the locals get up early and beat you to the powder and then get back in time to serve you breakfast. The town staged its first winter carnival in 1921. In 1933 the Civilian Conservation Corps cut

Two main peaks with long, narrow runs cutting into the forest make for a classic wild and winding New England ski experience. Stowe is renowned for its great steeps, boundless tree skiing, and bucolic charm. It is, perhaps, America's most romantic ski resort. The place has soul.

the first ski run. The winning formula came easy: Stowe offered fine lodging and dining, and the mountain provided challenges.

Two-hundred-year-old Stowe Village is classic Vermont, dominated by a white-steepled church and a historic Main Street against a ski-cut mountain backdrop. Many of its buildings are on the National Register of Historic Places. In the surrounding community, population 2,000, you'll find great lodging and dining. Surprisingly, there's no tony slopeside development at Stowe. At least not yet. A new base village is the evolving core of a $300 million, ten-year expansion.

The Trapp Family Lodge, America's first touring center, is a delightful European-style resort located along the rolling hills of the valley, a few scenic miles from Stowe Village. Along with the lodge and elegant spa, the resort offers more than 60 miles of cross-country ski trails winding through 2,700 acres of forest and grand mountain vistas. And yes, that's the von Trapp family of *The Sound of Music* fame. They came to America in 1939.

Traditions abound at Stowe. The April Sugar Slalom is one of the oldest ski races in the country. After racing down Nosedive, competitors slurp snow dipped in maple syrup at the finish area. Another spring happening is the nondenominational Easter sunrise service atop Mount Mansfield. The annual Stowe Winter Carnival runs the last week in January, featuring fun-in-the-snow competitions and a village block party.

But Stowe's key enticement is the resort's splendid ski and snowboarding terrain. Off the mountain, skiers find an enchanting town with an enduring classic look and feel that embraces winter and inspires its guests to do the same.

Stowe Mountain Resort
5781 Mountain Road
Stowe, Vermont 05672

Phone: (800) 253–4754

Web Site: www.stowe.com

E-mail: info@stowe.com

Elevation: Top—3,640 feet; base—1,280 feet

Vertical Drop: 2,360 feet

Total Area: 485 acres

Number of Trails: 48

Longest Run: 3.7 miles (Toll Road)

Terrain: 16% beginner; 59% intermediate; 25% advanced/expert

Average Annual Snowfall: 333 inches

Lifts: 12

Snowmaking: 350 acres

Central Reservations: (800) 253–4754

Snow Report: (802) 253–3600

Accommodations: A limited supply of slope-side hotel rooms and condos. A wide range of lodging in the surrounding area.

Getting There: Burlington International Airport is a 40-minute drive. I–89 (exit 10 to Route 100 north) and the Amtrak station are just 15 minutes away.

Keep in Mind: It can be cold.

BEST BETS

Beginners: Toll Road, more than 3 miles long.

Intermediates: Gulch on Mount Mansfield.

Advanced: The glades off Cliff trail.

Experts: The Front Four: National, Liftline, Starr, and Goat.

Lunch: Cliff House Restaurant.

Off the Slopes: Visit Stowe Village and historic Waterbury.

Best Hotel: The rambling 1833 Green Mountain Inn in the center of Stowe Village. Slopeside, the Inn at the Mountain.

STRATTON MOUNTAIN RESORT

Stratton Mountain, Vermont

Stratton was conceived as a resort community from the very beginning, which was outside-the-box thinking in 1960. No resort at that time combined skiing in winter with golf in summer. The lift-serviced skiing began at Christmas in 1961. The golf course opened a few years later. From early on, the resort was dubbed "Vermont's class act," even if it was mostly Austrian-kitsch architecture. It also broke ground with the first bona fide ski school for kids.

More than half of Stratton Mountain's ninety-one trails are tagged beginner or intermediate, and many of these are wide, groomed boulevards that foster Stratton's reputation as a cruiser's mountain. Even a beginner can ski down from the 3,875-foot summit. It's a one-mountain, four-area resort. Nothing is hidden, and it's easy to find your way around. There's even been some serious tree thinning to make it easier to slalom through ninety acres of nicely pitched glades.

Stratton hosts a high-end crowd attracted to its buffed slopes and pampering facilities. Many come here to feel good about their skiing. With its hero snow and ego-boosting terrain, intermediates can handle many of the black diamonds.

A quarter of the terrain is marked black diamond; six double-diamond trails are spread across the upper mountain, but the real steeps are found along Kidderbrook Ravine. Stratton's 2,000-vertical-foot drop puts it within the range of "big mountains," and a twelve-passenger high-speed gondola and four six-passenger chairlifts allow skiers to quickly rack up vertical. A computerized snowmaking system blankets 85 percent of the terrain.

At the base of the mountain, a beginners-only Ski Learning Park offers forty-five acres

of gentle terrain served by slow-moving ground lifts. The park utilizes specially made terrain features to help novices learn about steering, flexing, and edging.

Families flock to Stratton and its four-state view. It's their kind of skiing—manicured slopes with plenty of snowmaking and plenty of family-oriented programs. Many enjoy setting up day camp in the lovely seclusion of Sun Bowl with its friendly terrain. But the popularity of the resort is also partly due to its location in southern Vermont, which makes it easy to get to from Massachusetts, New York, New Jersey, and Connecticut.

Stratton has always been on the cutting edge of snowboarding. It was on Suntanner trail that local bartender Jake Burton Carpenter tested his prototypes under the cover of darkness. By 1983, snowboarders shared the mountain with skiers and Stratton launched the world's first snowboard school. Every March since 1985, Stratton Mountain has hosted the U.S. Open Snowboarding Championships, one of the biggest and rowdiest snowboarding events in the East. The mountain has five top-ranked terrain parks full of ever-changing hits, tabletops, spines, and rails. There's also a 400-foot-long halfpipe.

The base village is a hub of fine shops and restaurants lining pedestrian-only streets along the Village Square. The Austrian-like town has been experiencing a building boom in recent years. Intrawest is the parent company of Stratton Mountain Resort, and the place is a look-alike sibling to the brand that includes Whistler, Tremblant, and Copper Mountain.

Stratton's Nordic Center offers expertly manicured trails that wind over streams and through hardwood forests, offering jaw-dropping views. The resort also has a sports

One of the crown jewels of eastern skiing, and the birthplace of snowboarding, glitzy Stratton Mountain is the highest peak in southern Vermont's famed snowbelt. Its roots date back to the 1960s, when the community planned a resort so they'd "have something to do on Sunday." Novelist Pearl Buck was one of the original $500 investors.

center with indoor racquet sports and workout facilities. Other area activities include ice skating, snowtubing, sleigh rides, and cross-country tours to the Pearl Buck cabin. With Manchester nearby, nonskiers have plenty to do.

And there is music in these hills. The Stratton Mountain Boys originated with Stratton ski school founder Emo Henrich, who dreamed of bringing the music of Austria to the mountains of Vermont. On some days homegrown Austrian instructors sing in the base lodge.

Stratton Mountain Resort
R.R. 1, Box 145
Stratton Mountain, Vermont 05155

Phone: (800) 787–2886

Web Site: www.stratton.com

E-mail: infostratton@intrawest.com

Elevation: Top—3,875 feet; base—1,872 feet

Vertical Drop: 2,003 feet

Total Area: 583 acres

Number of Trails: 91

Longest Run: 3 miles

Terrain: 42% beginner; 31% intermediate; 27% advanced/expert

Average Annual Snowfall: 180 inches

Lifts: 16

Snowmaking: 400 acres

Central Reservations: (800) 772–8866

Snow Report: (802) 297–4211

Accommodations: Plenty of condos and a few good hotels at the resort. Manchester is just 30 minutes away.

Getting There: Manchester is the nearest airport. The Albany airport in New York is 1½ hours away.

Keep in Mind: Crowds on weekends and not a lot of expert terrain.

BEST BETS

Beginners: Middlebrook and Churchill Downs on Sun Bowl.

Intermediates: The Drifter trio in Snow Bowl.

Advanced: Upper Middlebrook.

Experts: World Cup.

Lunch: The Roost, in the base lodge.

Off the Slopes: Explore Manchester.

Best Hotel: Stratton Village Lodge.

SUGARBUSH RESORT

Warren, Vermont

This is as picturesque as skiing gets in Vermont. No malls, no fast food, no stoplights. Bucolic Mad River Valley, home to storied Sugarbush Resort and the infamous Mad River Glen ski area, is the last bastion of major old-time skiing. In this part of Vermont, residents live well on the ski economy, minus much hustle and bustle. The locals say the valley has funk and soul, and they believe in such things.

Sugarbush is vast, with a varied mix of trails that make it a good choice for groups with mixed levels of skiers. Its 111 trails, usually uncrowded, span six mountain areas. Strategically placed high-speed lifts make it easy to get around the ski area.

The storybook village setting and rural surroundings are part of the charm. Vistas include clapboard Yankee church steeples backdropped by steep, snowy slopes. It looks like a farming community. Near Sugarbush are the lovely towns of Waitsfield and Warren, rustic New England gems that appear to have changed little in a century. In actuality, Mad River Valley's natural attractions have largely replaced logging and dairy farming as the local industry. The views are worth more than the milk.

The valley's first ski area was quirky Mad River Glen, built in 1948 by a former Stowe investor. His plan was to create an area that would rival the tough slopes of the West, and he succeeded. It's a respected little area with a single-person chairlift to the summit that almost dares you to ski it. So do bumper stickers, which read: SKI MAD RIVER GLEN IF YOU CAN. The resort lives in the 1960s and does not allow snowboarding. Overnight guests at Sugarbush get lift tickets interchangeable between Sugarbush and Mad River Glen.

Ten years after Mad River, Sugarbush opened with gentler terrain and immediately achieved destination status. It quickly gained the nickname "Mascara Mountain"—a reference to the large number of movie stars and politicians, including the Kennedy clan, who came to revel in the skiing.

The area is wildly scenic. From the 3,975-foot summit of Lincoln Peak, you can view shimmering Lake Champlain, plus the Adirondacks of New York and the White Mountains of New Hampshire. A spectacular aerial tram spans the valley between North Lynx Peak on the shoulder of Castlerock Peak and Mount Ellen, commonly called Sugarbush North.

 It doesn't get much more New England than Sugarbush in central Vermont. The towns and surrounding rural landscape haven't changed that much in a century. The resort epitomizes big, varied, and picturesque eastern skiing played out on six mountains. Down-home Mad River Glen lingers next door like a throwback to the ski resorts of the 1950s.

The landscape is on an epic scale, too. The six-mountain area delivers a smorgasbord of varied terrain, including slopes that carry you along at your own comfort level or confront you with testy, in-your-face runs that demand more than you can give. Sugarbush snow crews make heaps of snow and can blanket the mountain in white from top to bottom.

The resort has a great reputation for easy slopes, and many eastern skiers learned the sport under blue Vermont skies. But Sugarbush also is stacked with loads of intermediate cruisers and terrifying expert terrain, ranging from the big bumps of Stein's at the south end to Upper FIS at the north end. Modern high-speed lifts quickly move skiers around the mountain.

One throwback to earlier years is Castlerock, with its signature narrow wrap-around-the-forest trails. Plans to modernize the lift, broaden the ski trails of the Castlerock area, and add snowmaking have always been met with protests from Sugarbush regulars, a band of old-school renegades who prefer narrow, steep faces with rock outcrops and the cover of natural snow. Skiing "the Rock's" 2,000 vertical feet carries a lot of nostalgia value in a place that values good skiing. It's a reminder of tougher days on the mountains. A few years ago, as a compromise, Sugarbush replaced the old Castlerock chairlift with a new model of the old one. One does not spit in church.

Other activities in the Mad River Valley include snowshoeing, sledding on a Mad River Rocket, horse-drawn sleigh rides, ice skating, and cross-country skiing. Sugarbush offers a popular outdoor instructional program called Perfect Kids. Day care is available.

Sugarbush Resort
1840 Sugarbush Access Road
Warren, Vermont 05674

Phone: (800) 537–8427

Web Site: www.sugarbush.com

E-mail: info@sugarbush.com

Elevation: Top—4,083 feet; base—1,483 feet

Vertical Drop: 2,600 feet

Total Area: 508 acres

Number of Trails: 111

Longest Run: 2.5 miles

Terrain: 22% beginner; 46% intermediate; 32% advanced/expert

Average Annual Snowfall: 262 inches

Lifts: 16

Snowmaking: 286 acres

Central Reservations: (800) 537–8427

Snow Report: (802) 583–7669

Accommodations: Luxurious slopeside town houses and condos. Also a wide range of inns, lodges, and condos in the valley.

Getting There: Sugarbush is 3½ hours from Boston, 5½ hours from New York City. Burlington International Airport is 45 minutes away.

Keep in Mind: Nightlife is limited.

BEST BETS

Beginners: Easy Rider and Push Over.

Intermediates: Jester and Downspout.

Advanced: Paradise and Organ Grinder.

Experts: Rumble on Castlerock.

Lunch: Chez Henri, across the covered walking bridge from the base area.

Off the Slopes: Explore Waitsfield and Warren.

Best Hotel: The Sugarbush Inn.

CRYSTAL MOUNTAIN
Crystal Mountain, Washington

Ever since 1998, when Boyne USA bought this big-mountain day area located ninety minutes from Seattle, Crystal Mountain has been experiencing a growth spurt. Every season brings something new.

But the skiing remains as dramatic as ever. It changes over the course of the winter as the heavy Northwest snows accumulate, giving the mountain the physique of a middle-aged, potbellied man. For the most part, Crystal Mountain is for advanced skiers. Its dramatic setting next to Mount Rainier gives it a real alpine feel, and the resort is both big enough—and small enough—to unravel in complexity over a day or two of skiing. No wonder Seattle has kept it a secret.

Crystal opened in 1962 and burst upon the world stage in 1965, when the little-known ski area hosted the National Alpine Championships and drew big names from the racing world, including up-and-coming French star Jean-Claude Killy, as well as Americans Billy Kidd and Jimmie Heuga.

Boyne USA, which owns a handful of other ski resorts, including Big Sky in Montana, made a commitment to invest heavily in Crystal Mountain. Immediately the company added high-speed lifts and spruced up the base facilities, finally giving the state of Washington a destination resort worthy of the extraordinary Coast Mountains. The area is scenic enough that the legendary Pacific Crest Trail, a popular summertime hiking route that runs from Canada to Mexico, crosses the ski runs.

Outstanding stashes of terrain are sprinkled throughout the resort's 2,300 acres of steep basins and bowls. It's an expert skier's dream. Cliffs and chutes tumble down the 3,100-vertical-foot face. Next door, Mount Rainier towers in a world

of white and rock more than a mile high above skiers. The high volcanic massif catches most of the heavy snow coming off Pacific storms. Crystal Mountain is on the leeward side, often getting light, dry snow that has drifted high over Rainier's snow trap.

Crystal is one of the best mountains in the West for challenging terrain. You'll find every conceivable type of advanced terrain—from moguls to crud to big air. But you'll also find lengthy cruisers and good beginner terrain. The ski area includes 1,000 acres of in-bounds backcountry skiing with its own world of glades, chutes, and powder bowls. Most of it requires some hiking to access the best lines, but it's worth the additional effort.

From the Summit House (Washington State's highest restaurant), there are several intermediate runs heading down the face bound for the base. The longest ride is Green Valley, which connects with Kelly's Gap Road to the base area. Expect talclike snow groomed to perfection on the main runs.

At the base, the Chinook Express lift is beginner territory. But try to work your way up to Queens, a nicely sloped 3.5-mile beginner run that democratizes the unbelievable vistas from high up on the mountain.

 The sprawling expanse of the ski terrain flows over half a dozen peaks and basins and lends itself to seemingly limitless variations. Its mountaineer's view of neighboring Mount Rainier, which towers overhead by more than a country mile, is as breathtaking to view as Crystal Mountain is to ski.

Snowboarders can shred anywhere on the mountain. There's also dedicated riding terrain under the Quicksilver lift that features jumps, slides, and a halfpipe. Most of the mountain's natural terrain rides like it's custom-made for boarders. Campbell Basin is particularly popular because of numerous drop-offs and natural hits. The mountain rewards skiers with all sorts of topographical pleasures.

Crystal offers more than 1,000 acres of easily accessed backcountry skiing when safe snow conditions permit. The South Backcountry area is reached from the High Campbell chair. Within a half-hour hike are steep couloirs sheltered by cliffs where the snow stays cold and fluffy. Pinball, a 50-degree chute off the top of King Peak, is one of the popular named routes. The North Backcountry, accessible from the Rainier Express lift and the Green Valley chair, offers deep-powder glade skiing for days after the snowstorms pass. At the bottom of the powder run, a regularly scheduled shuttle bus takes skiers back to the base area.

Skiers seeking help getting in and out of the steep and deep might want to consider the instructional Steep Skiing Camp offered at Crystal. The camps include three days of coaching and video analysis while exploring the mountain's most challenging terrain.

There are a handful of shops, hotels, and condominiums slopeside at the mountain's base. Nightlife is pretty much what you can make it in the handful of Crystal Mountain bars.

Crystal Mountain
33914 Crystal Mountain Boulevard
Crystal Mountain, Washington 98022

Phone: (360) 663–2265

Web Site: www.skicrystal.com

E-mail: comments@skicrystal.com

Elevation: Top—7,012 feet; base—4,400 feet

Vertical Drop: 3,100 feet

Total Area: 2,300 acres

Number of Trails: 50

Longest Run: 2.5 miles (Northway)

Terrain: 13% beginner; 57% intermediate; 30% advanced/expert

Average Annual Snowfall: 380 inches

Lifts: 10

Snowmaking: 35 acres

Central Reservations: (888) 754–6400

Snow Report: (888) 754–6199

Accommodations: There's a sprinkling of slopeside chalets and condos.

Getting There: Crystal Mountain is 76 miles from Seattle.

Keep in Mind: Potential for wet Pacific weather.

BEST BETS

Beginners: Queens.

Intermediates: Green Valley.

Advanced: Powder Bowl off High Campbell chair.

Experts: The Silver King.

Lunch: Crystal Summit House.

Off the Slopes: Very little nightlife.

Best Hotel: Crystal Mountain Lodging Suites.

JACKSON HOLE MOUNTAIN RESORT

Teton Village, Wyoming

Board the candy-apple-red aerial tram beneath the crisp blue dome of the Wyoming sky and twelve minutes later the greatest continuous vertical rise of all American ski resorts is at your feet. There is no need to traverse or skate long cat tracks: It's all straight downhill. Jackson Hole might have the best lift-serviced expert terrain in the country.

Close by the top tram portal is Corbet's Couloir, a narrow, rocky passage that requires a 5- to 20-foot leap of faith into a steep 50-degree chute. It's no place for the timid. Another option from the tram is to ski down Rendezvous Bowl, a steeply pitched paradise of snow that is either untracked or tracked-up crud. The bowls are perfectly pitched and make up a single, wide wall of the Teton Range.

Getting to know the Jackson Hole ski area by flying down chutes, dodging rock outcroppings, skipping along mogul fields, and threading through trees is a rite of passage for adventurous skiers. It can be a long and sometimes painful experience. Half the mountain is labeled single or double black diamond. And then there's the tempting

The mountain statistics are staggering. Consider the vertical drop—4,139 feet; or its sheer size—2,500 acres. But the numbers don't say that the vertical is continuous. Nor do they take in the acres and acres of Euro-style backcountry. And the rating of 50 percent expert terrain gives no hint of the perfectly groomed boulevards that skirt the chutes and cliffs.

backcountry, one of the largest, most easily accessible in the country. The mountain's policy of not roping off the backcountry exposes another 3,000 wild acres for experienced skiers equipped with avalanche transceivers, probes, and shovels. Upon leaving the ski-patrolled resort, signs bluntly state: CAUTION YOU ARE LEAVING THE JACKSON HOLE SKI AREA BOUNDARY—THIS IS YOUR DECISION POINT.

To help adventurers make the right choice, Jackson is unique among U.S. ski resorts in that it has a European-style, resort-based system of guides to accompany skiers in the unroped areas beyond the accordioned ridges of the resort.

Jackson Hole Mountain Resort has earned its reputation as one of the most challenging mountains on the continent. Bring your A game. It's also a place where the vastness and variety of the skiing combine with the wildness and beauty of the surroundings to inspire skiers and boarders to accept new challenges. The inspiration is everywhere.

Looming immediately to the north of the resort and rising from the valley floor are the Alps-like peaks of Grand Teton National Park. Farther to the north lies Yellowstone National Park, where you can cross-country ski past bison, elk, and the park's signature multihued geothermal pools and erupting geysers. The ski area is also on the edge of Bridger-Teton National Forest, one of the largest wilderness areas in the country and headwaters of the Snake, Yellowstone, and Green Rivers.

Named for an early fur trapper, the town is called Jackson; Jackson Hole is the name of the entire valley, which starts at the south entrance of Yellowstone National Park and runs 60 miles south through Grand Teton National Park to Jackson. The ski resort rises from Teton Village, 12 miles north of Jackson.

The skiing and snowboarding take place on two adjoining mountains, steep-faced Rendezvous and baby-faced Apres Vous. Most of the tough stuff is separate from the easier runs. Intermediates find plenty of ballroom-smooth slopes. Beginners have an entire fenced-in learning area called Fort Wyoming at the base of Apres Vous served by a moving-carpet lift. Once they get their legs, they're ready for Apres Vous. But there may not be enough beginner terrain to keep novices content. Snowboarders get a halfpipe on Apres Vous and fine freeriding terrain like the natural pipe on Upper Dick's Ditch.

But more than anything, hard-core snowriders come to test their mettle against the likes of high, windblown Rendezvous Bowl, the Hobacks, and, at least once, Corbet's Couloir. The dazzling sight of the jagged Teton peaks, the delicate early-morning frost on cottonwood trees, and the sunlit mist hanging over the Snake River convey a sense of an American wilderness as fresh as anything the early fur trappers laid eyes on. Even the air, bone-dry and often chilled to zero, is exhilarating.

Other nearby activities include cross-country skiing along the southern edge of the Yellowstone River to Huckleberry Hot Springs and sleigh rides in the National Elk Refuge, the wintering spot for 7,500 elk. There's also dogsledding through the black pine and quaking aspen of Bridger-Teton National Forest.

Jackson Hole Mountain Resort
P.O. Box 290
3395 McCallister Drive
Teton Village, Wyoming 83025

Phone: (307) 733–2292

Web Site: www.jacksonhole.com

E-mail: info@jacksonhole.com

Elevation: Top—10,450 feet; base—6,311 feet

Vertical Drop: 4,139 feet

Total Area: 2,500 acres

Number of Trails: 65

Longest Run: 4.5 miles

Terrain: 10% beginner; 40% intermediate; 50% advanced/expert

Average Annual Snowfall: 460 inches

Lifts: 11

Snowmaking: 160 acres

Central Reservations: (800) 443–6931

Snow Report: (888) 333–7766

Accommodations: There's a wide range of lodging available in Teton Village at the base of the ski area. There are also plenty of accommodations available in the cowboy town of Jackson, a 20-minute drive from the base.

Getting There: Jackson Hole Airport is served by several major airlines.

Keep in Mind: It can be cold.

BEST BETS

Beginners: Fort Wyoming and Apres Vous Mountain.

Intermediates: Gros Ventre.

Advanced: Hobacks—North, Middle, and South.

Experts: Corbet's Couloir.

Lunch: The Peak in The Four Seasons.

Off the Slopes: Explore Grand Teton National Park and nearby Yellowstone National Park. Toast the Old West at the Million Dollar Cowboy Bar in Jackson.

Best Hotel: The Four Seasons Jackson Hole.

LAKE LOUISE SKI AREA

Lake Louise, Alberta

Astonishing scenery is the hallmark of Banff National Park. And within this extraordinary setting, Lake Louise is the most famous, most visited, and most photographed region. Towering above the valley with views of the celebrated turquoise-colored alpine lake is the park's largest ski resort.

The views just don't get any better than those from Lake Louise Ski Area. The resort looks out on the Continental Divide, offering unsurpassed panoramas of hanging glaciers on the jagged peaks of Mounts Temple and Victoria, which appear as lacy and delicate as hoarfrost. Their summits are in excess of 11,000 feet and among the highest in the Canadian Rockies. Lake Louise, named for a daughter of Queen Victoria, can be seen across the valley as a patch of frozen white, surrounded by green Douglas fir, lodgepole pine, and Engelmann spruce.

Every skier and boarder visiting Lake Louise raves about the surrounding sea of glacier-draped peaks. But the ski terrain is pretty extraordinary, too. Louise's four mountain faces deliver 113 designated runs in a vertical drop of 3,365 feet, which can be skied nonstop. There are green, blue, and black runs off every lift, except the Summit Platter's expert-only terrain. Two-thirds of the resort consists of long, tree-lined trails; the rest is above the tree line. Six high alpine bowls offer 2,500 acres of lift-serviced backcountry terrain.

Louise is ideal for all ability levels of skiers. The south-facing front side, White-horn Mountain, has long, gently winding runs. It's also the site of one of the largest terrain parks in North America. Men's and women's World Cup downhill courses blaze down the mountain's front face.

On the back side of Whitehorn are steep and spacious alpine bowls—more than a mile long and pitched at 40 degrees. Their northern exposure on the lee side of the mountain ensures that even days after a storm, the wind continues to dump fresh powder into these chutes. Beginners avoid the steeps by windshield-wipering their way down the Saddleback run, while intermediates joyously fly down Boomerang. Climbing back up the back side is Paradise lift. Beneath the chair is the aptly named Diamond Mine, a series of take-no-prisoners, black and double-black runs that drop precipitously off Eagle Ridge. Here are some of the best steeps in Canada, and the lift makes lapping runs easy.

Continuing down the valley, past the base of Paradise lift, is the Larch area with its perfectly pitched intermediate trails bordered by forest. As you approach the base, gaze high across the valley to the fractured north face of Mount Temple. Resort owner Charlie Locke and a climbing partner were the first to climb this extraordinary rock-and-ice face.

Back on the slopes above the Larch area, the resort offers Beyond the Boundary guided tours for guests who want an introduction to backcountry skiing. The adventure starts with a one-hour hike to Purple Bowl on Lipalian Mountain, site of the Canadian Powder 8 Championships.

At the base of the Larch area is Temple Lodge, one of four magnificent pine lodges that offer a variety of dining experiences. No need to ride the lift back to the front of Whitehorn; the 5-mile-long gentle Ski Out lies waiting to glide you back to the front-side base.

The village at Lake Louise, across the Trans-Canada highway from the ski area, is small. You'll find a collection of motel-like lodges and the outstanding Post Hotel

The Canadian Rockies' largest ski area—and the second biggest in Canada—offers a whopping 4,000-plus acres of every conceivable type of ski terrain. Skiers and snowboarders consistently rank it as the most scenic resort in North America.

scattered around a small shopping center. Ten minutes higher up the road is the majestic lake itself. On the shoreline, and worthy of the setting, is the castlelike Chateau Lake Louise. The massive 487-room hotel was built in 1924 by the Canadian Pacific Railroad as part of a chain of luxurious hotels that stretch across Canada. Like its sister properties in Banff and Jasper, it has hosted royalty and countless foreign heads of state. Known to be rather formal in the British tradition, the Chateau is considerably more casual for its winter guests. Winter is low season. For action, go to the town of Banff 36 miles away.

Skating on the real Lake Louise is a winter treat. Other nearby activities include cross-country skiing (on almost 100 miles of groomed trails), dogsledding, and horse-drawn sleigh rides.

Lake Louise Ski Area
P.O. Box 5
Lake Louise, Alberta T0L 1E0
Canada

Phone: (877) 253–6888

Web Site: www.skilouise.com

E-mail: info@skilouise.com

Elevation: Top—8,765 feet; base—5,400 feet

Vertical Drop: 3,365 feet

Total Area: 4,200 acres

Number of Trails: 113

Longest Run: 5 miles

Terrain: 25% beginner; 45% intermediate; 30% advanced/expert

Average Annual Snowfall: 150 inches

Lifts: 10

Snowmaking: 1,700 acres

Central Reservations: (877) 754–5462

Snow Report: (403) 762–4766

Accommodations: There are lodges in the village and the storied Chateau Lake Louise up on the lakeshore. The widely ranging accommodations in the town of Banff are 45 minutes away.

Getting There: Lake Louise Ski Area is 36 miles west of Banff and 115 miles west of Calgary International Airport.

Keep in Mind: Midwinter can be cold.

BEST BETS

Beginners: Wiwaxy, a 2.5-mile cruiser.

Intermediates: Larch area.

Advanced: The men's and women's downhill courses.

Experts: The back bowls and the Diamond Mine area.

Lunch: Sawyer's Nook Restaurant at Temple Lodge.

Off the Slopes: Head up to the real Lake Louise for the scenery and down to Banff for the nightlife.

Best Hotel: The Fairmont Chateau Lake Louise.

SKI MARMOT BASIN

Jasper, Alberta

In winter when the high alpine areas surrounding Marmot Basin are buried deep in snow, the wide Athabaska Valley beneath the summits teems with wildlife. The river valley is the winter feeding ground in Canada's largest national park. At times it resembles a white Serengeti, flush with herds of elk, mule and white-tailed deer, and, higher up, bighorn sheep. There are moose, too, and late in the spring ski season, black bear.

Tucked within Jasper National Park's 4,200 square miles of pristine wilderness, Marmot Basin looks out over a wild pocket of Canada that has changed little in thousands of years. In winter even the waterfalls are frozen in time.

The family-friendly town of Jasper, 12 miles from the ski area and four hours from Alberta's capital city, Edmonton, can't seem to make up its mind if it's a resort town or a blue-collar railway town. The result is an unpretentious mountain berg and friendly ski area that draws fewer visitors than its glitzier and somewhat distant neighbors Lake Louise and Banff.

Marmot Basin, the only lift-served ski area in Jasper Park, is situated half above the tree line and half in the forest. The area's upper portion sits in a high, snow-filled basin ringed by snowcapped peaks. The lower half consists of classic tree-rimmed fall lines. All of it offers heavenly skiing. The snow is fluffy and light, and often deep. Lift lines are practically nonexistent, except on weekends.

Novice trails occupy a third of the mountain. The rest is split between intermediate and advanced terrain. Most lifts have access to all levels of terrain, making Marmot a fine place to ski for families and groups of differing abilities.

What's the catch? Marmot Basin, like Lake Louise and Sunshine Village in neighboring Banff National Park, is susceptible to arctic cold spells. The best months to ski are March and April, when winter is losing its grip but the snow is seldom slushy. Four mountain day lodges—two at the base and two at midmountain—offer warm refuges in the winter and open sundecks on warm days.

In recent years new lifts have greatly expanded the resort's lift-served black-diamond terrain. You'll find powder chutes, steep glades, and windswept bowls off the Eagle quad and the Knob chair. Beginners zigzag their way down high alpine bowls connecting tree-lined boulevards that end at the base lodge with few difficulties. Intermediates pretty much have the run of the place. And there's plenty of elbow room for everybody.

There are few flat spots, so snowboarders can easily move around the mountain. A terrain park features tabletops and all the other accoutrements that challenge and entertain boarders.

Marmot Basin has no on-mountain accommodations. Nor is there a base village. There are, however, plenty of digs to choose from in nearby, laid-back Jasper. A few miles from town is the rambling, low-

 Located in Jasper National Park, three hours from the town of Banff along the extraordinary Columbia Ice-fields highway, which is rimmed by more than 200 glaciers, Marmot Basin is a snowy paradise well worth the effort of getting to its out-of-the-way location.

rise but upscale Fairmont Jasper Park Lodge, one of Canada's great railroad-built resorts. Set in a winter wonderland of 900 pristine acres, the accommodations consist of a series of log cottages spread around a lovely alpine lake that is open for skating during the winter.

Some skiers combine a visit to Jasper with one of the great scenic train trips in the world. VIA Rail offers the Snow Train to Jasper from Vancouver, 550 miles to the west; and from Edmonton, 225 miles to the east. The closest major airport is Edmonton International.

Other activities include guided back-country ski trips, ice skating, cross-country skiing, and horse-drawn sleigh rides. Jasper National Park is gorgeous no matter how you see the sights.

Ski Marmot Basin
P.O. Box 1300
Jasper, Alberta TOE 1E0
Canada

Phone: (780) 852–3816

Web Site: www.skimarmot.com

E-mail: info@skimarmot.com

Elevation: Top—8,534 feet; base—5,534 feet

Vertical Drop: 3,000 feet

Total Area: 1,675 acres

Number of Trails: 84

Longest Run: 3.5 miles

Terrain: 30% beginner; 30% intermediate; 40% advanced/expert

Average Annual Snowfall: 160 inches

Lifts: 9

Snowmaking: No

Central Reservations: (800) 473–8135

Snow Report: (780) 852–3816

Accommodations: The town of Jasper offers a wide range of accommodations.

Getting There: Marmot Basin is 12 miles south of Jasper; 225 miles west of Edmonton; 255 miles northwest of Calgary; and 176 miles north of Banff.

BEST BETS

Beginners: Basin Run.

Intermediates: Paradise and Tranquilizer, top to bottom.

Advanced: Lift Line and Dromedary off the Eagle Express chair.

Experts: Chalet Slope.

Lunch: Eagle Chalet.

Off the Slopes: See as much as you can of Jasper National Park.

Best Hotel: Fairmont Jasper Park Lodge.

SUNSHINE VILLAGE RESORT
Banff, Alberta

The extraordinary UNESCO World Heritage Site of Banff National Park is reason enough to ski Sunshine Village. So is the storied town of Banff, just 10 miles and a gondola ride away from the resort.

In 1885 the Canadian government established the Banff Hot Springs Reserve after railroad workers building Canada's transcontinental railroad stumbled upon a soothing, natural hot springs in the Bow River Valley about 70 miles west of Calgary. Two years later the reserve was greatly expanded and awarded national park status.

 Located in Canada's oldest and most celebrated national park, Sunshine Village is surrounded by grand glacier-sculpted summits. The resort, which straddles the Continental Divide, is Canada's highest-elevation ski area. Its three mountains receive the most snow and sustain the longest season in the Canadian Rockies.

The park quickly became a popular destination when the Canadian Pacific Railway (CPR) built grand, castlelike hotels in Banff and nearby Lake Louise. At the time, mountaineering was a popular pursuit among the British gentry; the CPR stationed a number of Swiss guides, mostly from the Interlaken area, at their hotels to lead summer climbers on first ascents. By 1928, a log cabin was built at Sunshine (it still stands today), and the first ski tracks appeared the following spring. In 1938 the Canadian National Ski Championships were held at Sunshine,

even though the first rope tow didn't appear for another two years.

Yes, there's plenty of historical significance up at the oldest ski resort in the Canadian Rockies. But there's also great skiing and heaps of snow. And on sunny, see-forever days, it is one of the most beautiful places on the planet.

Until the 1970s, special ski buses from the parking lot ground their way up a 3-mile series of switchbacks through a box canyon to get to the resort's true base some 1,600 vertical feet higher. Eventually, a doglegged gondola replaced the buses; and in 2001, a quicker and larger gondola replaced it. The old bus route is now an appealing, intermediate-level ski run that leads to the parking lot.

The gondola ascends to a high meadow amid some of the grandest peaks of the Canadian Rockies, their sedimentary rock layered like a wedding cake. Sunshine Village gets softer and deeper snow than anywhere else in the region. For years, it was known as a pleasant intermediate and beginner area. But expansion onto Goat's Eye Mountain in the mid-1990s vastly increased the expert terrain and forever put an end to the what's-flatter-than-Saskatchewan jokes among derring-do Banff skiers. Boarders at Sunshine enjoy terrain parks and halfpipes and extraordinary freeriding. Most of the slopes are above the tree line, allowing boarders to carve wide swaths of arcs almost anywhere. Five high-speed quads move you quickly around the mountain.

The Great Divide chair on aptly named Lookout Mountain climbs the Continental Divide and crosses the provincial boundary between Alberta and British Columbia. On the back side of Lookout is the infamous Delirium Dive, a mile-wide, 1,800-vertical-foot cirque open to expert skiers and boarders with an experienced partner and avalanche safety gear. Transceivers, probes, and shovels are a bare minimum—you can rent them at the base. Access is through a control gate at the top of the Divide chair. From there, you follow steps down to the start, or huck off the cornice onto the 50-degree slope.

The resort's midmountain base area includes the charming and recently remodeled Sunshine Inn, the only downhill ski-in/ski-out lodge in a Canadian national park. But most visitors to Sunshine stay in the town of Banff, where winter brings low-season rates. There's a plethora of motels, hotels, and upscale lodges with roaring fireplaces, but the best of the lot is the venerable Fairmont Banff Springs Hotel.

The twenty-minute commute between town and the gondola affords frequent sightings of elk and deer, and sometimes bear in the springtime. On a high mountainside overlooking Banff, skiers soothe their aching muscles in the natural hot springs that first attracted tourism.

Late February to mid-April is the best time to ski in the Canadian Rockies. The daily winter average temperature is twenty degrees, but cold fronts can move in during December, January, and even February, dropping temperatures to minus-thirty degrees for several days at a stretch. Then, suddenly, a warm winter wind, known locally as a chinook, blows in and the temperature rises thirty degrees or more in a matter of hours, melting snow in the valley.

Except for the shops and restaurants in downtown Banff, there is scant commercialism within the national park. You won't find vacation resort developments here. Instead, you get enough raw beauty to cause a chinook in your heart.

Sunshine Village Resort
P.O. Box 1510
Banff, Alberta TOL 0C0
Canada

Phone: (877) 542–2633

Web Site: www.skibanff.com

E-mail: comments@skibanff.com

Elevation: Top—8,954 feet; base—5,440 feet

Vertical Drop: 3,514 feet

Total Area: 3,358 acres

Number of Trails: 107

Longest Run: 5 miles

Terrain: 22% beginner; 31% intermediate; 47% advanced/expert

Average Annual Snowfall: 324 inches

Lifts: 12

Snowmaking: No

Central Reservations: (877) 542–2633

Snow Report: (877) 542–2633

Accommodations: Sunshine Village Inn offers ski-in/ski-out rooms. A wide range of accommodations is available in Banff.

Getting There: Sunshine Village is 10 miles west of Banff town site and 110 miles from Calgary International Airport.

Keep in Mind: Potential for arctic weather.

BEST BETS

Beginners: The Jackrabbit chair.

Intermediates: Blue runs off the Angel Express or the women's World Cup downhill.

Advanced: The moguls and powder off the Continental Divide chair.

Experts: Delirium Dive.

Lunch: Eagle's Nest at the Sunshine Inn.

Off the Slopes: The town of Banff. The Sulphur Mountain hot springs is a must.

Best Hotel: The ski-in/ski-out Sunshine Inn.

FERNIE ALPINE RESORT

Fernie, British Columbia

Skiers have heard this story before. Every winter powder snow buries a nineteenth-century mining town, so the locals build a ski lift for the kids. People start coming from nearby cities, the mountain's reputation spreads, and an investor looking for the good life enters the scene and brings the ski area into the twenty-first century. The script has played in Crested Butte, Telluride, and Breckenridge, Colorado, to name just a few spots. And it has happened in Fernie before an alpine backdrop second to none.

A few years ago, the resort ranked high on the best-kept-secrets list of must-ski destinations. But the word has spread among skiers and snowboarders in search of the steep and deep. Families flock here for uncrowded slopes, hero-making snow, and exceptional value. The resort's owner, Charlie Locke (the same Charlie of Lake Louise and Kimberley fame), has pushed the standards—he is as aggressively proactive as surgery. Locke built new high-speed lifts, purchased a fleet of snow-grooming equipment, and constructed an ever-expanding base village. Fernie is now the fourth largest ski resort in Canada.

Fernie's coming-out party includes a glitzy new village at the base that greatly enhances the skiing experience. There are luxurious slopeside lodges and condos, gourmet dining, and great shopping. But the peripheral aspects of the ski experience have not subsumed the core of this place, which is the mountain. Skiing Fernie revolves around the excitement of the terrain and the high-quality snowpack.

There's also a real, working-class town just 3 miles away. Its down-home, friendly citizens feel as much a part of the mountain as the 350 inches of annual snow that blankets the slopes come winter.

Terrain highlights include five vast alpine bowls spilling down from the serrated limestone ridge of the Lizard Range. Countless configurations of cliffs, glades, and chutes overflow with powder, creating the possibility of endless adventure. The glorious bowls funnel into tree-lined runs that slide down the fall line. Intermediate skiers and snowboarders have a field day in the bowls. Experts find plenty of steep ridgelines with the look and feel of powder-covered wellheads.

Beginners have plenty of options, too. High on the mountain, they loop their way down Lizard Bowl beneath Polar Peak, the 7,000-foot summit of the resort. You'll also find more than a dozen green runs bordered by red cedar forests on the lower half of the mountain. All trails lead to the vicinity of the base area, where four quads (two of them high speed) and two triple chairs do most of the heavy lifting.

The relatively low elevation of the Canadian Rockies is physiologically less taxing than the higher-altitude American Rockies. Fernie sits at a mere 3,500 feet compared to Breckenridge's base at 9,600 feet. But breathe easy: You won't be cheated out of big vertical drops. The rise from base to summit is comparable to Breckenridge's.

In the late 1800s prospector William Fernie came to southeastern British Columbia (due north of western Montana) looking for gold. Instead he found heaps of coal. He founded the town that bears his name, and by 1908 Fernie's population had reached an all-time high of 12,000. Mines remain active in the area, but outsiders are drawn in by the quality and variety of Fernie's four-season recreational pleasures and vibrant mountain culture.

Cradled by the Canadian Rockies in the southeast corner of British Columbia, Fernie Alpine Resort has traversed a slippery slope from up-and-coming status to arrival on the international ski scene. This big mountain on the move offers bowls and glades and heaps of powder. Families love its low-key ambience and value. It's like Aspen, in about 1985.

If you want more powder, there are several first-class snowcat-skiing operations nearby. And Kimberley Alpine Ski Resort is only about an hour away. Your Fernie lift ticket is interchangeable.

Other winter activities include cross-country skiing, snowshoeing, snowmobile tours, horse-drawn sleigh rides, dogsled tours, and strolling historic downtown Fernie.

**Fernie Alpine Resort
5339 Fernie Ski Hill Road
Fernie, British Columbia V0B 1M6
Canada**

Phone: (250) 423–4655

Web Site: www.skifernie.com

E-mail: info@skifernie.com

Elevation: Top—6,316 feet; base—3,550 feet

Vertical Drop: 2,816 feet

Total Area: 2,504 acres

Number of Trails: 107

Longest Run: 3 miles

Terrain: 30% beginner; 40% intermediate; 30% advanced/expert

Average Annual Snowfall: 350 inches

Lifts: 10

Snowmaking: No

Central Reservations: (877) 333–2339

Snow Report: (250) 423–3555

Accommodations: Full-service hotels, lodges, and condos are slopeside. There's also a wide range of accommodations in the town of Fernie.

Getting There: Fernie is a 3-hour drive from Calgary International Airport.

Keep in Mind: There are some rowdy watering holes, but not much glitz in Fernie.

BEST BETS

Beginners: Falling Star.

Intermediates: Cedar Bowl.

Advanced: Sky Dive.

Experts: Diamond Black.

Lunch: Gabriella's.

Off the Slopes: Explore historic downtown Fernie with its local flavor.

Best Hotel: Lizard Creek Lodge.

KIMBERLEY ALPINE SKI RESORT

Kimberley, British Columbia

Kimberley Alpine Ski Resort remains a work in progress. Lake Louise owner Charlie Locke purchased the resort in the late 1990s, around the same time that he bought Fernie Alpine Ski Resort, just an hour's drive from Kimberley. New lifts emerged, and construction began on a luxurious base village centered on slopeside accommodations, restaurants, and shops. But the key ingredient is the magnificent mountain. (Charlie Locke knows mountains even better than he knows money. In his younger days as a mountain climber, the list of first ascents that he established in the Canadian Rockies numbered forty.)

Kimberley is located on Northstar Mountain at the foot of the Purcell Mountains in British Columbia's interior. It's a major snowbelt, and the resort receives an average of 12 feet of dry, powder snow every winter. The mountain's front side is a cluster of rolling intermediate and beginner trails named for the mining claims of early prospectors. The runs are long, tree lined, and finely groomed. The back side of the mountain caters to skiers and boarders who enjoy the adrenaline rushes of steep terrain and know how to finish their turns on black-diamond runs. Some of the steep pitches reach a mind-boggling, knee-wobbling 55 degrees. There also are infamous challenging mogul runs on the back side of the mountain, especially in the vicinity of Easter chair.

The resort is popular with snowboarders: partly because of the wide-open cruising, partly because of the quality of the snow, and partly because of the radical terrain park and halfpipe, which has lights for night riding. The park drops 700 vertical feet before a T-bar offers quick access back to the tabletops and other obstacles.

The town of Kimberley—"Bavarian City of the Rockies"—is a one-of-a-kind place. It presents a mélange of false-front ginger-bread architecture, hand-painted fire hydrants, and brightly colored footbridges. The carless, European-style town center is appropriately called the Platzl. It showcases the world's largest cuckoo clock, which yodels on the hour. It's tempting to think the place was dreamed up by the likes of Stephen King, but it was the brainchild of the town council back in the 1970s. What, you wonder, were they smoking?

Nonetheless, this pseudo-Bavarian village offers a special blend of fun and uniqueness uncommon to most North American ski towns. Kids love the place. Local restaurants have picked up on the European theme with specialties to match the ambience. Some of the best German food is served at the Old Baurenhaus Restaurant, an actual 350-year-old house built in Germany. It was dismantled, shipped to Kimberley, and reconstructed a few minutes from the base of Northstar Mountain.

Other off-mountain attractions include miles of groomed and illuminated double

 One of the emerging giants of British Columbia skiing, Kimberley Alpine Resort is tucked into the snow-rich Purcell mountain range. The town of Kimberley, which bills itself the "Bavarian City of the Rockies," is one of Canada's quirkiest ski towns. Yes, you'll hear some accordion music. Bring along your lederhosen and you'll fit right in. But most of all, bring your skis.

tracks and skating lanes for cross-country skiers. There's also ice skating and outstanding scenery in all directions.

For all its Bavarian trappings, the name *Kimberley* has its origins far from Germany. It's taken from the famous Kimberley gold mines of South Africa. The ore mines that sustained the Canadian town for the last century have pretty much run their course, however, and now Kimberley has bet the farm on its glorious mountain and the outstanding ski reputation of the province of British Columbia—with world-famous heli-skiing, the phenomenal success of Whistler-Blackcomb Ski Resort, and the stunning beauty of Vancouver. Interior jewels like Kimberley and Fernie have become part of the winter legend.

Kimberley Alpine Ski Resort
P.O. Box 40
Kimberley, British Columbia V1A 2Y5
Canada

Phone: (205) 427–4881

Web Site: www.skikimberley.com

E-mail: info@skikimberley.com

Elevation: Top—6,500 feet; base—4,035 feet

Vertical Drop: 2,465 feet

Total Area: 1,800 acres

Number of Trails: 68

Longest Run: 4 miles (Ridgeway)

Terrain: 20% beginner; 42% intermediate; 38% advanced/expert

Average Annual Snowfall: 144 inches

Lifts: 8

Snowmaking: No

Central Reservations: (877) 754–5462

Snow Report: (250) 427–7332

Accommodations: Slopeside lodges and condos. A few minutes away in Kimberley, there are hotels, lodges, motels, and bed-and-breakfast inns.

Getting There: Cranbrook Regional Airport is 12 miles from the resort. By car, Kimberley is 3 hours from Spokane, Washington, and 4 hours from Calgary.

Keep in Mind: Hard to get to. Limited shopping.

BEST BETS

Beginners: The Main.

Intermediates: The Dean.

Advanced: Easter.

Experts: Flush.

Lunch: Kootenay Haus on the mountain.

Off the Slopes: Plan on spending time in the historic, Bavarian-themed town.

Best Hotel: Trickle Creek Residence Inn by Marriott.

WHISTLER-BLACKCOMB RESORTS

Whistler, British Columbia

The two peerless ski mountains Whistler and Blackcomb knuckle up out of British Columbia's Coast Mountains 75 miles north of beautiful Vancouver. Each one is a terraced, snowy heaven offering skiers and boarders seemingly endless trails and glades and glaciers.

The chic village nestled beneath the two majestic peaks is as picturesque as a Swiss postcard, and, like the mountains, it changes character with the time of day. You'll find everything from coffee-and-homemade-muffin shops to unforgettable restaurants featuring exotic dishes like loin of wild Arctic caribou and wine cellars deep enough to boast verticals of Chateau Mouton-Rothschild dating back to the days of rope tows. And for better or worse, Whistler might be the best party town in all of Canada, winter and summer.

Ever since the resort schussed onto the alpine radar in the early 1980s, it has consistently captured glowing reviews. Readers of the glossy ski magazines often rank it the number one resort in North America.

Whistler surely is the most cosmopolitan ski resort in North America, with many visitors from Europe, Asia, Australia, and the United States. But save your furs for St. Moritz or Cortina d'Ampezzo; the scene is considerably more casual in environmentally correct British Columbia.

Whistler deserves high praise for its quality and range of terrain, abundance of snow and length of season, car-free central village and ski-in/ski-out accommodations.

The skiing and snowboarding terrain is vast beyond belief. You can't ski it all in a day. You won't ski it all in a week. Former U.S. Ski Team coach Bill Egan calls Whistler Mountain the best ski mountain in North America. "It's a bit long for our racers' legs," he said a few years ago, during one of the many World Cup downhill races held on Whistler's Dave Murray course, which is the venue for the 2010 Olympic Alpine Downhill event.

Considered individually, the two mountains, which are separated by a deep valley and linked at the village plaza, would each rank among the best ski resorts in the world. Respectively, they offer the highest and second highest vertical rise of all North American ski resorts. Taken together, they teeter skiers and snowboarders on the brink of nirvana.

With more skiable acres than any other North American resort, thirty-plus state-of-the-art lifts, and a mile-long vertical drop, the area offers a vast mix of beginner, intermediate, and expert terrain that includes plunging powder bowls, sheer couloirs, and gladed snowriding with views into glacier-draped Garibaldi Provincial Park. Lower runs are forested; mountaintops are crowned by steep bowls above the tree line. Whistler Mountain is enjoyed for its rolling, turning, and variable-pitch runs served by a scatter-shot lift network. Blackcomb Mountain touts its in-your-face fall line and the wildly scenic Horstman Glacier, which remains open for summer skiing. Both mountains have large, state-of-the-art terrain parks.

The summit elevations hover at just over 7,000 feet, compared to the 10,000-plus feet common in the American Rockies. If you're breathless in Colorado from the debilitating physiological effects of altitude, you'll be singing up the lift at Whistler.

What's the catch? Well, there is the weather. This is the Coast mountain range, not the Rockies. Whistler seldom has fluffy powder or as much sunshine as you'll find in the Rockies. The enormous bowls are frequently closed by Pacific storms, which are enough to throw skiers into a panic, sending them back to the village for a mug of hot, spiced glühwein. But snow conditions, especially at the higher elevations, are usually excellent.

On American holidays there are swarms of south-of-the-border college kids taking advantage of the favorable exchange rate and the lower legal drinking age. They can create the skiing equivalent of spring break in Fort Lauderdale. And lift lines are long on sunny weekends, when all of ski-mad Vancouver appears to be on the mountains.

The unifying principle behind Whistler Resort is its pedestrian-only central village, which combines the best elements of European plazas. There are shops, cozy cafes, and a variety of nightclubs featuring everything from raves to jazz. This is where megaresort developer Intrawest got its start.

For nonskiers—and there are many at Whistler—there's heli-flight-seeing, ice skating, snowshoeing, and sleigh rides, in addition to the shopping and nightlife. Covered tennis courts and spa facilities are available at several of Whistler's slopeside hotels. But visitors would be remiss not to spend a day in gorgeous Vancouver, an hour and a half away.

Accommodations at Whistler include more than 5,000 rooms ranging from ultradeluxe mountainside suites to dormitory-style hostels on the outskirts of the resort. There are no high-rise concrete monsters to darken the scene. Instead, a mixture of chalet-style apartments, inns, lodges, and condominiums fills the village and surrounding area. The premier properties include Chateau Whistler, Westin Resort and Spa, and Pan Pacific Lodge. In past years America's best-known travel magazine has ranked them the top three ski resort hotels in North America. But several smaller hotels in the village will treat you just as well.

Whistler and Blackcomb Mountain Resorts Ltd.
4545 Blackcomb Way
Whistler, British Columbia V0N 1B4
Canada

Phone: (866) 218–9690

Web Site: www.whistlerblackcomb.com

E-mail: info@whistlerblackcomb.com

Elevation: Top—7,494 feet; base—2,214 feet

Vertical Drop: 5,280 feet

Total Area: 8,171 acres

Number of Trails: 200-plus

Longest Run: 7 miles

Terrain: 20% beginner; 55% intermediate; 25% advanced/expert

Average Annual Snowfall: 360 inches

Lifts: 33

Snowmaking: 565 acres

Central Reservations: (888) 403–4727

Snow Report: (866) 218–9690

Accommodations: Lots of upscale hotels, lodges, and condos.

Getting There: Whistler Village is 75 miles north of Vancouver International Airport; regularly scheduled ground transportation is available.

Keep in Mind: Potential for wet, coastal weather.

Twin-peaked Whistler, the apparent gold-medal North American ski resort, boasts the continent's biggest vertical drop and the most terrain. The extraordinary range outruns the imagination of most skiers. Whistler Village offers some of the top-ranked hotels in the ski world, cuisine to match the terrain, and enough après-ski to draw nonskiers.

Beginners: Green Line on Blackcomb; Burnt Stew Trail on Whistler.

Intermediates: Cloud Nine on Blackcomb; Symphony Bowl on Whistler.

Advanced: Heavenly Basin on Blackcomb; Shale Slope on Whistler.

Experts: Sapphire Bowl on Blackcomb; the Couloir on Whistler.

Lunch: Christine's on Blackcomb; Round-house Lodge on Whistler.

Off the Slopes: Whistler Village offers great restaurants, intimate lounges, and first-rate shopping.

Best Hotel: Westin Resort & Spa.

MONT-SAINTE-ANNE
Beaupré, Quebec

Many of the local family names go back 300 years. Their language is French. And like France's Chamonix, there is paragliding off the snowbound summit of Mont-Sainte-Anne to the base of the ski area. The nearby city is a seventeenth-century fortress along the banks of the meandering St. Lawrence River. The setting is reminiscent of Europe. And the superb quality of the dining is the icing on the cake. Welcome to Quebec.

In North America you can't get much closer to European ski ambience than at Mont-Sainte-Anne—although the neighboring ski areas of Stoneham and Le Massif come close.

You might want to base yourself in unbelievably romantic Quebec City, which was founded in 1608. It's the site of Canada's oldest permanent European settlement, North America's only fortified city north of Mexico, and a UNESCO World Heritage Site. Hold the hands you love and stroll the ramparts. You're going to fall in love with French Canada.

There are shuttles from the city's hotels to Mont-Sainte-Anne and nearby Stoneham and Le Massif. The scene is not unlike culturally rich Innsbruck, Austria, with its backdrop of good skiing and boarding just a short distance away. A ski pass is valid at all three resorts, so skiers and boarders can create their own ski package depending on where they want to ski each day.

If you go in late February, you'll catch Quebec City's winter carnival, a seventeen-day extravaganza that is one of the largest winter festivals in the world. Along with skiing and hockey, it defines winter in Quebec.

But you might also decide to stay at the base of picturesque Mont-Sainte-Anne. The dining and lodging are posh, and you can ski in and ski out. There's also extensive night skiing.

Mont-Sainte-Anne's sixty-three runs slash down three mountain faces, dishing out some of the best skiing in the East. Steep black-diamond trails tumble down the 2,050-foot-vertical face. Long, winding intermediate trails amble over the contours of the mountain, rimmed by magnificent hardwoods that bleed maple syrup in the springtime when the trails morph into forgiving corn snow. Some of the runs are venues for World Cup events in both skiing and snowboarding. There's also advanced and intermediate glade skiing. More than a dozen trails and a mega terrain park with two halfpipes are open for night skiing. An enclosed gondola combats the northern cold. And you can get a taste of Quebec winter—snow soaked in maple syrup—at the sugar cabin on the La Pichard trail.

Located just 4 miles from the mountain's base is the largest cross-country ski facility in Canada. Mont-Sainte-Anne Cross-Country Ski Center features 135 miles of trails, including an 80-mile network for skating stride. The terrain is rated like alpine runs—green, blue, and black. Seven heated huts are spaced along the trails, and there's a cozy, ski-in/ski-out bed-and-breakfast inn called L'Auberge du Fondeur.

 One of eastern North America's finest resorts, Mont-Sainte-Anne is acclaimed for the quality and reliability of its snow conditions, for some of the best skiing terrain in the East, and for hosting numerous World Cups in both alpine skiing and snowboarding. The resort also has Canada's largest cross-country ski center. Two other alpine ski areas are close by.

STONEHAM MOUNTAIN RESORT

Stoneham Mountain Resort is set in a snow-trapping, wind-protected, horseshoe-shaped valley just twenty minutes north of Quebec City. Thirty trails sprawl across four mountains, making it easy to follow the sun. The terrain is perfect for families wanting to ski together. The resort is popular with snowboarders because of a large terrain park that includes halfpipes, rails, and other hits for X-minded snowriders. With its cozy slopeside accommodations, French Canadian joie de vivre, and enthusiastic nightlife, Stoneham is well worth the visit.

LE MASSIF

Le Massif, a little more than an hour from Quebec City, has the highest vertical drop in eastern Canada and an unforgettable view of the glacier-carved Laurentian Mountains tumbling down to the ice-choked St.

Lawrence River. It rises above a UNESCO World Biosphere Reserve. Its two ski mountains have few lifts, but they receive a yearly average snowfall of 260 inches and attract serious intermediate and advanced skiers away from Mont-Sainte-Anne's crowds.

Le Massif, together with Stoneham and Mont-Sainte-Anne, rounds out an enticing, family-friendly three-resort combo in the ski belt along the St. Lawrence River, which is Canada's Mississippi in history and lore.

The rolling, wooded mountain scenery will make you envious of the area's inhabitants, and the bonhomie of the Quebecois will draw you into their rich culture.

Mont-Sainte-Anne
2000, boul. Beau Pré
Beaupré, Quebec G0A 1E0
Canada

Phone: (418) 827–4561

Web Site: www.mont-sainte-anne.com

E-mail: info@mont-sainte-anne.com

Elevation: Top—2,625 feet; base—575 feet

Vertical Drop: 2,050 feet

Total Area: 450 acres

Number of Trails: 63

Longest Run: 3.5 miles

Terrain: 23% beginner; 46% intermediate; 18% advanced; 13% expert

Average Annual Snowfall: 160 inches

Lifts: 13

Snowmaking: 340 acres

Central Reservations: (800) 463–1568

Snow Report: (418) 827–4579

Accommodations: Ski-in/ski-out hotels, lodges, and condominiums are located at the base of the mountain. Quebec City offers a full range of big-city digs.

Getting There: Mont-Sainte-Anne is 25 miles from Quebec City. Montreal is 180 miles.

TREMBLANT
Mont-Tremblant, Quebec

What's the beef French-speaking Quebec has with the rest of Canada? It has to have something to do with the food. In a meat-and-potatoes country, Quebecois chefs are doling out carpaccio of Atlantic salmon. And that's just for breakfast. Here's a little secret from north of the border: Nothing warms a cold January morning like the smell of fresh-baked croissants and hot French-roast coffee.

At Tremblant, you'll find French alpine ambience on this side of the Atlantic. The mountain offers classic New England skiing; trails follow the rolls and dips of the mountain's contours, winding around the mountain and not just down the fall line. At the base, the pastel-colored old village has been meticulously restored while Tremblant's owner, mega ski resort developer Intrawest Corporation, has constructed a new, seemingly created-by-Disney village that appears lifted from Europe. It is studded with ski shops and boulangeries in Versailles-style buildings arranged around stone streets and courtyards. There's even a cabriolet, an open-air lift that transports skiers up the steep village streets to the ski lifts.

Located ninety minutes north of Montreal in the heart of the ancient Laurentian Mountains, Tremblant is one of the oldest ski resorts on the continent. It opened its first chairlift in 1939, shortly after Idaho's Sun Valley debuted the world's first. The panorama from Tremblant's summit showcases the icebound rivers and lakes used by early Canadian fur traders to traverse the time-worn but majestic humpbacked mountains.

Tremblant is one of those ski resorts where the heady atmosphere comes close to overshadowing the skiing. It's tempting to believe European ambience is the raison d'être—until you stand on top of the 3,000-foot mountain, that is. Engaging trails flutter down both sides of the summit, inviting you to ski in almost any direction. The diversity of the ninety-four runs is far reaching. Tremblant skis like a tall western mountain; there are no long, flat run-outs at the bottom. It boasts one of the largest snowmaking systems in Canada, with more than 800 snowblowers placed around the mountain.

Half of the runs are for advanced skiers, and the black diamonds are well distributed on the mountain. Unlike some resorts, Tremblant doesn't force expert skiers to the fringes of the ski area. Black runs take you anywhere on the mountain. And the glade skiing between named runs is out of this world.

You also can ski top to bottom on green trails on the mountain's south face. And there's a beginner area with two magic carpets so skiers can get comfortable on their skis before tackling the on-and-off skills necessary to ride a chairlift.

The mountain is ideal for boarders. There are two terrain parks with jumps, bumps, rails, and a humongous halfpipe.

Arctic weather is the only downside to Tremblant that you can't do anything about—though you can ride up the mountain in a heated, eight-passenger gondola. The best time to visit is late March when the weather is warmer, there's still plenty of snow, and crowds are minimal.

Pack your French dictionary. The lifties will love you for it. And bring the kids. Few resorts in the East do more to appeal to families. It even has a "baby" snow park for the tiniest snow rats. Ski lessons are offered for three- to twelve-year-olds and snowboarding for those seven years old and up. Canadians believe that if your children can climb stairs unassisted, they're ready to ski and ice-skate.

No kids? Tremblant is as romantic as the snowiest winter scene in the film version of *Doctor Zhivago.*

Other activities include cross-country skiing, snowshoeing, dogsledding, horseback riding, tubing, and skating on the village's frozen lake.

There's a joie de vivre at Tremblant that is uncommon at North America ski resorts. It feels like a trip to Europe.

Tremblant
3005, Chemin Principal
Mont-Tremblant, Quebec J0T 1Z0
Canada

Phone: (819) 681–2000

Web Site: www.tremblant.com

E-mail: info@tremblant.com

Elevation: Top—2,871 feet; base—870 feet

Vertical Drop: 2,116 feet

Total Area: 610 acres

Number of Trails: 92

Longest Run: 3.75 miles

Terrain: 17% beginner; 33% intermediate; 50% advanced/expert

Average Annual Snowfall: 150 inches

Lifts: 12

Snowmaking: 464 acres

Central Reservations: (866) 836–3030

Snow Report: (800) 461–8711

Accommodations: There's a large selection of ski-in/ski-out hotels, lodges, and condos.

Getting There: Tremblant is a 1½-hour drive from Montreal.

Keep in Mind: Arctic blasts of cold air.

BEST BETS

Beginners: La Crete, Bon Vivant, and Nansen.

Intermediates: Flying Mile, Tremblant's original run.

Advanced: Ryan Haut and Ryan Bas.

Experts: Dynamite, reportedly the steepest run in eastern Canada.

Lunch: La Legende at the summit.

Off the Slopes: The spa at Le Scandinave, 3 miles from the mountain. Also worth exploring is the charming old town of St. Jovite.

Best Hotel: Hotel Quintessence.

 Ah, the Frenchness of it all. During the Camelot years, even the Kennedys came. It's the crème de la crème of the East, offering classic Quebecois skiing above a luxury Euro-style village. Families are titillated by it. Cruisers, both the skiing and the partying kind, revel in it. *C'est magnifique!*

EUROPE

The prime Alpine nations of Europe—Austria, France, Switzerland, and Italy—offer the broadest range of skiing in the world. The mountains are bigger than North America's, and so are the ski resorts. The vertical drops are often twice what you'll find at many Rocky Mountain resorts.

But the major difference in the Alps is the large number of interconnected circuits that link resorts. The European term for these vast expanses of linked terrain is ski circus. Just knowing there's a word for it helps you come to grips with the sheer magnitude of it all. For example, Trois Vallées, a French ski circus incorporating Courchevel, Méribel, and Val Thorens, offers more than 200 lifts and 375 miles of trails spread across 70,000 acres. (Vail, the largest single ski mountain in the United States, covers 5,000 acres.)

In the Alps, skiers and snowboarders can cover vast horizontal distances traveling between resorts, sometimes even crossing national boundaries. The range of ski lifts is mind boggling; it includes aerial trams that span entire valleys and funicular trains traveling beneath glaciers to mountain summits.

Many of the lower slopes at European resorts are owned by farming cooperatives. Villages, or lift companies, build lifts to serve skiers bound for a nearby web of lifts. Even ski schools often invest their profits in building new lifts to stay competitive with other ski centers.

But the European experience is far more than just skiing and snowboarding.

Alpine ski resorts are usually centered at charming centuries-old villages that serve outstanding cuisine and dole out roaring nightlife. And Europe's gateway cities include rich cultural attractions that merit stopovers en route to the slopes.

Resorts vary greatly both among and within countries. Generally, France doles out some of the most dramatic terrain in the Alps, the most modern lifts, and the largest linked trail networks. Italy always offers a good time, as well as outstanding cuisine, sunny slopes, and the extraordinary beauty of the Dolomites. Switzerland has many of the most charming resorts—and some of the swankiest, which are often ancient, traffic-free villages reached via spectacular train rides. It also boasts some of the longest slopes in the Alps, with many cross-border opportunities. Austria has a well-founded reputation for bucolic settings and friendly villages, with quality midrange accommodations and fervent après-ski.

When searching for accommodations in the Alps you'll come across the term "apartments," which you can interpret as the equivalent of North American condos, meaning there is a kitchen and adequate facilities to set up housekeeping for the duration of your stay.

And finally, English speakers do just fine in Europe, thanks to the polyglot nature of most Europeans. Whatever the situation, you'll always find an English speaker nearby.

BAD GASTEIN
Bad Gastein, Austria

It is a clean, neat little town with mountains rising on three sides and the Gastein Valley stretching across the other. Elderly Austrians in woolen knickers roam streets that wind and curl back upon themselves, hairpinning up the mountains. A waterfall flows wild through the heart of the town and echoes off the gorgelike village. Castlelike hotels cling to forested hills and seem to be the doing of a mad architect.

Bad Gastein resembles a stage set. At any moment you expect a fat lady with a soprano voice to start singing. In fact, Franz Schubert and Johann Strauss both composed here. It is typical of the little Austrian towns that the young want to get away from and the older folks long to return to. But it's also Austria's most important spa town and one of Europe's leading ski centers.

In the fifteenth century the surrounding thermal waters put Bad Gastein on the map. The story goes that Frederick, duke of Styria, was dying of a gangrenous wound and so traveled to a miraculous spring in the Gastein Valley—where he was cured. Word quickly spread and a village grew around the town.

But the Alpine magic of the place also provides outstanding skiing and snowboarding. Winter snows blanket more than 125 miles of slopes, drawing all levels of skiers and boarders to the Gastein ski region, which is one of Austria's largest.

The slopes are separated into four areas spread across five mountains. Along with the year-round resort town of Bad Gastein, two other down-valley villages—Bad Hofgastein and Dorfgastein—offer accommodations in pleasant surroundings and quick access to the Gastein ski terrain. Bad Hofgastein, 3 miles from Bad Gastein, is an old spa town with considerable modern sprawl.

Dorfgastein, thirty minutes from Bad Gastein, is rustic and reminiscent of its farming roots.

The largest ski area is above Bad Gastein. Two mountains face each other across the village—Stubnerkogel and Graukogel. Stubnerkogel, the most popular area, appeals to high-end intermediate and advanced skiers. But it also has several sunny, easy slopes that wind back to the village. Graukogel has wide, tree-rimmed autobahns suitable for intermediates as well as steeper pitches that serve as venues for World Cup slalom and giant-slalom races.

One favorite ski and snowboarding route is a pleasant 7-mile journey for intermediates down the back side of Stubnerkogel to the Angertal Valley. From there, you can head up to the Schlossalm area above Bad Hofgastein, where there's a terrain park and halfpipe. The route from Schlossalm down to the village can be as easy or as difficult as you make it.

Dorfgastein has its own network of trails, which are accessed by lifts located outside the town. Its isolation means it's often overlooked. But a skier or boarder would be remiss not to explore its extensive slopes, which also link with another valley to the east.

The fourth area is Sportgastein, 6 miles from Bad Gastein. It's mostly a one-trail mountain with several side variations and off-piste options that appeal to expert riders and skiers. Two back-to-back eight-passenger gondolas rise to 8,810 feet, making it the highest and most snow-sure skiing in the valley. The vertical drop is a leg-tiring 3,500 feet with World Cup steeps.

The Gastein Super Ski Pass covers all the areas, but only Stubnerkogel and

Schlossalm (the Bad Gastein–Bad Hofgastein route) are linked via lifts. Trains and shuttles, included in the ski pass, connect all the areas. But the service isn't always convenient, so this is one resort where a car optimizes the experience.

The region also markets a lift pass called Ski Alliance Amadé, covering more than thirty resorts in eastern Austria as well as the buses and trains in between. The pass accesses an impossible-to-imagine 276 lifts serving 540 miles of trails. A complete trail map, if there were one, would look like a large city telephone book. But it is extremely good value for those interested in exploring a much wider region than the Gastein Valley.

Other activities include ice skating, curling, tobogganing, horse-drawn sleigh rides, horseback riding, snowshoeing, indoor tennis, and soaking in the legendary hot springs, just like Duke Frederick.

Cross-country skiers enjoy 56 miles of trails, mostly stretching along the valley from Bad Hofgastein. If snow is thin in the valley, the 6-mile loop at Sportgastein is almost always well maintained.

Bad Gastein Tourist Office
Kaiser-Franz-Josef-Strasse 27
A-5630 Bad Hofgastein
Austria

Phone: 43–6432–3393

Web Site: www.gastein.com

E-mail: info@gastein.com

Elevation: Top—8,810 feet; base—3,250 feet

Vertical Drop: 5,560 feet

Total Trails: 125 miles

Longest Run: 7 miles

Terrain: 24% beginner; 66% intermediate; 10% advanced/expert

Lifts: 50

Snowmaking: 37 miles

Central Reservations: 43–6432–3393

Snow Report: www.gastein.com

Accommodations: Four-star hotels in Bad Gastein and Bad Hofgastein, plus plenty of smaller hotels and lodges. There are rustic chalets at Dorfgastein.

Getting There: It's 1 hour from Salzburg, 2 hours from Munich.

Keep in Mind: A car helps in getting to and from the base areas.

BEST BETS

Beginners: Angertal area between Bad Gastein and Bad Hofgastein.

Intermediates: Höhe Scharte down to Bad Hofgastein.

Advanced: World Cup slopes high on Graukogel.

Experts: Sportgastein.

Lunch: Kleine Scharte at Schlossalm.

Off the Slopes: Thermal baths and spa treatments. Also, you're only an hour by train from Salzburg, one of the most beautiful small cities in Europe.

Best Hotel: Elisabethpark Hotel in Bad Gastein; Grand Park Hotel in Bad Hofgastein.

 Above the breathtaking spa town of Bad Gastein, the mountains of Austria's Gastein Valley offer 125 miles of unforgettable cruising for intermediate and advanced skiers and snowboarders. Add fifty ski lifts and you've got a day of high mileage. And at the end of your adventure, the thermal baths are waiting for you.

INNSBRUCK
Innsbruck, Austria

Early in the nineteenth century, the German poet Goethe lived at Innsbruck's Hotel Goldener Adler, one of the oldest hostelries in Europe. Today the owner of the 600-year-old hotel, Paul Cammerlander, tells this story: Goethe was known to love poetry, wine, and women, and was once asked if he had to abandon one, which it would be. Poetry, he replied. And if you had to abandon another? Depends on the age, Goethe said.

History is everywhere in the 800-year-old capital of Austria's Tyrol region. You can even stay in Goethe's room at the Hotel Goldener Adler.

The streets of Innsbruck's compact, car-free Old Town recall past centuries in which the city flourished. Located near the Brenner Pass, the lowest pass crossing the main region of the Alps, Innsbruck was already a trading post in the twelfth century. Many of the grandiose buildings date from Emperor Maximilian I, whose reign from 1490 to 1519 signaled the end of the Middle Ages.

But Innsbruck, with a population 130,000 (a quarter of them university students) and a lively cultural life, also is one of Europe's oldest ski centers and the site of the 1964 and 1976 Winter Olympic Games. The miracle of snow repeats itself every winter. Here, history, culture, and skiing blend together. It's hard to imagine a place in Europe that better combines great skiing with the richness of Old World culture. You can even ski in the summer on the Stubai Glacier.

The skiing and snowboarding play out in six nearby ski regions that include fifteen rustic villages, fifty-nine lifts, and 80 miles of trails. The six resorts are collectively marketed as Olympia Ski World Innsbruck, and consist of Seegrube-Nordkette, Patscherkofel, Axamer Lizum, Glungezer, Schlick 2000, and the Stubai Glacier. They are not linked by lifts, and by European standards they are not large areas. Each can be explored in a day. But taken together over the course of a week, they offer all the variety a skier or boarder could wish for. Various combinations of multiday lift passes offer good value. If you need more, Seefeld is only thirty minutes away, St. Anton is an hour west, Kitzbühel is a one and a half hours to the east, and Garmisch-Partenkirchen is an hour across the border in Germany. All are easily accessible by rail, bus, or car.

The areas around Innsbruck are extremely popular with snowboarders, and there are plenty of terrain parks, pipes, rails, tables, and every other type of obstacle to shred and get airborne off. Seegrube-Nordkette is known for its steep and sometimes deep freeriding terrain. The Stubai Glacier area has a large terrain park and racecourse, plus plenty of mellow runs for beginners. Schlick 2000 delivers extraordinary natural terrain for carving.

Advanced skiers can test their mettle at the Olympic downhill run on Patscherkofel,

Green domes and red roofs of centuries-old baroque buildings stand in contrast to the steep, sheer sides of the mighty Alps that rise from the edge of Innsbruck. The ski and snowboarding slopes of six different areas are easily accessed via a free shuttle bus, while the city's extraordinary architecture recalls the glory days of the great Austrian Empire.

site of Franz Klammer's extraordinary, on-the-edge victory in the 1976 Games. (Many former World Cup racers and coaches remember it as the most remarkable run they ever witnessed.)

The greatest variety of terrain is offered at Axamer Lizum, southwest of Innsbruck, where the other 1976 Olympic ski races were held—including the women's down-hill. The area consists of two peaks, Hoadl and Pleisen, offering mostly wide-open ski-ing and boarding above the tree line.

For cross-country skiers, there are 170 miles of maintained trails at various eleva-tions in and around Innsbruck, plus more than 30 miles of toboggan runs—one a whopping 7 miles long. You can also fly down the Olympic bobsled run at Igls behind a veteran driver.

Pick your pleasure, which is an adequate way to sum up the Innsbruck experience.

Innsbruck Tourist Office
Burggraben 3
A-6021 Innsbruck
Austria

Phone: 43–512–59850

Web Site: www.innsbruck-tourism.at

E-mail: office@innsbruck-tourism.at

Elevation: Top—10,530 feet; base—1,890 feet

Vertical Drop: 5,547 feet from the highest lift-served point

Total Trails: 160 miles

Longest Run: 9 miles

Terrain: 35% beginner; 42% intermediate; 23% advanced/expert

Lifts: 75

Snowmaking: 25 miles

Central Reservations: 43–5125–8376–6

Snow Report: www.ski-innsbruck.at

Accommodations: Innsbruck offers a wide range of hotels, including 4- and 5-star establishments. The ski villages close to the ski areas also offer hotels, lodges, and apartments.

Getting There: Innsbruck has an interna-tional airport and is linked to the rest of Europe by major railways and roads.

Keep in Mind: This is not a large lift-linked ski circus.

BEST BETS

Beginners: Stubai Glacier.

Intermediates: The wide-open terrain of Axamer Lizum.

Advanced: The Olympic men's downhill run at Patscherkofel.

Experts: The steeps at Seegrube-Nordkette.

Lunch: Each resort has charming, rustic restaurants.

Off the Slopes: Explore Innsbruck's Old Town and the dozen museums.

Best Hotel: Goldener Adler in Innsbruck.

ISCHGL

Ischgl, Austria

With its charming, car-free old village, spectacular intermediate slopes surrounded by 10,000-foot peaks, and the exciting opportunity to cross into neighboring Switzerland, you wonder why the four-star hotels of Ischgl seek to attract skiers by putting scantily clad dancing girls in their bars. Even Aspen doesn't do that—or at least it doesn't pay the women to do it.

Ischgl (pronounced *ish-gull*) was founded centuries ago by farmers in the Tyrol's isolated, steep-sided Paznaun Valley. The first cable car went up in 1963, and for years the area attracted a small following of skiers from nearby Innsbruck and Munich. But things changed in the early 1990s when the resort staged an end-of-season outdoor concert starring Elton John. It drew thousands, and overnight Ischgl developed a party-town reputation, much to the chagrin of the local farmers. The resort continues to hold year-end concerts with headline entertainers that have included Alanis Morissette, Madonna, and Sting. But during the ski season, Ischgl's party-town reputation draws rowdy German and Scandinavian males, who take over the village.

If that scene doesn't appeal to you, stay 6 miles higher up the valley in the traditional Tyrolean village of Galtür. With a population of only 700 clustered around a baroque church, several quality hotels, and twenty-some restaurants, it's a fine place for families or couples who want to enjoy the serenity of the Alps while indulging in Austrian mountain culture. The village's ski school has a good reputation, especially with kids. Galtür also offers quality accommodations that are less expensive; there are regular shuttles to the larger Ischgl.

The region offers a five-area Silvretta ski pass that includes Ischgl, Galtür, Kappl,

See, and Samnaun in Switzerland. But it is Ischgl that offers the best skiing and snowboarding. It also has the highest lift—topping out at over 9,400 feet—and most of the skiing lies above 6,600 feet.

Ischgl's youthful crowd is big on snowboarding, and the resort boasts one of the largest terrain parks in Europe, as well as a huge halfpipe. The slopes are mostly long, groomed, and rated intermediate, which makes for exhilarating carving and, for some, a surefire cure for hangovers. Most of the slopes are north facing and above the timberline.

Beginner terrain is in short supply, however. For the most part it's clustered around Ischgl's sunny midstation, called Idalp.

A favorite milk run for many is the mellow trail down to duty-free Samnaun, Switzerland, where the shops sell mostly low-priced liquor and backpacks in which to carry it home. But you'll also find some deals on duty-free ski equipment. (Confident novices can pick their way down if the snow is groomed.) The return journey is via Samnaun's Pendelbahn, the world's first double-decker tram, which is fitted with escalators to ease boarding.

Getting around the main ski runs of Ischgl is easy. The resort boasts Austria's most efficient lifts, including sixteen high-speed chairs (with six-seaters and an eight-seater), three gondolas, two trams, and twenty surface lifts. Even the village offers an underground, 600-foot-long moving sidewalk to assist skiers in getting from one end of town to the other.

Expert skiers and boarders have to go off-piste to find exciting challenges and deep powder. Like most of the resorts in the Alps, you should go with a guide when exploring the backcountry. This is particularly

This Austrian resort tucked next to the Swiss border is little known among North American skiers. Yet Ischgl is a charming old Tyrolean village with vast intermediate terrain and reliable snow. The lift system is one of the most modern in Europe. Many also consider Ischgl Austria's best party town.

important at Ischgl: The area gets more snow than any other Tyrolean resort, and the surrounding mountains harbor serious avalanche terrain. Rescues and body retrievals occur during the course of most winters. But rest assured, within the ski area boundaries it's safe.

Still, in 1999 a freak and fearsome avalanche destroyed much of the outlying village of Galtür, killing forty people. The village quickly rebuilt and fortified its location. Ischgl puts a lot of effort into avalanche control. But during most winters, there are times when slides cover the road, preventing people from getting in or out. (In that respect, it is somewhat like Utah's Little and Big Cottonwood Canyons.) Ischgl pays for your accommodation on either end of the road if you're trapped for more than twenty-four hours because of closures.

Off-slope activities include ice skating, curling, winter hiking, tobogganing on a 4-mile floodlit run, and a sports center with a pool. Ischgl also has a small museum and library, as well as a casino for gaming. Thirty miles of cross-country trails fan out from Galtür.

If you like hard skiing by day and hard partying by night, Ischgl might just be the best resort you've never heard of.

Ischgl Tourist Office
P.O. Box 9
A-6561 Ischgl 320
Austria

Phone: 43–5444–5266

Web Site: www.ischgl.com

E-mail: info@ischgl.com

Elevation: Top—9,423 feet; base—4,593 feet

Vertical Drop: 4,829 feet

Total Trails: 130 miles

Longest Run: 7.5 miles

Terrain: 25% beginner; 60% intermediate; 15% advanced/expert

Lifts: 43

Snowmaking: 40 miles

Central Reservations: 43–5444–5266

Accommodations: Four- and 3-star hotels in Ischgl and Galtür; also plenty of apartments.

Getting There: Ischgl is 1½ hours from Innsbruck and 3 hours from both Munich and Zurich. The nearest train station is Landeck; shuttles continue the 20 miles to the resort.

Keep in Mind: Some ski terrain can close because of avalanche risk.

BEST BETS

Beginners: Above the village of Galtür, or the Idalp area of Ischgl.

Intermediates: Palinkopf down to Gampenalp.

Advanced: The Hollspitz chair.

Experts: Fimba Nord.

Lunch: Paznauner Taya above Bodenalp.

Off the Slopes: Ischgl is Austria's main party town, but there also are 11 smaller hamlets in the area worth exploring.

Best Hotel: Trofana Royal.

KITZBÜHEL
Kitzbühel, Austria

Standing at the top of the Streif downhill course on Kitzbühel's Hahnenkamn ski area, you feel like a bridge jumper. Beneath you is a wall of ice where World Cup racers accelerate to 80 miles per hour in a matter of seconds. It's one of the most feared downhill courses in international competition.

Far below, the historic village of Kitzbühel sparkles in the sunlight and buzzes with activity. The fourteenth-century St. Andreas church bells toll, and the sweet, cinnamon scent of apfelstrudel drifts with the mountain air along the cobbled, car-free streets of the town's center. It's a poster pinup of everything North Americans hope to find when skiing Europe.

Surrounding Kitzbühel is a network of sixty-four lifts linking five Tyrolean villages with 100 miles of well-maintained runs. Dotting the mountainsides are rustic restaurants serving exquisite regional fare. The town has loads of Tyrolean ambience, outstanding luxury hotels, and a wide range of great family-run three-star hotels.

Skiing has a long history here. In 1892 a young man named Franz Reisch discovered a book about skiing and promptly ordered a pair of Norwegian skis. He later became the town's mayor, and by 1902 members of the Kitzbühel Ski Club were schussing the slopes above town. The first race on Hahnenkamn's terrifying downhill course was held in 1931. A tradition took hold, and strong village boys quickly rose to the top ranks of ski racing; soon the resort was attracting nobility and the idle rich. The most famous racers were the "dream team from Kitz" in the 1940s and 1950s, which included Anderl Malterer, Fritz Huber, Christian Pravda, Hans Leitner, Ernst Hinterseer, and Toni Sailer. They won dozens of Olympic- and world-championship medals. Toni Sailer alone won three gold medals at the 1956 Cortina d'Ampezzo Winter Olympics, and Austria usurped Switzerland's claim to fame.

Today skiing and snowboarding define winter in Kitzbühel. The slopes fan out across four main areas, two of them linked by trail. The other two areas are connected via shuttle bus.

 This Alpine classic is the most glamorous resort in Austria. It's also one of the largest and has produced more Olympic- and world-champion skiers than anywhere else in the world. The slopes sprawl across humpbacked mountains for miles along the valley. The medieval town center offers outstanding accommodations, Tyrolean restaurants, and lively bars and clubs.

The most popular and the largest ski area is Hahnenkamn, which rises immediately above Kitzbühel. Don't worry: You can avoid the extreme slopes like Streif downhill course. Most of the terrain is ideally suited to intermediate skiers and riders.

The other major ski area is Kitzbüheler Horn, which rises from the other side of town. Its elevation is higher, and it usually has the best snow on a nice variety of trails that lead back to town. The smallest area is Bichlalm, located a few miles away via a shuttle bus. It features a high, sunny bowl and a delightful rustic Tyrolean restaurant called Rosi's.

One of the most exciting ski or snowboarding routes involves a daylong outing between Kitzbühel and the Pass Thurn ski area. The route covers 9 horizontal miles and twice that distance yo-yoing up and down the snowy peaks. A shuttle bus returns you to Kitzbühel.

Snowboarders mostly prefer the Kitzbüheler Horn area and its high-energy terrain park featuring pipes, table jumps, and a loud sound system. There's also a slalom course.

When the snow is deep, there are guides available to lead you to exciting off-piste terrain. But snow can be a sore point at Kitzbühel. High elevations are often the determining factor for quality snow in the Alps, and Kitzbühel's top elevation is less than 7,000 feet.

If you're looking for a smaller, quieter, and less expensive place to base yourself, there are two nearby romantic villages, Reith and Aurach. Both contain many outstanding restaurants and alpine inns. Another nice spot is Kirchberg, just 3 miles away.

There are more than 70 miles of cross-country trails in the surrounding area. Off the slopes are miles of maintained walking trails, sleigh rides, and horseback riding. There's also a sports center in Kitzbühel with ice skating, swimming, and tennis. The shopping is renowned, and the nightlife is almost as legendary as the slopes.

Kitzbühel Tourist Office
Hinterstadt 18, Box 164
A-6370 Kitzbühel/Tyrol
Austria

Phone: 43–5356–62155–0
Web Site: www.kitzbuehel.com

E-mail: info@kitzbuehel.com

Elevation: Top—6,560 feet; base—2,620 feet

Vertical Drop: 3,937 feet

Total Trails: 100 miles

Longest Run: 4 miles

Terrain: 50% beginner; 42% intermediate; 8% advanced/expert

Lifts: 64

Snowmaking: 35 miles

Central Reservations: 43–5356–62155–0

Snow Report: www.kitzbuehel.com

Accommodations: There's a wide range of hotels, lodges, and apartments in the village.

Getting There: Major rail line to the village. Both Innsbruck and Salzburg are 1 hour away. Munich's airport is 2 hours.

Keep in Mind: The Hahnenkamn race in mid-January draws 100,000 ski-race-crazy Europeans to Kitzbühel.

BEST BETS

Beginners: Hagstein on the Horn.

Intermediates: Raintal on the Horn.

Advanced: The bowl on Ehrenbachgraben.

Experts: The Streif downhill run.

Lunch: Hochkitzbühel at the top of the Hahnenkamn gondola, or Rosi's on Bich-lalm.

Off the Slopes: Innsbruck and Venice are just an hour away.

Best Hotel: Romantik Hotel Tennerhoft.

LECH

Lech am Arlberg, Austria

The slopes above the ancient village's domed church and covered wooden bridge are as well groomed as the mostly silver-haired folks who ski here. Lech's Old World charm has always been popular with the well-to-do and the well known, including royalty. The village retains much of its centuries-old history—aside from opulent new hotels frequented by the fur-coat crowd. But Lech is also the only town that has spawned four Olympic gold-medal winners in Alpine skiing. The top skiers include Patrick Ortlieb, Olympic downhill champion at Albertville in 1992.

Postcard-pretty Lech lies in a high sheltered valley blanketed by deep snowfalls. In winter the only road in is over the Flexen Pass from St. Anton via Stuben. The thirty-minute route crosses two 6,000-foot mountain passes and burrows through six tunnels. Winter conditions or avalanches can close the road for days.

Above Lech, just below Flexen Pass, is the village of Züers, which also offers luxury digs and has a reputation as one of the most exclusive ski destinations in the world. Understated elegance and quiet comfort are reflected in its four- and five-star hotels (many of them ski-in/ski-out). The two villages of Lech and Züers are the most chic and expensive resorts in Austria. Along with impeccably groomed intermediate slopes, skiers and snowboarders enjoy a high concentration of sunny days, cosmopolitan ambience, and, in Lech, lively nightlife.

On the trail above Lech is its car-free suburb of Oberlech, connected via tram and an underground tunnel. It houses a collection of upscale chalets and four-star hotels. Oberlech also is the name of the main ski area. The trails here are mostly intermediate, but, like everywhere in the Arlberg ski region, experts have plenty of off-piste possibilities. Across from Oberlech rise the slopes of Rüfikopf, which lead to Züers.

Lech is the prettiest of five villages that make up the Arlberg ski region; the others are Züers, Stuben, St. Christoph, and St. Anton. With a guide, it's possible to ski the vast reaches from St. Anton to Lech. On the return journey, however, adventurers must ride a shuttle back over the Flexen Pass from Züers to Stuben, before picking up the ski lifts again. In total, the Arlberg ski pass accesses more than 165 miles of trails served by eighty-plus lifts.

Lech and Züers share a system of bowls and ridges that stretch 75 miles and are served by thirty-four lifts on the Vorarlberg side of the Arlberg region. A popular route for intermediate skiers and boarders is the Weisse Ring (White Ring), or Madloch tour, which circumnavigates the ski area.

The route begins in Lech on a cable car that rises to the slopes on Rüfikopf. From there, two long and winding intermediate runs lead to the Trittkopf cable car above Züers. Or you can get there by skiing or boarding off-piste. From the top station, you ski down to Züers and cross the Flexon Pass highway on a snow-covered bridge to the

This elegant resort village in Austria's Vorarlberg state is endowed with a magnificent setting, varied terrain, and superbly groomed runs. Together with its neighbor Züers, Lech is the last bastion of five-star skiing in Austria. It links with St. Anton in Tyrol and is included on the Arlberg ski region lift pass.

high-speed Muggengrat lift serving the Züers See area. From its 8,000-foot summit, there are endless off-piste options as well as a lovely cruiser dropping 2,500 feet back to Züers. Another high-speed lift from the Züers See area climbs the Madloch Joch. From there, the Weisse Ring drops thousands of vertical feet to Lech via the hamlet of Zug, which is isolated in a lovely side valley 2 miles from Lech. Ski trails link it to Lech, but so does a narrow road used by horse-drawn sleighs. Cross-country ski trails and hiking paths also connect this romantic hideaway to Lech.

Despite its tony trappings, Lech doesn't deter snowboarders. The groomed slopes are popular with beginner and intermediate freeriders. Experts head to St. Anton or go off-piste. For tricksters, there's a terrain park and halfpipe above Lech.

Off-slope activities include ice skating, curling, and tobogganing. Cross-country ski trails loop around the Ferwall and Zuger Valleys. Lech is small, but it offers enough ambience for those who don't ski.

Lech Züers Tourism Office
A6764 Lech am Arlberg
Austria

Phone: 43–5583–21610

Web Site: www.lech-zuers.at

E-mail: info@lech.zuers.at

Elevation: Top—8,730 feet; base—4,760 feet

Vertical Drop: 3,960 feet

Total Trails: 165 miles

Longest Run: 6 miles

Terrain: 25% beginner; 50% intermediate; 25% advanced/expert

Lifts: 85

Snowmaking: 40 miles

Central Reservations: 43–5583–21610

Snow Report: 43–5583–1515

Accommodations: A few dozen 4- and 5-star hotels in Lech and Züers; also a collection of private lodges.

Getting There: The nearest major airport is Zurich, 125 miles away, with excellent rail and road connections.

Keep in Mind: This is as exclusive as Austrian skiing gets.

BEST BETS

Beginners: Oberlech.

Intermediates: Rüfikopf.

Advanced: Züers Tali down from Muggengrat.

Experts: Off-piste with a guide.

Lunch: Goldener Berg at Oberlech.

Off the Slopes: Soak up the romantic ambience of Lech, Züers, Zug, and Stuben.

Best Hotel: Gasthof Post in Lech.

MAYRHOFEN
Mayrhofen, Austria

The heart of the Ziller Valley's enormous ski terrain is the 200-year-old village of Mayrhofen. The icing on the cake, however, is the 10,000-foot Hintertux Glacier, which offers year-round skiing on challenging terrain. These two areas, along with Zell am Ziller and eight other villages and their adjacent slopes (Fügen, Hippach, Lanersbach, Finkenberg, Gerlos, Kallenbach, Vorderlanersbach, and Hochfügen), add up to more than 300 miles of ski and snowboarding runs creating an enormous ski region called Zillertal 3000.

The valley's main mountain is Penken, which is accessed via a huge, high-speed gondola from the edge of Mayrhofen; it delivers vast pistes of intermediate terrain. You also can reach Penken via an eight-passenger gondola from the village of Hippach. Lifts and trails link Penken to the neighboring resorts of Finkenberg, Vorderlanersbach, and Lanersbach. Snowmaking covers most of the slopes. But you can't ski from Penken back down to the village of Mayrhofen. You must download on the lift or ski to one of the other villages and ride the shuttle back.

Mayrhofen also is home to the small ski area of Ahorn, which offers perfectly pitched slopes for the beginners and children who come to Austria's Tyrol to partake in the legendary scenery and the joy that skiing and snowboarding offer. Most of them begin this lifelong journey on the right foot by enrolling in any of the area's storied ski schools. Peter Habeler directs one of them. In the 1980s he became an overnight legend when he, together with fellow Tyrolean Reinhold Messner, completed the first ascent of Mount Everest without supplemental oxygen, a feat that was considered impossible at the time.

Mayrhofen is at the crossroads of four side valleys of the Ziller that lead to the other ski areas. One of the valleys, the Tux, ends at the breathtaking glacier above the tiny village of Hintertux, which gives its name to the 10,600-foot-high snow-sure glacier. It offers an unusually high quality of advanced terrain for a year-round glacier. Steep runs on- and off-piste, as well as long intermediate boulevards, continue on through the forest and down to the valley, covering more than a vertical mile. To reach the summit, three high-speed gondolas rise one above the other and cover the distance from the valley to the glacier in just twenty minutes.

For high-octane snowboarders, Europe's highest World Cup–caliber halfpipe and a terrain park complement an enormous variety of freeriding terrain. The village at the foot of the glacier has a few quality hotels, apartments, and modest pensions—but it's nothing like the wide range of facilities offered at Mayrhofen.

Another top-tier ski area of the Ziller Valley is lift-linked to the villages of Zell am Ziller (ten minutes from Mayrhofen) and Gerlos (on a nearby mountain pass at 6,200 feet). The vertical drop is a whopping 4,700 feet of long intermediate runs and steep chutes. Gerlos attracts large numbers of boarders with slopeside speakers pounding out music to put riders in the groove.

Peter Habeler advises skiing the Ziller Valley from mountain to mountain, using linking lifts and the shuttles to create your own adventures rather than simply making laps up and down the same mountain. In other words, ski the European way.

The village of Mayrhofen is fairly large and offers a full complement of services. Nonetheless, the architecture is mostly in traditional style with cobblestone alleys, wrought-iron balconies, and candlelit windows. The many quality hotels are located away from the noisy pockets of nightlife. The resort is popular with families. The ski school and day care have excellent reputations.

Off-slope activities in Mayrhofen include ice skating, curling, horseback riding, sleigh rides, and winter walking trails. A sports center offers a swimming pool; spa treatments are available at several hotels. Day trips to 800-year-old Innsbruck, little more than an hour away by train, offer a rewarding break from the slopes.

Thirteen miles of cross-country trails are located at Lanersbach.

Mayrhofen Tourist Office
Dursterstabe 225
A-6290, Mayrhofen
Austria

Phone: 43–5285–67600

Web Site: www.mayrhofen.com

E-mail: info@mayrhofen.com

Elevation: Top—7,380 feet; base—2,066 feet

Vertical Drop: 5,314 feet

Total Trails: 319 miles in the Zillertal 3000

Longest Run: 3.5 miles

Terrain: 29% beginner; 59% intermediate; 12% advanced/expert

Lifts: 149 in the Ziller 3000

Snowmaking: 48 miles

Central Reservations: 43–5285–67600

Snow Report: www.mayrhofen.com

Accommodations: Many upscale hotels and budget-priced pensions.

Getting There: Innsbruck is 1 hour away, Munich, 2 hours.

Keep in Mind: Slopes and restaurants can be crowded. Lower runs often lack snow, and beginner terrain is limited.

BEST BETS

Beginners: Ahorn area.

Intermediates: Penken area.

Advanced: Hintertux Glacier.

Experts: Tour off-piste with a guide.

Lunch: Vroni's on Penken.

Off the Slopes: Explore Innsbruck, easily reached by train.

Best Hotel: Elisabeth in Mayrhofen; Hintertuxerhof in Hintertux; Sport Vital Hotel Theresa.

 The largest of a dozen small villages in the Ziller Alps, Mayrhofen is a beauty of a resort offering genuine Tyrolean hospitality. The slopes favor intermediate skiers, and the area is home to many of Austria's best snowboarders. The nightlife can test the limits of almost anyone. But it's also a great resort for families.

SAALBACH-HINTERGLEMM
Saalbach, Austria

In 1991, when the area was the venue for the World Alpine Ski Championships, Saalbach and Hinterglemm were almost 3 miles apart. Since then they've both grown—now they almost touch. The marriage has taken a hyphenated name, with the resort called Saalbach-Hinterglemm.

But for skiers and boarders, the ideal way to get from one village to the other is the scenic and exhausting long way around, taking advantage of the lift-linked ski circus that includes fifty-five lifts. En route, forty mountain huts offer opportunities to relax and enjoy regional cuisine served within the log walls of rustic, wurst-scented huts and sunny outdoor decks. It's one of the finest ski circuses in Austria.

The ski and snowboarding runs are mostly intermediate trails on sparsely wooded north- and south-facing slopes. But even though the runs are aimed at midlevel skiers, they're never boring for experts. North-facing slopes are long; south-facing slopes bask in the sunshine. Ski the southern slopes in the morning, the northern slopes in the afternoon.

The mountain ski route from village to village, which must be followed counterclockwise to get up all the slopes, hits seven major areas—Bernkogel, Kohlmaiskopf, Wildenkarkogel, Schattberg, Zwölferkogel, Hochalm, and Reiterkogel.

Saalbach's main street connects to the south-facing Bernkogel and Kohlmaiskopf lifts. The two mountains are divided by a deep gorge and link only at the village. On the other side of Kohlmaiskopf, moving counterclockwise, is the Wildenkarkogel area, with trails down the back side leading to a small third village called Leogang, which is older than Saalbach and Hinterglemm and oozes genuine rural ambience

with ornately stuccoed charm and gingerbread architecture. An eight-passenger gondola brings skiers back to the top of Wildenkarkogel with its trails down to Saalbach.

Across from Saalbach, on the north-facing slopes, the largest aerial tram in Austria climbs to the sunny slopes of Schattberg. Beneath the lift is a long moguled run for experts. At the top station, another lift traverses across the mountaintop to the Zwölferkogel area, offering long runs down to Hinterglemm, where you can access lifts to the final two areas, Hochalm and Reiterkogel.

 Almost all Austrian ski resorts are picture-postcard pretty, but they aren't always convenient to the slopes. At Saalbach, though, the slopes ramble down to the car-free streets of the village. The ski circus that links with Hinterglemm totals 120 miles of trails served by fifty-five lifts.

All seven areas have their own network of lifts serving myriad beginner and intermediate runs. It's one of the most remarkable ski circuses in the Alps for lower-level skiers—though again, the terrain also is varied enough for experts.

For snowboarders, halfpipes are positioned at Bernkogel and Hochalm, and there's a terrain park on the north-facing slopes above Hinterglemm. Eight miles of carving-only zones are positioned on the mountain, open to both boarders and skiers. Most of the lifts are chairs or gondolas, with only a few surface lifts to negotiate.

More than half the runs of the ski circus face south, however, and they can quickly lose their snow during warm weather. To combat this, an artillery of snowmaking cannons blows snow on most of the lower slopes. The resort also engages in excellent slope maintenance.

The two villages of Saalbach and Hinterglemm are squeezed among the 6,500-foot peaks of the beautiful, big-shouldered Glemmtal Valley. Saalbach is larger, more upscale and offers more services. It's also livelier, another one of Austria's great party towns. Most of the buildings are in the traditional style of the Tyrolean Alps, even though many have been built in the last twenty years. The village almost has a theme-park quality to it. But the mustard-colored onion-domed church is authentic, and Saalbach is one of the prettiest villages in Austria. With its proximity to the slopes, it is reminiscent of a purpose-built French resort. The main street is car-free and rimmed with top-tier hotels and stylish shops.

Hinterglemm mostly consists of unimaginative hotels scattered in distant areas away from the small town center. It's not as pricey as Saalbach, but it's still a pretty village, offering easy access to the north-facing slopes. Several nearby ski resorts are easy day trips via shuttle, including Bad Gastein and Zell am See.

Off-slope activities include ice skating, tobogganing, horse-drawn sleigh rides, and winter walking trails. There's also swimming, indoor tennis, and spa treatments.

Cross-country ski trails are limited, but there are 120 miles of trails at nearby Zell am See.

Saalbach Tourist Office
Glemmtaler Landesstrasse 550
A-5753 Saalbach
Austria

Phone: 43–6541–6800

Web Site: www.saalbach.at

E-mail: contact@saalbach.at

Elevation: Top—6,870 feet; base—3,050 feet

Vertical Drop: 3,290 feet

Total Trails: 120 miles

Longest Run: 4 miles

Terrain: 50% beginner; 40% intermediate; 10% advanced/expert

Lifts: 55

Snowmaking: 19 miles

Central Reservations: 43–6541–6271

Snow Report: www.saalbach.at

Accommodations: You'll find a wide range of hotels and pleasant pensions in both villages.

Getting There: Innsbruck is 2½ hours away; Munich, 3 hours.

Keep in Mind: Snow is often in short supply, especially on the south-facing lower runs. Expert terrain is in short supply, too.

BEST BETS

Beginners: Blue runs on Bernkogel and Schattberg.

Intermediates: The long run from Limbergalm to Vorderglemm.

Advanced: World Cup downhill run from Zwölferkogel.

Experts: Beneath the Schattberg tram.

Lunch: Waleggeralm on Hochalm.

Off the Slopes: Both Innsbruck and Salzburg are easy day trips.

Best Hotel: Krallerhof.

SCHLADMING
Schladming, Austria

Schladming is all about feeling good and being excited by the sheer beauty of the place, which is surrounded by gorgeous mountains holding up bowls of snow to toast your presence. It's about soaring down vast intermediate slopes with the sunshine filtered by pine trees. Like the mantra of an Eastern mystic, 600-year-old Schladming puts you in a be-here-now mind-set. It's a mellow kind of place that tugs at your emotions.

The chief product of Austria is scenery. And Schladming is located in the center of the nation, in the federal state of Styria, which itself is the heart of the mother lode of spectacular sights. A friendly and ancient town with 4,400 inhabitants, it serves as the regional capital. There are more residents than beds for tourists, which is unusual in such a well-known resort. The main square is car-free and is the focal point of most of the nightlife.

 This classic four-mountain resort with 100 miles of trails served by eighty-six lifts is paradise for intermediate-level skiers and boarders. Snowmaking blankets all the main runs; a nearby glacier offers year-round skiing. The town is steeped in tradition and regularly plays host to World Cup races.

Lording over the town are the twin peaks of Planai and Hochwurzen, two perfectly pitched mountains made for swooping turns and linked via a lift that travels through a tunnel. The slopes also connect in the valley at opposite ends of the town. Most of the trails are forested, north facing, and groomed to corduroy perfection. But there also are wide-open bowls above the tree line near the summits.

Lifts and trails on Planai's summit slopes link to a neighboring mountain called Hauser Kaibling. From its 6,600-foot summit, you can ski and snowboard broad, sheltered runs down to the valley. At the base of Hauser Kaibling is the rustic village of Haus, which offers several quality hotels and restaurants, and a much quieter après-ski scene than Schladming.

The fourth linked mountain is Reiteralm, which connects with Hochwurzen at the valley. Shuttle buses also link each of the mountain bases to Schladming.

All four mountains offer mostly broad intermediate trails that zigzag through the forest. Snowmaking covers all the main runs to the valley floor, ensuring good early-season skiing. Schladming hosts a World Cup downhill race almost every January.

But considering its stellar reputation as a World Cup venue, there are surprisingly few expert slopes on the main runs of the four areas. Both Planai and Hauser Kaibling have some steep, if short, bump runs near their summits. The World Cup men's downhill course has a steep section at the finish, which also has been used as a venue for World Cup slalom races.

Snowboarders groove on terrain parks that include pipes and rails. A few of the slopes are floodlit for night riding.

In a high, nearby side valley is the Rohrmoos ski area, which links to year-round lifts on the Dachstein Glacier, a forty-five-minute shuttle ride away. Rohrmoos is an ideally pitched hill for first-time skiers and boarders. After a few days, they're ready for the other mountains, particularly the easy slopes at the top of Planai.

Schladming appeals to kids in a big way. It has a snow playground with a magic carpet lift, snow caves, and other distractions to keep their minds busy while they learn to get comfortable on their skis or snowboards. The play is supervised by instructors who get the kids higher up the mountain as soon as they're ready.

Schladming is part of the Ski Alliance Amadé ski pass, which covers more than 400 miles of trails at thirty ski areas in eastern Austria.

Off the slopes, you'll find ice skating, curling, horse-drawn sleigh rides, winter hiking trails, and an exciting 4-mile-long toboggan run. Schladming also has a sports center with a swimming pool, indoor tennis, and spa treatments. The splendid city of Salzburg is an easy train ride away.

Schladming rivals Seefeld as one of the best cross-country ski resorts in Austria. It has more than 200 miles of trails and was the venue for the 1999 World Cross-Country Ski Championships.

Schladming-Rohrmoos Tourist Office
Rohrmoosstrasse 234
A-8970 Schladming
Austria

Phone: 43–3687–22777

Web Site: www.tiscover.at/schladming

E-mail: info@schladming-rohrmoos.com

Elevation: Top—6,610 feet; base—2,440 feet

Vertical Drop: 4,170 feet

Total Trails: 104 miles

Longest Run: 5 miles

Terrain: 29% beginner; 61% intermediate; 10% advanced/expert

Lifts: 86

Snowmaking: 104 miles

Central Reservations: 43–3687–22268–0; www.schladming.com

Snow Report: www.schladming.com

Accommodations: There's a wide range of apartments, pensions, and a few upscale hotels.

Getting There: Schladming is 56 miles south of Salzburg.

Keep in Mind: Not much variety or expert terrain.

BEST BETS

Beginners: Upper bowl on Planai.

Intermediates: Hauser Kaibling has several excellent top-to-bottom trails.

Advanced: The men's and women's World Cup runs.

Experts: Off-piste with a guide.

Lunch: Onkel Willi's on Planai.

Off the Slopes: Salzburg is an easy day trip.

Best Hotel: Sporthotel Royer.

SEEFELD
Seefeld, Austria

Sometimes, from up on the ski mountains, it's easy to forget that the picture-postcard villages of the Alps are not just extravagant settings concocted as backdrops to please visitors. Indeed, amid these hulking mountains is a world of rich cultures, traditions, and proud people. Many of them depend on tourism, but they also live well without it. For visitors, skiing and snowboarding are ways to glimpse their world. Villages like Seefeld give you that opportunity.

Imagine, for instance, the radiant Austrian brides who have ambled down the aisle of Seefeld's ancient church in the last 500 years. Think of proud, barrel-chested fathers clutching their daughters' white-lace-covered arms.

Located just 15 miles south of Innsbruck near the border of Germany, Seefeld is one of the prettiest spots in the Alps. It's also long lived. The village is ancient. Mention of Seefeld first appeared in Roman documents in the year 1022. In the fourteenth century it was an important pilgrimage site after a reported miracle took place in the church. During the Middle Ages, it was a major market town along a major trade route.

The fifteenth-century St. Oswald church dominates this fairy-tale village. Beneath its red steeple are more five-star hotels than you'll find at any other resort in the Alps. Austria's Seefeld is all charm and scenery. The slopes are pleasant, and dozens of other major resorts are within easy striking distance, including Garmisch-Partenkirchen in Germany.

The railway linking Seefeld to Munich and Innsbruck arrived in 1912, and the village quickly became a popular summer resort. Lift-serviced skiing developed after World War II, and *Seefeld* became a household name throughout the Alps in the 1950s, when local boy Tony Seelos became a world-champion skier.

At the heart of the village is a car-free, cobblestone center rimmed by steep roofs, ornate balconies, and the post-and-beam craftsmanship typical of Tyrolean architecture. Hotels are small, intimate, and upscale. There are more than half a dozen five-star hotels, and about thirty four-star hotels. Ninety-eight percent of them are family run, and guests are treated like family.

And the skiing? It's worthy of the village and the setting. The slopes run the gamut from easy blues to wide-open intermediates and expert pitches that separate the lookers from the doers. In recent years the resort has hosted some of Europe's biggest snowboarding competitions. The area is part of the stunning Karwendel nature preserve, stretching along a high, sunny plateau and surrounded by three mountain ranges.

The resort is also internationally famous as the site of most of the Nordic cross-country skiing events in the 1964 and 1976 Innsbruck Olympics. It also was the venue for the 1985 Nordic skiing world championships. Almost 150 miles of expertly groomed trails loop across the spectacular landscape. It might be the best cross-country ski resort south of Scandinavia.

The two main Alpine ski areas— Gschwandtkopf and Rosshütte—are located just beyond the village and are reached by free shuttle buses. Gschwandtkopf is an ideal beginner mountain. Shaped like a huge mogul, with perfectly pitched learning terrain, it offers almost 1,000 vertical feet of ballroom skiing and snowboarding. The main slopes are at the much larger Rosshütte area, which sports plenty of ego-boosting intermediate terrain. A funicular from the base rises to midmountain, connecting to other lifts that fan out and access the resort's 6,700-foot summit.

Rosshütte boasts a 3,000-foot vertical drop, as well as a terrain park and halfpipe. A cable car spans a small valley accessing another area named Harmelekopf, which serves up the resort's most challenging runs. The exciting off-piste routes are best explored with a local guide.

But for the skiers and snowboarders who travel to Europe chasing big, challenging verticals, Seefeld is the perfect base for exploring many other great, close-by resorts. A multiday lift pass covers twelve surrounding resorts in Austria and Germany. And if the weather is bad for a day, or you need to rest that old high school volleyball injury, jump the train for a thirty-five-minute journey to the Old World pleasures of Innsbruck.

Seefeld's sports center offers ice skating, swimming, indoor tennis, curling, and fitness facilities. There also are winter walking trails and romantic sleigh rides.

Seefeld is a great place to ski—but there are many other reasons to visit. And they all contribute to making this one of the best ski resorts in the world.

Seefeld Tourismusverband
A-6100 Seefeld
Austria
Phone: 43–5212–2313

Web Site: www.seefeld.at

E-mail: info@seefeld.tirol.at

Elevation: Top—6,775 feet; base—3,937 feet

Vertical Drop: 2,953 feet

Total Trails: 20 miles

Longest Run: 3 miles

Terrain: 40% beginner; 40% intermediate; 20% advanced/expert

Lifts: 25

Snowmaking: 3 miles

Central Reservations: 43–5212–2313

Snow Report: www.tiscover.com/seefeld

Accommodations: Eight 5-star and 30 4-star hotels, plus many other lower-rated hotels, and private chalets.

Getting There: Munich is the nearest international airport (2 hours). Innsbruck is 15 miles away. Seefeld is on a major European rail route.

Keep in Mind: There isn't a great deal of variety on the local slopes.

BEST BETS

Beginners: Gschwandtkopf.

Intermediates: Rosshütte.

Advanced: Rosshütte.

Experts: Harmeleabfaht.

Lunch: Rosshütte at midmountain.

Off the Slopes: The Schloss Ambras castle is nearby, and the cultural richness of Innsbruck is just 15 miles away.

Best Hotel: The 5-star Klosterbrau, a former sixteenth-century monastery.

SÖLDEN
Sölden, Austria

The Ötz Valley and its spectacular 2-mile-high mountains have attracted visitors for a long time. Sölden's ski club dates back to 1910, but people were up on the glaciers long before that. Nearby is the site of the well-publicized 1991 discovery of the 5,000-year-old frozen man preserved in glacier ice. The corpse was named Ötzi the Iceman and is permanently on display in Bolzano, Italy. (Austrians found him, but the glacier site is just across the border in Italy.)

Located near the Italian border, 56 miles southwest of Innsbruck, Sölden lies in the Ötz Valley and offers high-altitude skiing and snowboarding on two snow-sure glaciers. Away from the glaciers, most of the slopes are above 6,800 feet, which is usually high enough to trap and keep snow. The combination of glaciers and altitude makes Sölden one of the most snow-reliable ski resorts in Austria.

The village consists of Tyrolean architecture but lacks the Alpine charm of resorts like Saalbach and Lech. Hotels, restaurants, and bars stretch along the bustling valley floor for 2 miles. The place is crowded with traffic and lacks a town center. Still, the resort does have a lively atmosphere. Its party-town reputation almost rivals that of Ischgl or Saalbach; it's one of the rowdiest resorts in the Alps.

But you can get away from the noise. Above Sölden, there is a quiet alternative in the tiny village of Hochsölden. Along the valley floor, within a few miles of Sölden, there also are two compact villages—Vent and Zwieselstein—both offering fine accommodations and restaurants.

And just 8 miles away is the resort of Obergurgl, a classic Tyrolean village with fewer lifts than Sölden and outstanding off-piste terrain.

At Sölden, the ski and snowboarding terrain beneath razor-sharp peaks is split into two main sectors linked by lifts. One sector consists of Gaislachkogl and Giggijoch, two mountain faces that are reached by lifts from opposite ends of the village. Both of these areas consist of wide-open skiing near their summits. In powder snow you ski almost everywhere. Lower down are intermediate-level, tree-rimmed runs leading back to the village. Gaislachkogl offers an exciting variety of intermediate and advanced terrain. Giggijoch has some high beginner slopes and several intermediate trails.

The other sector includes the Tiefenbach and Rettenbach Glaciers, which are connected by a tunnel and ski lifts, making this the only linked glacial ski area in the Alps. The slopes are perched between 8,800 feet and 10,600 feet, and both glaciers offer summer skiing.

Milelong Tiefenbach Glacier is nicely pitched for intermediate skiers. Beginner and advanced trails also are part of the mix. Rettenbach Glacier offers some gentler runs plus a World Cup training center and racecourse. During the month of October, many of the national ski teams from Europe and North America train here as a final tune-up before the World Cup season, which traditionally begins with a race on the Rettenbach Glacier.

For snowboarders, there are terrain parks and halfpipes at Giggijoch and on the Rettenbach Glacier. The park at Giggijoch is large, containing several pipes, rails, and jumps.

But overall, there is little in the way of expert terrain on the main slopes at Sölden. Off-piste, it's another matter. Experts can hire a guide in the village and enjoy exciting off-trail options at both

Two glaciers linked to the two-mountain ski area above the village add up to Austria's largest glacier ski area, making Sölden one of the most snow-sure of the 119 ski resorts within an hour or so of Innsbruck. The vertical drop is more than 6,000 feet. The village also has a reputation for wild nightlife.

Sölden and Obergurgl. And the mountain-top ridges of the Ötz Valley offer some of Austria's best ski touring.

Off the slopes, there's ice skating, horse-drawn sleigh rides, tandem hang gliding, and a 4-mile-long floodlit toboggan run. There's also a sports center with a swimming pool and spa treatments. Innsbruck is an easy day trip, and perfect for a bad-weather day.

Sölden offers 10 miles of cross-country ski trails. Nearby Langenfield, accessible via a shuttle bus, has 30 miles of trails. Winter walking trails are also in the area.

Sölden Tourist Office
P.O. Box 80A
A-6450 Sölden
Austria

Phone: 43–5254–5100

Web Site: www.soelden.com

E-mail: info@soelden.com

Elevation: Top—10,660 feet; base—5,495 feet

Vertical Drop: 6,136 feet

Total Trails: 88 miles

Longest Run: 6 miles

Terrain: 52% beginner; 32% intermediate; 16% advanced/expert

Lifts: 34

Snowmaking: 17 miles

Central Reservations: www.soelden.com

Snow Report: www.soelden.com

Accommodations: There is a good selection of quality hotels, lodges, and apartments in the village.

Getting There: Regular bus service from Innsbruck to Sölden. Also trains to Ötztal station, 25 miles away, with shuttles to Sölden.

Keep in Mind: Wild nightlife and not much for experts.

BEST BETS

Beginners: The Giggijoch area and the Rettenbach Glacier.

Intermediates: Gaislachkogl.

Advanced: Tiefenbach Glacier.

Experts: Off-piste with a guide.

Lunch: Gampealm at Rettenbachtal.

Off the Slopes: A swimming pool at the sports center. A day trip to Innsbruck.

Best Hotel: The Central.

ST. ANTON AM ARLBERG

St. Anton am Arlberg, Austria

There is a carnival atmosphere when the train pulls into the station at the storybook village of St. Anton. Late on a winter afternoon, brightly clothed skiers and boarders slide through the crowds on the main street, looking for warm taverns in which to recount the thrills of the day played out on the high slopes above.

At some of the hotels, the usual group of ski instructors is drinking with their clients from pitcher-size mugs. It is a ritual that is part of the lore of St. Anton, which boasts one of the best and largest ski schools in Europe and has a tradition going back to the beginning of the sport.

In a sense downhill skiing was invented at St. Anton, when a young villager named Hannes Schneider turned skiing from horizontal labor into vertical enjoyment, and came up with effective ways of teaching it. The year was 1901, and his method became known around the world as the "Arlberg technique." The strong village boys of St. Anton have been cashing in ever since.

Nestled in the spectacular snow-draped Arlberg range in western Austria, St. Anton is where people who prefer quaintness to massive sprawl come to ski vast and exciting runs. It is one of the most famous addresses in the world for winter sports—an age-old settlement whose cultural and social traditions date back centuries.

The village is showcased by Tyrolean architecture. Hotels are privately owned. There are no high-rises, no condo sprawl. St. Anton's ancient onion-domed church still dominates the human-made horizon, dwarfed by nature's work rising steeply above it. The emphasis is on good, hard skiing by day and hard partying by night. The quality of both is uncommonly high.

A sweeping ski circus links St. Anton and the lovely nearby villages that make up the Arlberg ski region, which includes eighty-two lifts and 165 miles of prepared slopes—plus all the easily accessible off-piste skiing. For boarders, the steep terrain yields quality freeriding and a trickster's bag of natural hits.

The 8,000-foot-high jagged summits that loom above the valley offer every kind of skiing imaginable. The terrain is sprawling and wide ranging. You can snowride anywhere and find nice, long steep runs. There are no glacier crevasses to cross or 500-foot cliffs that come out of nowhere. You see it and you ride it.

St. Anton is one of four fairy-tale villages linked along a winding 10-mile road, crossing two mountain passes and forming the Arlberg ski region. The other resorts are St. Christof, Züers, and Lech. Taken together, these snowbound gems offer some of the finest skiing in Europe. The snowfall is plentiful, and the season stretches to the end of April—uncommon in Europe. The region is so perfectly laid out that after spending the day skiing the Arlberg from one end to the other, you can catch a regular train that goes under the mountains to return you to St. Anton in five minutes.

 This is a wonderland of fairy-tale villages set among some of Europe's most captivating alpine scenery. The Arlberg region has Austria's most famous ski terrain. Some say its ski instructors taught the world to ski, moving to new mountain ranges like missionaries.

The mountain pass near St. Anton, which connects Western Europe with Austria and Central Europe, has been a trading route since at least the fourteenth century. A herdsman built a hospice here in 1386, and in 1884 the railway came, putting Arlberg on a line connecting Paris and Vienna.

If you haven't been to St. Anton for a few years, you won't recognize the place. The railway that once split the town has been rerouted to a new station on the valley's edge. Ski slopes now flow into the traffic-free village center. There's a lot of commercialism, but it hasn't spoiled the alpine charm. Unless you long to ski the vertical cliffs of Chamonix or the steep chutes of Verbier, European skiing really doesn't get any better than St. Anton.

Ernest Hemingway, during his Paris years in the early 1920s as a reporter for the *Toronto Star,* spent two winters in Schruns, not far from St. Anton. He wrote: "Towards spring there was the great glacier run, smooth and straight if our legs could hold it, our ankles locked, we running so low, leaning into the wind, dropping forever and ever in the silent hiss of the crisp powder. It was better than any flying or anything else."

St. Anton am Arlberg
Tourist Office St. Anton am Arlberg A-6580 Austria

Phone: 43–5446–22690

Web Site: www.stantonamarlberg.com

E-mail: info@stantonamarlberg.com

Elevation: Top—9,222 feet; base—4,278 feet

Vertical Drop: 4,944 feet

Total Trails: 165 miles

Longest Run: 6.3 miles

Terrain: 26% beginner; 42% intermediate; 32% advanced/expert

Lifts: 82

Snowmaking: 40 miles

Central Reservations: www.stantonamarlberg.com

Snow Report: www.stantonamarlberg.com

Accommodations: A wide range of privately owned lodges and hotels in the village.

Getting There: St. Anton is 3 hours by train and car from Zurich, Salzburg, Innsbruck, and Munich. Train station at the village.

Keep in Mind: It fills up on weekends. Intermediate heaven, but slim pickings for beginners.

BEST BETS

Beginners: The base area of St. Christof.

Intermediates: From the Valluga summit to the valley floor.

Advanced: Moguls off the Tanzboden lift.

Experts: The off-piste bowls.

Off the Slopes: Visit the ski museum in St. Anton.

Best Hotel: St. Antoner Hoff.

STUBAI GLACIER
Neustift im Stubaital, Austria

In the 1964 and the 1976 Innsbruck Winter Olympics, not a single alpine event was held on the Stubai Glacier, just forty-five minutes from the capital of Austria's Tyrol. And yet it would be hard to find an international-caliber ski racer or snowboarder who hasn't trained here. For racers, running gates at Stubai is like going to grad school. It might be August, or October, midwinter, or even nighttime under the lights, but sooner or later every national ski team member from around the world will spend at least a few days working on technique at the perfectly pitched river of ice that is the Stubai Glacier.

There are five glacial ski resorts in Austria's Tyrol region; Stubai is the biggest and best, offering snow-riding on four separate glaciers. The terrain offers vast intermediate runs made for autobahn-like cruising with some tough, don't-let-fear-hold-you-back steeps. There also are plenty of trails for beginners to zigzag their way down to the valley. The summit approaches 10,600 feet, and one run stretches more than 6 miles on this snow-sure, 10,000-year-old glacier.

Innsbruck's top-gun ski instructor Bernhard Schlechter takes most of his clients to Stubai. "The runs are wide open and the snow is always good," he says.

A gondola whisks skiers from the base to a midmountain point on the glacier high above tree line. Overhead, the mountain and its glacier rise like the crest of a flood. Lifts fan out serving a wide variety of runs geared to every level of snowrider. The summit is reached via a six-passenger, state-of-the-art gondola. In some places boulders as big as boxcars perch on the glacier to bring perspective to a world awash in blinding white snow and deep blue sky. But stay on the trails. The off-piste areas are littered with

dangerous crevasses bridged by snow. Like Central Park after midnight, it's no place for amateurs. Local guides are available to take you on spectacular back-of-beyond adventures that will have you writing postcards to every skier you know back home.

 The Stubai Glacier, the largest in Austria, offers year-round skiing. A training ground for the world's best ski racers for more than twenty-five years, it shares a lift ticket with five other resorts less than an hour's drive from Innsbruck.

In recent years the Stubai Glacier, like many of Innsbruck's surrounding resorts, has become a paradise for snowboarders, offering exciting freeriding and a terrain park featuring rails, halfpipes, tabletops, and more. At Daunferner there's a carving run with a traffic light to let you know when the coast is clear to soar down the mountain. There also are two giant-slalom runs set for your pleasure—or demise, if you don't round off your turns.

Beyond the lower reaches of the glacier, the valley has a rich skiing tradition. Traveling overland by skis was the way of winter long before the notion of a ski vacation ever took hold. The ski is to Tyrolean farmers what the canoe was to Native Americans, or what the snowshoe was to the French trappers.

A string of Christmas card–like Tyrolean villages lies in the bucolic Stubai Valley below the glacier. The main town is Neustift, 12 miles from the skiing at Stubai. You'll find a nice selection of quality hotels and sufficient dining facilities. A few small ski hills sit next to the village. And the cultural riches of Innsbruck are just thirty minutes away.

Off the glacier, activities include ice skating, tobogganing, horseback riding, indoor swimming, hiking, and bowling. Ice climbing is popular, and introductory courses are offered.

More than 60 miles of well-maintained cross-country ski trails lace the Stubai Valley.

Neustift im Stubaital Tourist Office
A-6167 Neustift im Stubaital
Austria

Phone: 43–5226–2228

Web Site: www.stubaital.at

E-mail: tv.neustift@neustift.at

Elevation: Top—10,502 feet; base—5,300 feet

Vertical Drop: 4,756 feet

Total Trails: 32 miles

Longest Run: 6 miles

Terrain: 20% beginner; 35% intermediate; 45% advanced/expert

Lifts: 23

Snowmaking: 6 miles

Central Reservations: 43–5226–2228

Snow Report: 43–5226–2228

Accommodations: There's a wide selection of 3- and 4-star hotels in Neustift.

Getting There: Easy access from Innsbruck via the Stubaital railroad and shuttle buses.

Keep in Mind: This is high-altitude skiing. In bad weather, whiteout conditions make skiing near impossible.

BEST BETS

Beginners: Trail 1 down the glacier's bowl.

Intermediates: Trail 17 off the Sesselbahn.

Advanced: The 6.5-mile-long Trail 14 to the valley.

Experts: Trail 18 to the base of the Rotadl chairlift.

Lunch: Zur Goldenen Gams.

Off the Slopes: Explore 800-year-old Innsbruck.

Best Hotel: Sonnhof in Neustift.

ZELL AM SEE
Zell am See, Austria

A tenth-century tower overlooks the medieval town center. Skaters wearing bright scarves move like Brueghel figures on the frozen lake, which rims one side of Zell am See. On the other side, skiers and snowboarders rise in an aerial tram bound for the sugarcoated slopes of Schmittenhöhe. An electric train whines along the track and stops at the station, then departs on its hour-long journey to the spectacular city of Salzburg.

Zell am See is one of Austria's prettiest resorts, drawing visitors from all over Europe to its four-season playground. Skiers and snowboarders even journey here in summer to enjoy the high slopes of the Kitzsteinhorn Glacier above the resort town of Kaprun, which is just ten minutes up the valley. During the winter season, the most popular slopes are on Schmittenhöhe. The two areas are separated by a steep-sided

The lovely lakeside resort of Zell am See offers sunny slopes and the snow-sure bowls of a neighboring glacier. The town is a mix of Old World charm and modern sport-crazy Austria. The Grossglockner—Austria's highest mountain—towers nearby.

valley and linked via a common lift ticket and shuttle buses.

Schmittenhöhe tops out at 6,500 feet. The skiing and snowboarding begin on long, gently pitched ridges above the timberline. The views are stunning. Far below is the lovely town, backdropped by the stillness of the frozen lake and the panorama of the surrounding Alps. The scene is reminiscent of Heavenly Ski Resort in California, with its wild views of Lake Tahoe. Skiers can keep doing laps on the summit lifts of Schmittenhöhe or head for more challenging terrain, where the ridge trails suddenly swoop into the forest and morph into New England–style cruisers that hairpin their way down the contours of the mountain. The longest run rambles for 4 miles.

Over on the 9,900-foot Kitzsteinhorn Glacier, the high runs drop into vast snow-filled bowls scoured by beginner and intermediate runs. Short, challenging mogul-filled pitches also dot the area, while fresh-faced fields of powder entice freeriders to explore the perimeters. Beginners enjoy a nice smorgasbord of mellow trails lower down on the mountain.

And like most of Austria's resorts, both Kaprun and Zell am See have acres of challenging off-piste skiing—and guides available to lead you down the best routes and then back to the lifts. Both areas have terrain parks and halfpipes.

Zell am See is one of the sunniest areas of the Alps. And that's the problem. Too often the lower slopes lack snow.

Snowmaking supplements many of the runs, but in dry times it barely yields enough snow to keep the main freeways skiable; rocks emerge like the treads of a well-worn carpet.

The glacier at Kaprun is always snow-sure. But if the snow is bad at Zell am See, it's bad at other nearby ski areas, which also shuttle skiers to the glacier and diminish the ski experience, mostly because of long lift lines. Neither the glacier nor Schmittenhöhe is large in relation to many of the other popular ski areas in the Alps.

Still, no one can deny that Zell am See is a jewel of a resort. The town center is a car-free medieval treasure, but it's no rustic village. The small vibrant city has a population of 10,000, and even a few traffic lights. An excellent range of two-, three-, and four-star hotels, outstanding restaurants and shops, as well as lively nightspots lines its warren of crooked streets. The spectacular lake and mountain setting appeal to everyone. Couples come looking for a romantic holiday, families come seeking a memorable ski vacation, and singles come to chase whatever they can find. It is one of Austria's earliest resorts, dating back to 1893. The Kitzsteinhorn was Austria's first glacier ski area. Zell am See also has served as the venue for the World Alpine Ski Championships. And as in Chamonix, France, visitors can't help but absorb the mountain heritage when they stroll the town or cruise the slopes.

Zell am See also is a good base to explore other nearby areas. Bad Gastein, Kitzbühel, and Saalbach are easily reached by bus and train.

Off-slope activities at Zell am See include ice skating, tobogganing, horse-drawn sleigh rides, indoor swimming and tennis, and scenic flights in hot-air balloons and gliders.

The broad valley offers more than 120 miles of cross-country ski trails and more than 60 miles of winter walking paths.

Zell am See Tourist Office
Brucker Bundesstrasse
A-5700 Zell am See
Austria

Phone: 43–6542–7700

Web Site: www.zellamsee.com

E-mail: welcome@europasportregion.com

Elevation: Top—6,569 feet (Kaprun 9,938 feet); base—2,490 feet

Vertical Drop: 4,000 feet

Total Trails: 81 miles

Longest Run: 4 miles

Terrain: 38% beginner; 50% intermediate; 12% advanced/expert

Lifts: 57

Snowmaking: 38 miles

Central Reservations: 43–6542–2032

Snow Report: www.zellamsee.com

Accommodations: There's a wide range of hotels and lodges in Zell am See. Kaprun offers good budget accommodations.

Getting There: Train station at the resort. Salzburg is 56 miles away; Munich, 120 miles.

Keep in Mind: The ski terrain is not enormous, and snow quantity is often a problem.

BEST BETS

Beginners: The lower slopes next to Kaprun.

Intermediates: Standard run.

Advanced: Trass run.

Experts: Off-piste with a guide.

Lunch: Glocknerhaus.

Off the Slopes: Take the train to Salzburg.

Best Hotel: Salzburgerhof.

ALPE D'HUEZ
Alpe d'Huez, France

The resort is an easy hour east of the Olympic city of Grenoble. Its craggy peaks often jut out from a sea of clouds high above the Romanche Valley in a range of the Alps called the Grandes Rousses. Alpe d'Huez is one of the highest and sunniest ski resorts in Europe. Its marketers call it "the island in the sun," and on many days that's a fair assessment. On a clear day, they say you can see a fifth of France from the summit.

The resort dates back to the 1930s but was little known until its slopes served as a venue for some of the skiing competitions at the 1968 Olympic Winter Games. A growth spurt followed in all manner of

architectural styles. Alpe d'Huez is now one of the largest single resorts in the Alps, offering more than 140 miles of linked trails served by eighty-seven lifts.

But it was American cyclist Lance Armstrong who brought Alpe d'Huez to the wide screens of North American sports fans. Armstrong garnered victories in the Tour de France, the world's most grueling road race, by winning big in the mountains. The switchbacks up to Alpe d'Huez are as challenging as any he had ever encountered.

The skiing and snowboarding are on an equally grand scale. The resort is defined by five linked villages—Alpe d'Huez, Vaujany, Oz-en-Oisans, Villard-Reculas, and Auris. All have deep local roots but have been taken over by developers, giving the entire resort a modern, purpose-built appearance. Tiny Vaujany is perched across from its own ski area and links to the Alpe d'Huez lifts via a 160-passenger tram. Oz is a purpose-built collection of apartment blocks and attractive chalets above the older village of the same name. Villard-Reculas is secluded on a small plateau with good lift access to Alpe d'Huez. And Auris is a series of attractive chalet-style apartments hugging the forest above its old town.

The skiing divides into four areas. The main slopes directly above the central village are south facing and stretch up the 2-mile-high Serenne Glacier on Pic Blanc. Another ski area, Signal de l'Homme, is separated by a deep gorge and accessed by a quick, down-and-up chairlift. Its north-facing runs offer a reprieve when the spring sun turns the resort's south-facing slopes to slush. In the other direction from Signal de l'Homme is the small Signal area, which leads down to the old village of Villard-Reculas. The fourth area, Vaujany-Oz, consists largely of northwest-facing slopes.

The best-known run is 10-mile-long Sarenne, which starts at the top of Pic Blanc and drops 6,500 feet. The top section is steep and worthy of its black trail designation, but the bottom half flattens on the skirt of the mountain. In fact, *steep up top, tame at the bottom* describes most of the skiing on Pic Blanc. Beginners rarely have it so good. A large network of green trails climbs upward directly next to the village.

Intermediate-level skiers and boarders have plenty of variety throughout the resort. There's a nice mix of blue and red trails accessed from the gondola above the main village. (France color-codes advanced trails red and expert trails black.) There are also long, leg-tiring intermediate runs dropping down to Villard-Reculas.

For boarders, there are plenty of challenges on- and off-piste. Near the main lift base is a long terrain park that includes a demanding halfpipe and go-for-broke hits, rails, and tabletops. There's also another terrain park at Auris.

If you want more time on the snow, a slalom course is floodlit three nights a week. There are also twenty off-piste trails. During July and August, the Sarenne Glacier is open for summer skiing.

 A popular venue at the 1968 Grenoble Olympic Winter Games, Alpe d'Huez offers sunshine and plenty of variety with big vertical drops, including 10-mile-long Sarenne, the longest maintained run in the Alps. There are steep expert trails on- and off-piste, as well as pleasant beginner runs alongside the village.

Snow cover at the area's lower elevations has always been the resort's Achilles' heel. In recent years they've added extensive snowmaking to blanket many of the main runs above Alpe d'Huez, Vaujany, and Oz.

Off the slopes there's a sports center with ice skating and a swimming pool. You'll also find a movie theater, a library, 20 miles of walking trails, and an ice-driving school. Alpe d'Huez offers 30 miles of groomed cross-country ski trails.

Les Deux Alpes links by gondola to La Grave, which has a cult following among hard-core skiers. The rustic village fronts the high glaciers of 11,650-foot La Meije, which has just four ski lifts and 3 miles of trails. But almost all the skiing and snowboarding happen off-piste, dropping more than 6,000 vertical feet into the steep and deep. Local guides are strongly recommended.

Alpe d'Huez Tourist Office
38750 Alpe d'Huez
France

Phone: 33–476–11–44–44

Web Site: www.alpedhuez.com

E-mail: info@alpedhuez.com

Elevation: Top—10,926 feet; base—6,100 feet

Vertical Drop: 7,317 feet

Total Trails: 142 miles

Longest Run: 10 miles

Terrain: 36% beginner; 29% intermediate; 25% advanced; 10% expert

Lifts: 87

Snowmaking: 33 miles

Central Reservations: 33–476–11–44–44

Snow Report: www.alpedhuez.com

Accommodations: An enormous range of apartments and many hotels, mostly in the 1- and 2-star range.

Getting There: Alpe d'Huez is 5 hours from Paris, 40 miles from Grenoble.

Keep in Mind: The resort is famous for sun, not snow.

BEST BETS

Beginners: Green runs directly above the village.

Intermediates: Couloir from the top of the gondola.

Advanced: Sarenne from Pic Blanc.

Experts: Off-piste with a guide.

Lunch: Chalet du Lac Besson.

Off the Slopes: Heli-sightseeing trips are popular. Explore the old village of Villard-Reculas.

Best Hotel: Royal Ours Blanc.

AVORIAZ-MORZINE
Avoriaz, France

Set in a dramatic mountain landscape a few miles above the traditional French Alpine village of Morzine, Avoriaz is a modern, traffic-free purpose-built resort that forms part of the sprawling Portes du Soleil ski region in the northern French Alps near Mont Blanc. Avoriaz usually offers the best snow in the region due to its relatively high elevation. You can ski in and out from your accommodation—and that's rare in the Alps.

Avoriaz is well positioned on the main circuit of the Portes du Soleil, with easy access to runs covering the gamut from beginner to expert. The car-free village is set on a steep slope with horse-drawn carriages clip-clopping along snowy streets. The high-rise apartments that dominate the architecture are built with chocolate-colored wood and sloping roofs that don't distract from the appealing Alpine scenery.

The lifts fan out in all directions from Avoriaz. Facing the resort are the slopes of 8,090-foot Hauts Forts, offering long and varied runs perfect for carving swooping parabolas all the way to Les Prodains, which lies 2,000 vertical feet below Avoriaz. Directly above the resort, from the top of the Chavanette area, you can cross the border and ski the infamous Swiss Wall down to Champéry. But the slopes on the north-facing French side usually have much better snow than the south-facing Swiss runs. They also offer some of the steepest pistes in the Portes du Soleil, although that's not saying much—skiers with solid intermediate skills can ski the entire circuit.

Avoriaz was one of the first European resorts to encourage snowboarding, and it boasted the first terrain park on the Continent in 1993. New, state-of-the-sport terrain parks have been added. And it remains a mecca for riders. The parks are served by three lifts, and you can purchase a special lift ticket if that's where you want to spend all your time. There's also a smaller, less challenging park for younger children.

But like all of France's purpose-built resorts, Avoriaz lacks Alpine charm. The apartment blocks are functional rather than attractive, and there is little traditional atmosphere or history—resort workers are seasonal and come in from far away.

Nearby Morzine is just the opposite. A lovely old village typical of the Haute Savoie, it maintains much of its Alpine charm with chalet-style buildings spread along a river gorge. Like Avoriaz, it appeals to families. It's less expensive and

low-key compared to highly charged Avoriaz, which is linked by gondola. The slopes directly above Morzine offer mellow runs rimmed by forest that favor beginner and intermediate skill levels and attract large numbers of snowboarders. Quads have recently replaced old chairlifts, and there are few surface lifts to trouble beginners on snowboards.

From the top lift stations, there are breathtaking panoramas of the Mont Blanc Massif, with the Aiguille du Midi, the Dru, and the Grandes Jorasses piercing the sky.

A free bus service links Morzine with the outlying lifts. It also goes to Avoriaz, a few miles away and higher up the valley, leading to the main circuit of the Portes du Soleil. You can also approach the circuit from Morzine via the nearby resort of Châtel.

Besides Châtel, the bus also travels to other French resorts of the Portes du Soleil, including Les Gets, Abondance, La Chapelle d'Abondance, Montriond, and La Grande Terche. The resorts on the Swiss side include Champéry, Les Crosets, Morgins, Champoussin, Torgon, and Val d'Illiez. A single lift ticket covers more than 400 miles of ski and snowboarding trails served by more than 200 lifts. And like all European resorts, a six-day pass to the Portes du Soleil is an incredible bargain compared to higher-priced North American resorts.

From the top of the Pleney ridge above Morzine you can ski down to the resort of Les Gets, where five beautiful mountains fold into a range of hanging valleys and the vast sweeps of seventy ski trails through the pines. Les Gets alone has fifty-four lifts.

Off-slope activities at Avoriaz and Morzine include guided nature walks, sledding, horse-drawn sleigh rides, snowshoeing, snowmobile excursions, and a complete sports center.

The high, north-facing slopes above the two villages often boast the best snow in the seemingly endless Portes du Soleil, which spans the French-Swiss border. The low-key atmosphere attracts families and entices snowboarders with the best terrain park in the region. The scenery couldn't be finer.

Office du Tourisme d'Avoriaz
F-741 10 Avoriaz
France

Phone: 33–450–74–72–72

Web Site: www.morzine-avoriaz.com

E-mail: info@morzine-avoriaz.com

Elevation: Top—7,874 feet; base—3,085 feet

Vertical Drop: 4,789 feet

Total Trails: 400 miles

Longest Run: 4.5 miles

Terrain: 51% beginner; 40% intermediate; 9% advanced/expert

Lifts: 212

Snowmaking: 522 acres

Central Reservations: 33–450–74–72–72

Snow Report: www.morzine-avoriaz.com

Accommodations: Few hotels but plenty of condos.

Getting There: Avoriaz-Morzine is less than 50 miles from Geneva's airport.

Keep in Mind: Lower slopes of the Portes du Soleil often lack snow.

BEST BETS

Beginners: Several excellent novice runs down Hauts Fort to the village.

Intermediates: The slopes of Chavanette.

Advanced: The World Cup women's downhill on Hauts Forts.

Experts: There are challenging runs down from Hauts Forts to Les Prodains.

Lunch: Crémaillière at Les Lindârets.

Off the Slopes: Explore the rustic villages that link to the resort via trail or shuttle bus.

Best Hotel: Dahu in Morzine; Dromonts in Avoriaz. (Slim pickings given all the apartments.)

CHAMONIX-MONT-BLANC
Chamonix-Mont-Blanc, France

Traveling from village to village along the paper-clip bends in the mountain roads and rails, it sometimes seems like all the Alps live on pastry and tourism. Until you arrive at Chamonix, that is, and behold a resort with heart and soul and heritage.

In the history of mountaineering, Chamonix is as imposing as the surrounding granite and ice summits of the high French Alps. To make an entrance worthy of the setting, travel there from the Swiss border town of Martigny on the narrow-gauge train called the Mont-Blanc Express. To call it express vastly overstates its velocity, but then nobody should rush through country like the Chamonix Valley.

Located at the foot of 15,770-foot Mont Blanc, Western Europe's highest summit, Chamonix lies in the center of a U-shaped, 14-mile-long valley rimmed by mountains sculpted for skiing, where you can carve until the cows come home. Surrounding the valley are 95,000 acres of national park.

The nineteenth-century town is all atmosphere, and perhaps the best ski town in all Europe. The car-free center attracts shoppers and diners, who are always staring up at the extraordinary summits and glaciers high above.

The valley's population of 10,000 sometimes doubles during peak ski periods. Many come to ski the Vallée Blanche, the longest ski run in Europe (12 to 14 miles, depending upon snow conditions). Skiers and boarders also come for the extreme skiing found in the elevator shaft–like couloirs, so narrow that only a sliver of sunlight reaches the snow each day.

Of course, a place with as much ski terrain as Chamonix has something for everybody. Beginners enjoy the gentle slopes at La Vormaine, Les Chosalets, Les Planards, and Le Savoy. Le Tour, Le Brévent, and La Flégère areas are ideal for intermediates. A tram links Le Brévent to La Flégère, but otherwise the areas are not interconnected. Shuttle bus access is part of the ski pass.

The best snow is frequently on the north-facing slopes above the nearby postcard-pretty village of Argentière. The area has a terrain park and halfpipe, and there is usually skiing and boarding well into May. The most challenging slopes are the steeps at Les Grands Montets above Argentière. The area teeters between two glaciers and delivers serious black runs and hair-raising off-piste challenges that are best explored with a guide. With fresh, deep snow you can drop more than 7,200 feet. Argentière is also the starting point for the famous and extraordinary Haute Route, taking guided skiers from Chamonix to Zermatt and Saas-Fee in Switzerland.

Every visitor should ride the airy tram to the rockbound beauty of the Aiguille du Midi, part of the Mont Blanc Massif that pierces the sky at more than 12,000 feet. The tram covers the vast distance from town to summit in two airy spans—one of them the longest of any aerial tram in the world. The views peer down to France, Italy, and Switzerland.

Many of these peaks served as the petri dish for the evolution of mountaineering and extreme skiing and boarding. The summit of Mont Blanc has lured climbers (with sometimes deadly outcomes) since its first ascent by two Chamoniards in 1786.

The Aiguille du Midi is the start of the Vallée Blanche, widely acknowledged as one of the world's greatest ski runs. Given the right conditions, any intermediate-level skier with derring-do can cruise its 9,200-foot vertical drop with an experienced Chamonix mountain guide leading the way. The main route down is the Mer de Glace, the largest glacier in the French Alps. But don't ski it without a local guide. It is littered with crevasses, hopefully safely bridged by snow. Other dangers include train-car-size seracs—large masses of ice isolated by intersected crevasses—that can shift and tumble and crush a skier. Hazards not withstanding, the route exposes some of Europe's most imposing summits. The history of twentieth-century alpinism is written on the steep granite faces that rise here—Le Dru, La Verte, and the Grandes Jorasses.

The final escape into Chamonix is through the woods at the bottom of the glacier. The run is the longest lift-served vertical descent in the world. If snow is sparse in the final stretch, skiers can bail out near the toe of the glacier at the Montenvers ice cave, where a tourist train travels back to Chamonix.

Elsewhere in the valley, much of the skiing and boarding is for the hard-core. Particularly prized are the snow-filled couloirs that tumble down from all directions. But remember: Off-piste, you ski at your own risk. The backcountry is neither maintained nor patrolled. Again, a local guide is strongly advised.

Along the valley floor exists a great cross-country ski network. And if you get

Site of the first Winter Olympic Games in 1924, handsome and refined Chamonix is France's original ski resort. It remains a legend for new generations of skiers and boarders who seek challenging, off-piste carving and charming French ambience steeped in mountaineering tradition.

carried away, you can always hop the train back to Chamonix.

Off the slopes, heritage guides from the Chamonix Tourist Office lead a two-hour walking tour. The discussion centers on the legends of Chamonix's great mountain history. The tour takes in numerous heritage buildings. Also worth a stop is the Alpine Museum, with its inspiring collection of old photos of guides and equipment, including a jury-rigged sling that Edward Whymper, the first person to climb the Matterhorn, was carried down Mont Blanc on. The town's sports center contains a library, national school for skiing and alpinism, and an outdoor and indoor swimming pool.

Office de Tourism de Chamonix-Mont-Blanc B.P. 25
85, place du Triangle de l'Amitié
F-74401 Chamonix-Mont-Blanc Cedex France

Phone: 33–450–53–33–450

Web Site: www.chamonix.com

E-mail: info@chamonix.com

Elevation: Top—12,600 feet; base—3,400 feet

Vertical Drop: 9,200 feet

Total Trails: 94 miles

Longest Run: 14 miles (Vallée Blanche)

Terrain: 21% beginner; 31% intermediate; 35% advanced; 13% expert

Lifts: 47

Snowmaking: 6 miles

Central Reservations: 33–450–53–23–33

Snow Report: www.chamonix.com

Accommodations: There's a wide range of hotels and lodges in the valley.

Getting There: The Geneva airport is less than 60 miles away.

Keep in Mind: Getting to the lifts involves long walks, driving, or buses.

BEST BETS

Beginners: There are beginner lifts at La Vormaine, Les Chosalets, Les Planards, and Le Savoy.

Intermediates: Le Brévent, La Flégère, and Le Tour.

Advanced: Les Grands Montets.

Experts: Hire a guide and go off-piste.

Lunch: Le Brévent at midstation of Le Brévent.

Off the Slopes: Visit the Alpine Museum in Chamonix.

Best Hotel: The 4-star Hotel Mont Blanc.

COURCHEVEL
Courchevel, France

Every lover of great skiing should visit France's sunny Trois Vallées ski region. Its huge sawtoothed hulks of mountains offer everything from ballroomlike beginner slopes to hair-raising chutes. And they offer them over and over again in an area that would hold half a dozen of America's largest resorts, with plenty of white space in between.

There are several resorts that serve as a jumping-off point for the Trois Vallées (Three Valleys), but you can hardly do better than the resort of Courchevel, three hours from both Lyon and Geneva. It's the swankiest of the ski areas in the region and may even be France's most exclusive resort. The clientele consists of what the French call "pipole"—the hip, the beautiful, and the famous. The skiing on the surrounding well-maintained slopes is vast and varied. The Courchevel ski area alone has sixty-three lifts and 117 trails. The snow is reliable at high elevations, and on the lower slopes there are batteries of snowmaking cannons. Most of the lifts are top-shelf. The accommodations are close by, and the Courchevel ski school is the largest in Europe, with more than 500 instructors.

Created on virgin snowfields in 1946, Courchevel was the brainchild of Savoyard civic leaders and a few deep-pocketed developers. They hired French Olympic champion Emile Allais to plan the slopes. The resort consists of four self-contained villages ascending the valley, linked by lifts and roads and known by their elevations. A shuttle bus operates among them. The lowest is the original Savoyard village of Le Praz, site of the ski-jumping competitions at the 1992 Albertville Winter Olympic Games. It's also known as Courchevel 1300, as in 1,300 meters (4,270 feet) in elevation. Expert tree-lined slopes run to the edge of town, and there is excellent lift service to the higher slopes. It's a peaceful setting, even though it's bursting at the seams with post-Olympic growth.

The next village is Courchevel 1550, the low-rent area, with economical accommodations and restaurants, and easy slopes for the visiting French families who like to make it home. The third village is Courchevel 1650. It's a nice nest of chalets and bars with an old and pretty village center, even though the road runs through it. Nearby is a stimulating mix of beginner and intermediate slopes.

The highest village is Courchevel 1850. Yes, it's located at 1,850 meters (6,013

The Trois Vallées ski region of France is enormous. Three main ski resorts—Courchevel, Méribel, and Val Thorens—link with 375 miles of trails, 200 lifts, and about fifty mountain villages to form the world's largest truly interconnected ski domain. But it is Courchevel, with its ski-in/ski-out hotels, that offers the most extensive and varied slopes in the entire region.

feet), and it is the penthouse. It's the largest, has the best views, and is high rent. It's upmountain and upscale. Parisians are smitten with it. There are fine restaurants, high-watt nightlife, and upper-crust shops. Consider it the Deer Valley or Beaver Creek of France.

Courchevel 1850 also is where the seemingly endless skiing begins. Lifts and runs spread across the white faces in all directions; you can easily access the immensity of the Trois Vallées. The impressive resorts of Méribel and Val Thorens are within easy striking distance. (At 7,450 feet, Val Thorens is the highest ski area in Europe.) From Courchevel to the far reaches of the Trois Vallées, you'll cover 25 miles on skis.

Snowboarders flip over the terrain parks above and below 1850. There's also an Olympic-caliber halfpipe. And the slopes of Courchevel are a great place to learn. There are thirteen free beginner lifts and slopes varying from molehills to mountains.

The runs at Courchevel are extensive and varied enough to suit every level of skier or boarder. Many skiers never leave the area. But you would be remiss not to head off into the wild white yonder of the Trois Vallées.

For cross-country skiers, Courchevel offers more than 40 miles of maintained trails that wind through the woods from Le Praz to 1650 and 1850.

Off the slopes, there's ice skating, tobogganing, snowshoeing, sleigh rides, and 10 miles of walking paths. There's also a swimming pool. The Olympic city of Grenoble is an hour away.

Office du Tourisme
B.P. 37
73120 Courchevel
France

Phone: 33–479–08–00–29

Web Site: www.courchevel.com

E-mail: info@courchevel.com

Elevation: Top—10,500 feet; base—4,270 feet

Vertical Drop: 6,230 feet

Total Trails: 370 miles (Trois Vallées)

Longest Run: 5 miles

Terrain: 17% beginner; 34% intermediate; 37% advanced; 12% expert

Lifts: 200 (Trois Vallées)

Snowmaking: 56 miles

Central Reservations: 33–479–08–14–44

Snow Report: www.courchevel.com

Accommodations: A wide range of hotels and condominiums, many of them ski-in/ski-out.

Getting There: It's 3 hours from Geneva and Lyon. The nearest train station is Moutiers, a 15-mile bus ride away.

Keep in Mind: Plenty of skiing and après-ski, and not much else.

BEST BETS

Beginners: Pyramide and Grand Bosses above 1650.

Intermediates: Combe de la Saulire.

Advanced: The Grand Couloir off the Saulire tram.

Experts: Vallée des Avals, which is off-piste above 1650. Go with a guide.

Lunch: Chalet de Pierres on the Verdons trail.

Off the Slopes: Shops and a sportscenter at 1850.

Best Hotel: Bellecôte at 1850.

FLAINE
Flaine, France

The colossal concrete buildings are functional and designed to mirror the shadow and light of the rocks and crags at the base of the slopes, say defenders of the 1960s Bauhaus style of architecture that the French resort of Flaine so perfectly represents. Others say its square, car park–like appearance makes it one of the ugliest resorts in the Alps. Not even the outdoor Picasso sculpture sways their opinion.

But even Flaine's detractors agree that the skiing is excellent and varied, with an abundance of snow that more than compensates for the surrounding architecture. For skiers, a world covered in powder snow always softens the harsh edges of life.

The reality is that Flaine's architecture is functional. The ski lifts, accommodations, restaurants, and parking lots are all laid out to make village life easy—especially if you have children in tow. The village is positioned high enough to offer the luxury of ski-in/ski-out convenience. And in recent years new developments next to the village were built in the traditional chalet style.

But if you must have Alpine charm, stay at one of the traditional villages elsewhere in the Grand Massif ski circus. Nearby Samöens, with its medieval fountains and rustic buildings, is the only French ski resort officially listed as a "Monument Historique." You can also find real Haute Savoie ambience by skiing down to the nearby village of Sixt.

Flaine is at the heart of the Grand Massif, an interconnected ski region that includes the resorts of Samöens, Les Carroz, Morillon, and Sixt. The ski circus offers more than 160 miles of well-maintained trails served by seventy-eight lifts. It is the third largest interconnected ski region in France and has an excellent reputation for fine skiing and an integrated lift system, including the first detachable, high-speed eight-passenger chairlift.

Flaine has miles and miles of appealing intermediate runs. It also offers a well-rounded complement of beginner and expert slopes, and loads of challenging off-piste. The annual snowfall is plentiful, and a battalion of snowmaking guns supplement the powder dumps that drift in over the Haute Savoie. The resort encourages beginners with four free lifts at the beginner slopes next to the village. Children under five and seniors over seventy-five ski free throughout the Grand Massif.

From Flaine's base at 5,200 feet, a gondola rises over a huge, white north-facing bowl to the 8,140-foot summit of Grandes Platières, the highest point of the Grand Massif. The sheer beauty of what can be seen from so high is breathtaking. The mountains grow like dreams, one out of the other, dominated by Mont Blanc, the highest peak in Western Europe. Beneath the summit, lifts fan out in the vast snowy bowl and connect with lifts from the other four snowy resorts of the ski region.

Most of the runs in the Grandes Platières bowl are rated intermediate to advanced. There's a short beginner area near the summit served by its own lift and an expert trail called Diamant Noir tumbling directly down the face. The tops of trails are above the tree line, but there are several stands of forest lower in the bowl that are woven with runs. An intermediate trail called Cascades winds its way down for 9 miles, dropping almost 6,000 vertical feet.

The other four traditional villages of the Grand Massif sit in hanging valleys at a lower elevation than Flaine. Each has its own network and variety of trails and lifts that link to the Grand Massif.

Snowboarders find plenty of interesting terrain, especially off the trail. There's a huge terrain park ideally located on Grandes Platières, and the French ski school runs a smaller park for kids. But there are few inescapable surface lifts for boarders to negotiate.

Off the slopes, Flaine offers just about every conceivable activity available at the base of a ski area. From dogsledding to ice skating to the latest English films, Flaine has it all. There's even a school sponsored by a European auto manufacturer that teaches skiers techniques for driving on winter's icy roads.

Flaine Tourist Office
Galerie Marchande forum
74 300 Flaine
France

Phone: 33–450–90–80–01

Web Site: www.flaine.com

E-mail: welcome@flaine.com

Elevation: Top—8,202 feet; base—5,250 feet

Vertical Drop: 5,840 feet (in Grand Massif)

Total Trails: 162 miles (Le Grand Massif)

Longest Run: 9 miles

Situated in France's Haute Savoie, this high-altitude, purpose-built resort is ideal for all levels of skiers and snowboarders. Flaine has a well-deserved reputation for fine skiing and an efficient lift system. It is the highest resort in the Grand Massif ski circus.

Terrain: 12% beginner; 41% intermediate; 38% advanced; 9% expert

Lifts: 78 (Le Grand Massif)

Snowmaking: 40 miles

Central Reservations: www.flaine.com

Snow Report: www.flaine.com

Accommodations: Tour operators book all hotels; independent skiers choose from a wide range of condominiums.

Getting There: Nearest airport is Geneva, 44 miles; nearest train station is Cluses, with bus transfers the final 19 miles to Flaine.

Keep in Mind: Not much nightlife and lots of children.

BEST BETS

Beginners: Four free beginner lifts next to the village; also nice runs above the village of Morillon.

Intermediates: Cascades.

Advanced: Méphisto.

Experts: Diamant Noir.

Lunch: Michet, located in a chalet across from the gondola.

Off the Slopes: Explore the authentic Haute Savoie villages of Samöens and Morillon.

Best Hotel: The Grand Massif condo offers hotel facilities.

LA CLUSAZ–LE GRAND-BORNARD

La Clusaz, France

There's a popular nightclub in old La Clusaz that has a floodlit stream running beneath the glass dance floor. It seems perfectly in tune with this centuries-old village, which embraces the modern while never relinquishing its extraordinary natural heritage.

France offers much of the best skiing and après-ski in the Alps. The snow is reliable, and the colossal vertical drops seemingly stretch all the way to Paris. So how do you decide which resort to ski and snowboard? For the most part, the purpose-built resorts consist of functional, concrete villages like Flaine, but they deliver extraordinary skiing. The traditional villages of the French Alps ooze charm but often lack variety on the slopes. Take your pick. Or go to La Clusaz.

Savoyard charm and modern ski facilities are part of the mix at La Clusaz. The vast and interesting slopes that surround the pretty village are perfectly pitched for beginner and intermediate skiers and boarders. Above the village are five linked areas offering mostly wide-open cruising. The even more charming village of Le Grand-Bornard is just down the road. La Clusaz offers the tougher slopes. But you'll find expert pitches at both. Together, they market themselves as the Aravis Massif and share a common lift ticket.

Like most of the storybook villages around the Alps, a central church and its high steeple dominate La Clusaz. Next to the old stone-and-wood Sainte-Foy church

The traditional sixteenth-century village of La Clusaz has been a popular mountain resort for a century. The ski pass includes the neighboring resort of Le Grand-Bornard, linked by shuttle bus. The result is 130 miles of trails served by ninety-nine lifts offering excellent beginner and intermediate-to-advanced terrain, just one hour from Geneva.

is the ancient cemetery. It was here, in November 2001, that a popular young local woman named Regine Cavagnoud was laid to rest after tragically dying from an accident incurred during a ski race training run. At the time, she was the reigning Super-G world champion. More than 3,000 people, in a village with a permanent population of 1,800, jammed the square surrounding the church to pay their respects. A rustic church, an ancient cemetery, and an outpouring of grief by villagers and farmers from miles around are not things you experience at a purpose-built resort. There are rich lives lived in these mountains, and many things more important than skiing.

The atmosphere at La Clusaz is all French. Villagers are extremely heartwarming and welcome visitors every Monday night with an open wine and cheese party at the main square. There's also a weekly farmers' market. And on weekends the place is packed with families of skiers.

The atmosphere is even more intimate at Le Grand-Bornard, which is linked by a free, ten-minute shuttle bus. It has its own extensive network of lifts and slopes.

The first ski lift was constructed at La Clusaz in 1935. Today there are five main ski areas wrapping around La Clusaz. The two areas of L'Aiguille and La Balme, linked by a gondola and ski runs, stretch up to 8,000 feet and offer long, advanced-intermediate runs with white-domed Mont Blanc visible in the distance. The other three areas—L'Etale, Beauregard, and Manigod—offer more variety, including some of the best beginner and expert terrain. Most of the slopes face northwest, so they keep their snow. This is particularly so on La Balme, which also has the best terrain of the region. On the lower runs extensive snow-making guns blanket the slopes.

At Le Grand-Bornard, the gentler slopes serve as summer pastures for the cows of the region. But there's also plenty of steep terrain where even the agile cows of the Alps fear to tread. Many of the lifts serve both beginner and intermediate trails that meet at the bottom, allowing families and groups of mixed abilities to stay together.

For snowboarders, there's a terrain park and a halfpipe on the Aiguille slopes and another at Le Grand-Bornard. Riders also head for the playful terrain of La Balme. The resort's beginner terrain is mostly served by chairlifts, so it's a great place for learning to ride.

The cross-country ski trails are excellent. La Clusaz offers 45 miles of trails; there are 38 miles at Le Grand-Bornard. Another 8 miles of skiing links the two areas.

Off-slope activities include ice skating, horse-drawn sleigh rides, snowshoeing, and an open-air swimming pool. The resort is easily accessible in less than one hour from Geneva, which means it's hopping on weekends.

La Clusaz Office of Tourism
74220 La Clusaz
France

Phone: 33–450–32–65–00

Web Site: www.laclusaz.com

E-mail: info@laclusaz.com

Elevation: Top—8,200 feet; base—3,610 feet

Vertical Drop: 4,590 feet

Total Trails: 130 miles

Longest Run: 3 miles

Terrain: 29% beginner; 32% intermediate; 29% advanced; 10% expert

Lifts: 99

Snowmaking: 149 acres

Central Reservations: 33–450–32–28–33

Snow Report: www.laclusaz.com

Accommodations: A wide range of 2- and 3-star hotels, as well as chalets and apartments at both resorts.

Getting There: Geneva is 30 miles; the nearest train station is in Annecy, 12 miles away.

Keep in Mind: Weekends are busy.

BEST BETS

Beginners: La Joyère above Le Grand-Bornard.

Intermediates: La Balme.

Advanced: Combe du Fernuy.

Experts: Noire du Lachat at Le Grand-Bornard.

Lunch: Bercail, midway on L'Aiguille.

Off the Slopes: Wednesday farmers' market in Le Grand-Bornard.

Best Hotel: Beauregard at La Clusaz.

LA PLAGNE
La Plagne, France

When La Plagne turned forty, for its birthday, it got some new high-tech lifts and celebrated the arrival of middle age by hosting the French skiing championships. It even got married. In 2003 a 200-passenger tram linked La Plagne with neighboring Les Arcs. For snowriders, it's a marriage made in a snowy heaven. La Plagne is best suited to intermediates; Les Arcs has extraordinary expert terrain.

La Plagne consists of a necklace of ten villages linked by lifts and, hopefully, trails of white. The four villages on the lower fringes of the resort—Montchavin, Montalbert, Champagny-en-Vanoise, and Les Coches—are often short on snow. But they do have charm. They developed around traditional old hamlets set among the pastoral farming community of the Tarentaise Valley.

The other six are high-altitude purpose-built villages that began taking shape in

the 1960s. They were designed with the form-follows-function logic employed at modern French resorts, but there are elements of Savoyard chalet–style wooden architecture in the styling.

The first to be built was Plagne Center at 6,463 feet. It remains the focal point for life off the slopes, but unfortunately consists of blocky, concrete apartments with indoor shopping plazas that are the signature architecture of these purpose-built resorts.

About 300 vertical feet higher is Plagne Villages, with a more traditional look and handy to the slopes. Higher up the valley at Plagne 1800 are wooden chalets and a fitness center featuring court sports. Higher yet is Aime Plagne, with quality apartments and a movie theater. Next up is the principal aesthetic offender, an eyesore called Plagne Bellecôte. It's a cluster of high-rises that, well, works. To say more would be to tax the limits of charity. The highest and the last to be built is Belle Plagne. And it's not bad. The Savoyard chalet–style village center is integrated with the apartment buildings, each with its own beginner area and network of interconnected lifts.

There is little good shopping or fine dining at La Plagne. The bulk of the guests are French families, and self-catering apartments comprise the majority of accommodations. There are several three-star hotels, however.

When the snow cover on the lower slopes is adequate, you can ski more than 6,000 vertical feet from the lift station on the glacier of Bellecôte to the rustic restaurant verandas of Champagny and Montchavin.

The top of the resort is more than 10,000 feet high, and the scenery is spectacular in every direction. Thirty miles to the north, Mont Blanc, the highest peak in the Alps, thrusts out of a frozen landscape on the French-Italian border. Even beginners find snow to their liking at these snow-sure heights—unlike so many resorts, where novice riders can only grind up and down the skirt of the mountain, dreaming of one day reaching the summit.

From the village levels, the lifts fan out to a broad bowl and climb the Bellecôte Glacier. Some slopes descend into woodlands around the villages, but most of the skiing and snowboarding is on wide-open cruisers above the tree line. Most of what you see you can ski. It's a tame and fun area, where you can work on improving technique while enjoying the surroundings.

Limited expert terrain is probably the only reason La Plagne is not better known. But if skiing elevator-shaft runs is not an essential part of your ski day, then La Plagne has more than enough of everything, including great facilities for beginners, especially children. There are terrain parks at Plagne Bellecôte, Belle Plagne, and above Montchavin–Les Coches. With a guide, backcountry skiers wander the wide expanses of Vanoise National Park.

The new 200-passenger cable linking La Plagne to Les Arcs creates one of the largest ski circuses in Europe. Paradiski covers more than 250 miles of trails in 34,000 skiable acres—as large as all major Colorado slopes combined. But the link is mostly a marketing vehicle for competing with other vast ski regions like Trois Vallées and Portes du Soleil. The reality is that there is more than enough terrain at both huge resorts to stick with one or the other.

La Plagne was a venue for the 1992 Albertville Winter Olympic Games. The best-known remaining legacy is the bobsled run. Courageous visitors can careen down the icy track on a specially modified and padded bobsled or ride a real bobsled behind an experienced driver.

Val d'Isère, Tignes, and the Trois Vallées are doable as day trips. A six-day La Plagne lift ticket covers all.

For cross-country skiers, La Plagne offers more than 50 miles of prepared trails.

La Plagne Office du Tourisme
B.P. 62
73211 Aime Cedex
France

Phone: 33–479–09–79–79

Web Site: www.la-plagne.com

E-mail: bienvenue@la-plagne.com

Elevation: Top—10,660 feet; base—4,100 feet

Vertical Drop: 6,560 feet

Total Trails: 250 miles (Paradiski)

Longest Run: 9 miles

Terrain: 12% beginner; 48% intermediate; 33% advanced; 7% expert

Lifts: 141 (Paradiski)

Snowmaking: 50 acres

Central Reservations: 33–479–09–79–79

Snow Report: www.la-plagne.com

Accommodations: Mostly self-contained apartments, some 3-star hotels.

Getting There: Geneva is 90 miles north, Lyon 120 miles west. The nearest train station is Bourg St. Maurice.

Keep in Mind: Limited off-slope activities.

BEST BETS

Beginners: High on Bellecôte.

Intermediates: Roche de Mio to Belle Plagne.

Advanced: Kamikaze and Hara-Kari from Grande Rochette.

Experts: Off-trail with a guide.

Lunch: Le Sauget above Montchavin.

Off the Slopes: Try the Olympic bobsled run.

Best Hotel: Balcons might be the best of the 3-star hotels.

 This colossal ski resort—one of the largest in Europe—lies in the Savoie region of France. La Plagne climbs to more than 10,000 feet, offering big vertical drops and a linked ski circus with 250 miles of slopes. The runs fall in favor of intermediate-level skiers and snowboarders and are well suited to families and groups of mixed abilities.

LES ARCS
Bourg Saint Maurice, France

The high-speed TGV train running between Paris and Geneva can whisk you to Les Arcs at 200 miles per hour. From the station at Bourg Saint Maurice, a funicular grinds up to the mile-high purpose-built resort, where more than seventy ski lifts operate. They also link with the 250-mile ski circus known as Paradiski, stretching all the way to La Plagne.

Les Arcs dates back to 1968, when the most famous Frenchman in the world was Jean-Claude Killy, the peerless Olympic three-way champion. His success at nearby Grenoble kick-started a building boom of ski resorts in the virgin, snowbound valleys of France's Savoie region. The slopes proved to be made for skiing, and they quickly morphed into destination resorts, flaunting megalifts the way the nouveau

riche flaunt jewelry. Old World style was as out of fashion as European royalty. The French wanted ski weeks at family apartments with access to vast terrain. Les Arcs was purpose-built for that, sacrificing charming ambience for big skiing and slopeside convenience.

Les Arcs' location could hardly be more convenient. The intercity TGV is just six minutes away via the funicular. Bourg Saint Maurice, the main market town of the region, is well stocked with budget accommodations. Half a dozen other major resorts are easily accessible by car, train, or bus.

The funicular from Bourg Saint Maurice climbs to the cluster of buildings called Arc 1600 (its metric height), which connects with two other villages, Arc 1800 and Arc

2000. They are mostly self-contained groupings of apartments, hotels, and commercial vendors. But each has a different feel: 1600 is low budget, 1800 is action central, and 2000 appeals to the more alpine minded who want quick access to the highest and best slopes.

Changes recently came to Arc 2000. Intrawest, the Canadian-based developer of Whistler and Tremblant, among other North American resort villages, built a new village center aimed at bringing a fresh face to the middle-aged resort. It is bound to be a big improvement. Imagine, Europe importing North American ski ambience.

Even in a sea of massive resorts, Les Arcs stands out like Gulliver among the Lilliputians, with a vertical that dwarfs anything in North America. And much of what's there is tough. The long slopes above the village are punctuated its own network of lifts and trails. But Les Arcs also connects with La Plagne and the gigantic ski circus called Paradiski.

 This is one of the largest stand-alone ski resorts in the Alps. Its milelong vertical descents are easily reached from a trio of modern villages located above high-speed intercity rail service. What Les Arcs lacks in ambience it more than makes up for in skiing and snowboarding opportunities.

The best skiing and snowboarding starts at 10,000 feet on the Aiguille Rouge, where glacier-filled basins provide miles and miles of varied snowriding. You'll find everything from cruisers to headwalls to natural bowls, where freeriders bank like bobsledders while careening all the way down to Arc 1600. With a guide, there are infinite possibilities off-piste. Les Arcs even has an internationally known speed-skiing track called Kilometre Lancé, where racers reach speeds of 140 miles per hour.

Les Arcs is very popular with French snowboarders. It was the first European resort to permit boards, and there is a high ratio of riders to skiers on the mountain. The terrain park is a maze of tricksters— and the halfpipe rips.

Off the slopes, you can chase thrills at the speed-skating oval and the luge track. If the snow is low in the valley and your group can handle intermediate terrain, ski down to the rustically charming village of Le Pré and enjoy lunch in one of its fine old restaurants. You should also visit the cluster of five small villages called Peisey-Vallandry, which dates back 1,000 years into Savoyard history.

Les Arcs Tourist Office
B.P. 45
73700 Arc 1800 Cedex
France

Phone: 33–479–07–12–57

Web Site: www.ski-lesarcs.com

E-mail: info@ski-lesarcs.com

Elevation: Top—10,580 feet; base—5,250 feet

Vertical Drop: 6,976 feet

Total Trails: 250 miles (Paradiski)

Longest Run: 4 miles

Terrain: 8% beginner; 45% intermediate; 33% advanced; 14% expert

Lifts: 141 (Paradiski)

Snowmaking: 8 miles

Central Reservations: 33–479–07–68–00

Snow Report: www.ski-lesarcs.com

Accommodations: There's a handful of 3-star hotels and plenty of apartments. Budget hotels in Bourg Saint Maurice.

Getting There: A funicular runs from Bourg

Saint Maurice, a major rail destination served by high-speed trains from Paris and Geneva.

Keep in Mind: Not much activity off the slopes; lacks Alpine charm.

BEST BETS

Beginners: Arc 2000 and Vallandry.

Intermediates: Renard, high on Vallandry.

Advanced: Aiguille Rouge–Le Pré run.

Experts: Off-piste with a guide.

Lunch: La Ferme at the bottom of the Villaroger lift.

Off the Slopes: Explore Bourg Saint Maurice.

Best Hotel: Mercure Coralia at Arc 1800.

LES DEUX ALPES/LA GRAVE
Les Deux Alpes, France

From the top of Glacier du Mont de Lans to the low-lying village of Mont de Lans is an easy ski trail descending 7,400 vertical feet. It is the longest drop of any maintained ski run in the world. Slow skiers might consider packing a lunch.

But the glacier above the resort of Les Deux Alpes also connects by gondola to the dramatic resort of La Grave, where the off-piste experience is everything, because there are no marked runs. Together, the two resorts offer some of the wildest and most satisfying skiing in Europe.

Les Deux Alpes is not well known outside the circle of French skiers and British tour operators who frequent the resort. It teeters on a high saddle in a remote valley of the Grands Oisans, less than an hour from the Olympic city of Grenoble. Like Alpe d'Huez, which is forty-five minutes away, Les Deux Alpes started resort life in the 1930s, but it didn't really get out of the starting gate until the 1968 Grenoble Winter Olympic Games put the Grands Oisans on the ski map. Regrettably, purpose-built architectural weeds took root, and the place blossomed with apartments. But no architect can completely spoil a place where the natural world so overshadows the human-made.

Les Deux Alpes wallows in a sun-splashed landscape of rugged summit ridges that sweep up from protected valleys. The skiing stretches to heights of 12,000 feet, where snow is guaranteed. Les Deux Alpes is slightly larger than Alpe d'Huez and much livelier at night. It can get downright rowdy when a lot of Brits are in town.

The village stretches along a narrow valley with mountains rising steeply on both sides. The slopes, which offer something for everyone, are mostly south facing, and the sun shines most of the winter. In some areas the runs are ridged with 6-foot steps, bearing testimony to the efforts of previous generations who scratched a living from terraced farming.

The arrival of mass tourism after the 1850s changed life. Locals discovered that harvesting the beauty of the Alps had greater value than growing crops. The growth of skiing paralleled the growth of winter resorts, and vice versa. The only agricultural products to survive are wine and cheese. The vineyards are low on the south-facing slopes, and the ski runs pasture cows in summer. During ski season, cows winter on hay in the ground floor of traditional elevated homes.

Below Les Deux Alpes and connected by gondola is the hamlet of Venosc, where Old

Known as one of France's great après-ski resorts, Les Deux Alpes also offers high-altitude snow, state-of-the-art lifts, and long vertical drops amid extraordinary scenery. A lift links Les Deux Alpes with La Grave, one of the most dramatic resorts in the world.

World charm oozes from the cobbled streets. Watch village life unfold at the local bakery and delicatessen, while enjoying a drink at an outdoor table, or as you dine at one of the fine rustic restaurants.

If you want more of those this-could-only-happen-in-Europe experiences, and if you're a skilled skier or boarder, ride the gondola to La Grave, population 512, a village of narrow streets and stone houses. The skiing here offers 7,000 vertical feet of glaciers, cliffs, and couloirs with no marked trails and only four lifts. Nothing in North America comes close to this much vertical, not even Whistler.

The slopes above Les Deux Alpes are generally long and narrow, with a few standout runs for every ability level. All but a few are above the tree line. Experts will find plenty of bumps and sun-softened snow frozen overnight into icy lumps. Beginners have the good fortune of having compatible slopes at the top of the mountain, making the splendid view extremely egalitarian. More beginner slopes are down low next to the village.

The resort is popular with boarders, especially at the Toura area of the mountain where there's a terrain park, halfpipe, and bordercross, along with a constant carnival-like atmosphere that includes barbecues and music.

Off the slopes, Les Deux Alpes offers plenty of raucous nightlife centered on the village's bars. But not much else.

Les Deux Alpes Tourist Office
B.P. 7
F-38860
France

Phone: 33–476–79–22–00

Web Site: www.les2alpes.com

E-mail: les2alp@les2alpes.com

Elevation: Top—11,810 feet; base—4,270 feet

Vertical Drop: 6,397 feet

Total Trails: 137 miles

Longest Run: 5 miles

Terrain: 24% beginner; 39% intermediate; 24% advanced; 13% expert

Lifts: 60

Snowmaking: 60 acres

Central Reservations: 33–476–79–24–38

Snow Report: www.les2alpes.com

Accommodations: About three dozen mostly 2- and 3-star hotels and lots of apartments.

Getting There: Lyon's airport is 3½ hours; Geneva's is 4½ hours. The nearest train station is Geneva, 43 miles.

Keep in Mind: Not much to entertain non-skiers.

BEST BETS

Beginners: The top of the glacier on sunny days.

Intermediates: La Toura area.

Advanced: Combe de Thuit.

Experts: La Grave with a guide.

Lunch: Chalet de la Toura.

Off the Slopes: Explore the old hamlet of Venosc, reached via gondola.

Best Hotel: The 4-star Berangère.

MEGÈVE
Megève, France

Courchevel may have usurped Megève as France's most fashionable winter address, but not for the old-money crowds. The storybook village at the foot of Mont Blanc first attracted an influential clientele in the 1920s, when St. Moritz became crowded. The French upper crust tossed that Swiss resort a snub and reinvented rustic Megève as the height of French fashion. The village, which has a medieval church as a focal point, maintains its elitist cachet. It is among a handful of resorts that rank as the most romantic and charming in the ski world.

 There are still French aristocrats who wouldn't be seen anywhere else. Stylish Megève is as much a state of mind as a place, and like all great ski towns it attracts nonskiers. The sunny Mont Blanc neighborhood is all you can ask of the Alps, and the mountain restaurants are the best in France's Haute Savoie.

But visitors to Megève also witness many of the clichés concerning highfalutin European ski resorts. Among them: Skiers who show up for après-ski with small dogs and big fur coats seldom spend the day on steep, shadow-filled couloirs. And so it is at Megève. Skiing the tame, snow-covered pastures is like riding in a luxury European sedan. Still, in fairness to all those Megève skiers who actually can ski, it should be noted that there's enough variety to keep everyone feeling snobbish. The resort's high areas have steep pitches where experts can strut their Ferrari-like legs. Off-piste, powder often remains untouched for days. And

no wonder. After all, what's the point in skiing at Megève if you can't be seen?

The skiing and snowboarding play out on three mountain faces, with the trails of Megève seamlessly connecting with those above the old village of St. Gervais. The slopes offer mile after mile of forgiving intermediate terrain. The more challenging runs overlook St. Gervais on Mont Joly and Mont Joux, where there's also a terrain park and halfpipe. Beginners enjoy gentle slopes both around the valley and high on the slopes, with a nice progression to longer and longer green runs. There really is something for everyone.

What's the downside? The elevation is too low for reliable snow. The solution has been an armory of snowmaking cannons, more than 250 at last count, which keep the lower runs open, but the ski-in/ski-out advantages of Megève are seldom a reality. Nonetheless, there are plenty of options to ski elsewhere.

Megève is a partner in the Evasion Mont Blanc lift pass that covers many of the resorts in the shadow of Western Europe's highest peak. The resorts include Rochebrune, Mont d'Arbois, St. Gervais, Le Bettex, St. Nocolas, Le Jaillet, Combloux, Les Contamines, and Bellevue. In total, the Evasion Mont Blanc pass covers 117 lifts serving 270 miles of trails.

The medieval-style village of Megève, population 4,700, offers luxury accommodations, fine French cuisine, and swank shops. Nonetheless, the horses that clip-clop away the winter pulling sleighs along the village's narrow streets come from working stock. There are some eighty farms keeping rural Savoyard traditions alive in the valley. One of the pleasures of European skiing is the opportunity to rub shoulders with Europeans. Megève yields plenty of these chances.

Neighboring St. Gervais, population 5,000, is a nineteenth-century, museum-piece spa village preserving the fantasy version of the Alps we all carry in our imaginations. You can still take the waters at the historic thermal baths, and a gondola links the village with Mont d'Arbois, where the terrain favors cautious skiers and the slopes receive plenty of winter sunshine.

Like Zermatt, Megève is famous for its mountain restaurants and the views they provide. To ensure a table, reservations should be made when you ski by in the morning.

Off-slope activities include ice skating, curling, and tobogganing. There's also a swimming pool and indoor tennis. The après-ski is centered on lively bars and clubs. There's also a casino and a cinema.

Megève Office de Tourisme
B.P. 24-74120
Megève, France

Phone: 33–450–21–27–28

Web Site: www.megeve.com

E-mail: megeve@megeve.com

Elevation: Top—7,710 feet; base—3,658 feet

Vertical Drop: 4,100 feet

Total Trails: 270 miles (including Combloux and St. Gervais)

Longest Run: 2 miles

Terrain: 17% beginner; 29% intermediate; 40% advanced; 14% expert

Lifts: 117 (including Combloux and St. Gervais)

Snowmaking: 160 acres

Central Reservations: 33–450–21–27–28

Snow Report: www.megeve.com

Accommodations: Lots of luxury hotels in Megève, many ski-in/ski-out when the snow is adequate.

Getting There: Geneva is 1 hour away; Lyon is 2½ hours. The nearest rail station is Sallanches, 7 miles away.

Keep in Mind: Snow is often in short supply on the lower runs.

BEST BETS

Beginners: Green runs on Cote 2000.

Intermediates: Mont d'Arbois area.

Advanced: Alpette downhill course.

Experts: Mont Joly.

Lunch: The Alpage at Les Communailles.

Off the Slopes: Explore the thermal baths at St. Gervais.

Best Hotel: Mont Blanc.

MÉRIBEL
Méribel, France

Above the honey-colored wood-and-stone chalets of Méribel, starting from the top of Mont Vallon, is a 3-mile-long run plunging more than 7,000 vertical feet to an old spa town in the valley. None of the lift-serviced slopes of North America comes even close to this much vertical.

Take the top half of Blackcomb Mountain and pile it on top of neighboring Whistler, and you get a part of the picture. But there's much more. The huge surrounding ski region of the Trois Vallées (Three Valleys) has enough acreage to sprout more than half a dozen resorts the size of Jackson Hole.

Ski-in/ski-out Méribel sits in the middle of this expansive ski region between the more exclusive Courchevel and the wilder landscapes of Val Thorens. The Trois Vallées offers more than 375 miles of ski and snowboarding trails, plus all the off-piste you can handle. Most of it lies in a national park. If you want more, Méribel's six-day lift ticket includes a day at nearby Val d'Isère, La Plagne, and Les Arcs.

The ambience at Méribel is mostly English. The ski resort dates back to 1938, when a Scotsman named Peter Lindsay began developing the place. It's nothing like the nearby French enclave of Courchevel. But don't worry: The English are not foolish enough to do away with the French chefs. You can blissfully dine on Savoyard specialties and enjoy exquisite regional wines while reliving moments of magic or misfortune from the day on the mountain.

In the Allues Valley you won't find the high-rise concrete slabs common to France's purpose-built resorts. Méribel is built in traditional Savoyard architectural styles, with a high concentration of luxurious ski-in/ski-out chalets, complete with chefs and nannies if you so desire. The valley also is home to other smaller and older hamlets like St. Martin de Belleville, where you can enjoy village squares lined with pleasant, informal cafes. The locals welcome you and go about their business.

Like most of the French Alps, the lifts at Méribel are state-of-the-art. And it has its own complement of fifty-one lifts serving seventy-five mostly intermediate runs. It is the only resort in the world with fourteen gondolas. The French don't fool around when it comes to high-tech lifts—but they do like to joke that they sell the old stuff to Switzerland. Méribel supplements the local slopes with snowmaking and does an adequate job of grooming. Some 400 ski instructors work the slopes, which are tilted to the morning and afternoon sun.

The snow is often better in Courchevel and Val Thorens, and there's good ski access to both areas. Between them is the wild white yonder of the Trois Vallées.

Snowboarders enjoy two terrain parks at Méribel; one is a mile long. There are half-pipes, and smaller pipes and tables and rails that defy description. Several of France's top riders train at Méribel.

 Located in the extraordinary Allues Valley of France, Méribel consists of a string of fourteen rustic villages that form one of the most picturesque resorts in the French Alps. It is also the epicenter of the world's largest ski region—Les Trois Vallées—and was the venue for the 1992 Olympic women's downhill.

Like all French resorts, Méribel welcomes and pampers young ones. There are a host of facilities and programs for children of all ages. A fitness center houses an ice-skating rink and a heated pool. There also are 20 miles of cross-country ski trails. But one of the nicest winter diversions is a simple walk with someone you enjoy along the peaceful network of footpaths cut through the snow.

Méribel Office du Tourisme
B.P. 1
73551 Méribel
France

Phone: 33–479–08–60–01

Web Site: www.meribel.net

E-mail: info@meribel.net

Elevation: Top—10,500 feet; base—4,270 feet

Vertical Drop: 6,230 feet

Total Trails: 375 miles (Trois Vallées)

Longest Run: 4 miles

Terrain: 17% beginner; 34% intermediate; 37% advanced; 12% expert

Lifts: 200 (Trois Vallées)

Snowmaking: 56 miles

Central Reservations: 33–479–00–31–19

Snow Report: www.meribel.net

Accommodations: A wide choice of high-quality hotels, chalets, and condominiums.

Getting There: Méribel is 90 minutes from Geneva.

Keep in Mind: Life centers on the slopes.

BEST BETS

Beginners: Blanchot.

Intermediates: The women's Olympic downhill run.

Advanced: La Combe on Vallon.

Experts: Off-piste from the summit of Mont Vallon.

Lunch: Chardonnet, midstation at the Mottaret gondola.

Off the Slopes: Visit the 13 historic chapels in the lower valley.

Best Hotel: Chalet at Belvedere.

TIGNES
Tignes, France

Few have ever complained about the skiing at Tignes. The village is another matter. The cluster of high-rise condos would be at home in many a nondescript American city. The village is no wisp of Alpine charm clinging to a mountainside.

But this is the lofty Savoie region of France, and Tignes is one of the highest resorts in the Alps. The 2-mile-high glaciers glisten. Even throughout the summer, skiers and boarders barrel down the slopes, every fiber of their bodies tuned up to high.

Tignes was built after construction of the nearby Chevril dam flooded the original village of Tignes in the 1950s. High-rise apartments started going up in the late 1960s—not exactly a decade of flaunted style and elegance (except, of course, for Jacqueline Kennedy). It was an era of bell-bottoms, Afros, and purpose-built resorts in the French Alps. Concrete jungles in virgin,

It's not the prettiest French ski resort. But you don't go to Tignes for the ambience. You go for the vastness of the skiing and snowboarding. The high altitude ensures great snow, and the varied slopes appeal to all levels. Tignes links with Val d'Isère to form the off-piste paradise called L'Escape Killy.

snowy valleys were all the rage. And Tignes did the times proud.

But the ambience is improving. In recent years some of those stark walls have been warmed by wood, some of the roads have gone underground, and new buildings have adopted the traditional Savoyard style. It's also worth remembering that the driving force behind purpose-built design was function. And Tignes is functional.

The resort consists of buildings laid out in villages at elevations varying between 5,000 and 7,000 feet. The highest is ski-in/ski-out Val Claret, where an underground funicular whisks skiers and snowboarders to the 9,850-foot level on the Grand Motte Glacier in just six minutes. The top station connects with a mid-mountain restaurant featuring a wraparound view of dazzling snow-covered summits and swooping long runs leading back to the valley. You also can head over to Tignes's sister resort of Val d'Isère on an enormous ski circus called L'Escape Killy, after Val d'Isère's most famous son, Jean-Claude Killy, who swept all the gold medals in alpine skiing at the Grenoble Olympic Winter Games in 1968.

Carving up the slopes between the two resorts involves covering 6 horizontal miles and as many vertical miles as your thighs can handle. The area is so large you could dump several Sun Valleys within its boundaries. The ski region has 135 named runs served by almost one hundred lifts. Given

safe avalanche conditions, you can ski almost anywhere.

For experts, it is the off-piste delights and dilemmas that are a major part of the Tignes appeal. First-time visitors should consider hiring a guide to get their bearings and find the best fall lines. It's important to size up factors such as sun exposure, weather, and quality of snow in determining where to ski on the mountain.

Snowboarding is big at Tignes. Even freeriders staying at Val d'Isère gravitate to the wide glacier slopes above Tignes. There are few surface lifts and often acres and acres of powder. There also are dynamite terrain parks, and you can buy a less expensive lift ticket if that's where you want to spend all your time.

What you can't find at Tignes—long beginner trails and Alpine-village ambience—you'll find at Val d'Isere. But one potential problem is the limits imposed by bad weather. High winds and dangerous avalanche conditions can close much of the area. The lack of trees makes flat-light days a dizzying and sometimes daunting experience.

Back in the village clusters of Tignes, there are not a lot of activity options. You can roll a few strikes at Europe's highest bowling alley, or throw curling rocks down the ice. And of course, there are plenty of bars and restaurants.

If you like big ski areas with excellent slopes and guaranteed snow, however, you could hardly do better than Tignes.

Tignes Tourist Office
B.P. 51
F-73321
Tignes, Savoie
France
Phone: 33–479–40–03–03
Web Site: www.tignes.net
E-mail: info@ski-tignes.com

Elevation: Top—11,647 feet; base—6,070 feet

Vertical Drop: 4,290 feet

Total Trails: 186 miles (L'Escape Killy)

Longest Run: 3.5 miles

Terrain: 17% beginner; 47% intermediate; 26% advanced; 10% expert

Lifts: 97 (L'Escape Killy)

Snowmaking: 15 miles

Central Reservations: 33–479–40–03–03

Snow Report: www.tignes.net

Accommodations: Mostly ski-in/ski-out, high-rise condos and a handful of 3-star hotels.

Getting There: Geneva is 110 miles away; Lyon, 120 miles. The nearest train station is Bourg St. Maurice, 16 miles.

Keep in Mind: Lacks village charm and sustained beginner terrain.

BEST BETS

Beginners: Several free chairs above Tignes-le-Lac, Val Claret, and the first stage of the Bollin chair.

Intermediates: The Grand Motte Glacier.

Advanced: The Col des Ves chair.

Experts: Hire a guide and explore L'Escape Killy.

Lunch: The Savouna, above Tignes-le-Lac.

Off the Slopes: Explore the villages of Le Fornet, Le Joseray, Le Manchet, Le Chatelard, and La Daille et le Laisinant.

Best Hotel: Campanules might be the best of the 3-star hotels.

VAL D'ISÈRE
Val d'Isère, France

The wooden chalet where 1968 Olympic champion Jean-Claude Killy grew up still stands in the old town of Val d'Isère. Surrounding the village, the Alps leap so abruptly and theatrically as to appear rendered instead of real. Killy calls his hometown "the most beautiful winter playground in the world." He's biased, of course, but thousands of skiers from faraway mountains agree. Winter visitors have been coming for more than sixty-five years. It is a truly classic European resort, and a must-ski on any traveling skier's tick list.

The nearby city of Albertville hosted the 1992 Olympic Winter Games, and Val d'Isère was the venue for the men's downhill. The course remains one of the most exciting challenges on the World Cup circuit. It's also yours to ski.

Directly above the 6,000-foot-high village, the slopes are treed, but most of the serious skiing takes place above the tree line. The cleverly laid-out lifts offer thigh-burning vertical drops. Arctic cold spells are rare. In recent years the resort has responded to critics of European skiing by hiring charming lift attendants and unleashing a daily flotilla of snow-grooming machines. But there remain thousands of acres of quiet, untrammeled mountain and deep snow easily accessed from the lifts.

Unfortunately, Val d'Isère offers little in the way of sustained beginner terrain. The best bets for true novices are the mellow runs directly above town served by free lifts. The top pitch is a bit steep, but the rest of the terrain is ideal for novices.

For the most part, the skiing at Val d'Isère is neatly divided into three areas rising above the villages that spread across the remote valley. They link by ski lifts; each appeals to skiers of different abilities. La Daille area is teeming with broad, long intermediate cruisers that get the juices flowing. The second area includes the more advanced terrain of Bellevarde and Solaise peaks, with the higher regions offering more gentle slopes. The third has its base in the old village of Le Fornet and offers a high-Alpine experience with plenty of off-piste possibilities in a wilderness with spectacular scenery and peerless skiing.

Much of the terrain is ideally suited to snowboarders, but they must endure the hassle of a few surface lifts and some flat stretches. Otherwise it's clear sailing. Nonetheless, nearby Tignes attracts more boarders.

But the real ski appeal of Val d'Isère is L'Escape Killy, one of the most far-reaching lift-served backcountry skiing venues in the world. It is a 6-mile-long stretch of ridges, valleys, and peaks that rise as high as a vertical mile and connect Val d'Isère with neighboring Tignes. The area is five times larger than Vail, with many of its 136 named runs lying in Vanoise National Park.

It's a mistake not to hire a guide, at least for the first couple of days. Much of the ski experience hinges on timing, and a guide who can evaluate factors such as sun exposure, weather, and type of snow can position you in the right place for the time.

But never follow a set of tracks if you don't know where they lead. As at most European resorts, a rescue by the Val d'Isère ski patrol costs anywhere from $30 for a toboggan rescue to $1,000 or more for a helicopter evacuation. Buy the Carte des Neiges, an insurance card offered whenever you buy a lift ticket in France. It covers the cost of carrying you down when injured or if you need to be rescued off-piste.

 For skiers who seek vast expanses of lift-serviced, backcountry-type skiing, this is one of the great resorts of Europe. But Val d'Isère also delivers miles and miles of groomed intermediate trails, close to one hundred lifts, and impeccable French ambience. It's linked with Tignes, and the high altitude ensures good snow.

Val d'Isère offers plenty of small, charming lodges serving superb French cuisine. Free shuttles ferry skiers to the base of the lifts. Off-slope activities include dogsledding and winter hiking in the national park.

A multiday lift ticket at Val d'Isère includes a day at nearby Les Arcs or La Plagne, plus access to the enormous Trois Vallées, the large ski circus that includes Courchevel and Méribel resorts.

To the north of Val d'Isère are the spectacular Grandes Jorasses and the white crest of Mont Blanc, the highest mountain in Western Europe, looming above Chamonix and Courmayeur, Italy.

Val d'Isère Tourist Office
B.P. 228
73 155 Val d'Isère Cedex
France

Phone: 33–479–06–06–60

Web Site: www.valdisere.com

E-mail: info@valdisere.com

Elevation: Top—11,647 feet; base—6,070 feet

Vertical Drop: 4,290 feet

Number of Trails: 186 (L'Escape Killy)

Longest Run: 3 miles

Terrain: 17% beginner; 47% intermediate;

26% advanced; 10% expert

Lifts: 97 (L'Escape Killy)

Snowmaking: 15 miles

Central Reservations: 33–479–06–06–60

Snow Report: www.valdisere.com

Accommodations: Many small, family-run chalets in the area.

Getting There: Val d'Isère is 112 miles from Geneva and 137 miles from Lyons, France. From Paris, the high-speed TGV train goes to Bourg St. Maurice; a bus continues the 21 miles to Val d'Isère.

Keep in Mind: High-season crowds.

BEST BETS

Beginners: Madeleine on Solaise.

Intermediates: La Daille area.

Advanced: The Olympic downhill run at Bellevarde.

Experts: Hire a guide and explore the backcountry of L'Escape Killy.

Lunch: Le Signal at the top of the Fornet cable.

Off the Slopes: Stroll the villages of Le Fornet, Le Joseray, Le Manchet, Le Chatelard, and La Daille et le Laisinant.

Best Hotel: The Blizzard or the Hotel Christiania.

GARMISCH-PARTENKIRCHEN
Garmisch-Partenkirchen, Germany

Located beneath the 9,718-foot Zugspitze, Germany's highest mountain, the combined town of Garmisch-Partenkirchen is the picture-postcard image you imagine when you think of the Bavarian Alps. The pretty town, with outdoor frescoes beaming from pastel stuccoed buildings, is surrounded on three sides by glacier-carved summits. Even the wild baroque castles of Bavarian King Ludwig II are nearby, including the fairy-tale Neuschwanstein.

Garmisch-Partenkirchen also is at the heart of four widely varying ski areas and is Germany's best and best-known ski resort.

Adolf Hitler decreed that the two towns of Garmisch and Partenkirchen join forces to host the 1936 Olympic Winter Games. Both towns have a long history. Partenkirchen dates to 15 B.C. Its warren of Old World streets defines Bavarian architecture, especially in the old Ludwigstrasse section of town. The town's museum itself is located in a museum piece, a fifteenth-century home.

Garmisch was first mentioned in ninth-century documents. It's a little more commercial, and a little livelier than its elder sister city, with a downtown jam-packed with popular watering holes and nightclubs. Garmisch also is the site of the Olympic Ice Sports Center.

The location has always been strategic. Italian goods, along with Roman armies, moved north over the Brenner Pass to Innsbruck and then into Germany via Partenkirchen. Garmisch had its own trade links. The Partnach River flows into the Loisach River, which runs through Garmisch and historically provided a shipping lane to the Black Sea. Today it remains a major rail and road hub between Germany, Innsbruck, and the Brenner Pass to Italy.

German composer Richard Strauss lived in Garmisch for most of his life and died there in 1949. The extraordinary setting must have influenced his grand symphonies and operas. Today the combined population of 28,000 is large enough to support a rich endowment of cultural activities, including an annual Richard Strauss Festival of chamber music, song recitals, and symphony concerts.

It's almost enough to make you bypass the slopes—but don't. There is a world of high-end intermediate terrain for skiers and boarders in the four areas, which are not linked by lifts, but connected by shuttle buses and trains from town.

 With fifty-seven lifts, four separate ski areas, and access to a dozen more, Germany's winter sports capital ranks among the top resorts in Europe. But there's only one Bavaria, and Garmisch-Partenkirchen is at its heart. You'll find plenty of Old World architecture and charm, along with varied and often challenging skiing.

The biggest and most popular ski area is the Hausberg/Alpspitz, directly above town, but still a bus ride away. Alpspitz lies above the Hausberg area and above the tree line. Both areas offer long, paperclip runs that will have intermediates soaring down the 4,000 vertical feet of nicely pitched terrain. For ski racing fans, a run down the infamous Kandahar, one of the toughest courses on the men's World Cup tour, is a must ski. For boarders, the gigantic bowl at the base of the mountain offers rolling terrain with lots of natural windlips and pipes.

The highest area is Zugspitzplatt. Its intermediate and advanced slopes snake down from 8,400 feet to 6,000 feet. Near its summit, the Schneeferner Glacier guarantees snow when conditions are bad elsewhere. To get to its tangle of lifts, which are mostly above the tree line, you ride a scenic aerial tram or a slower but interesting cog-

wheel train that tunnels through the mountain and emerges near the summit.

On the edges of town are the lesser slopes of Wank and Eckbauer. A cable car leads to five surface lifts on Wank Mountain and a lovely 5-mile trail winding through the forest back to town. The Eckbauer ski area is the site of the Olympic ski-jumping facilities and is connected to the Hausberg area by gondola. Its claim to fame is a steep World Cup slalom run.

Garmisch-Partenkirchen also markets a lift pass good at twelve nearby resorts in Germany and Austria, including Seefeld.

Garmisch comes alive at night with clubs, taverns, and a casino (jacket and tie required). Day trips include visits to the surrounding Wagnerian countryside of mountains, castles, and baroque churches.

Hotels provide visitor cards entitling guests to free bus shuttles, reduced admissions to some venues, and accident insurance for the duration of the stay.

The resort offers more than 25 miles of prepared cross-country trails and 60 miles of maintained winter walking trails. There's also ice skating, curling, and a swimming pool with a wave machine.

The rich folklore and traditions of Bavaria are showcased throughout the region. Interesting side trips include King Ludwig II's castles at Linderhof and Neuschwanstein, the passion play theater in Oberammergau, and the cities of Munich and Innsbruck.

Garmisch-Partenkirchen
Tourist Office
Richard Strauss Platz la
D-82467 Garmisch-Partenkirchen
Germany

Phone: 49–88–21–180–700

Web Site: www.garmisch.de

E-mail: tourist-info@gapa.de

Elevation: Top—9,732 feet; base—3,362 feet

Vertical Drop: 4,347 feet (Alpspitz area)

Total Trails: 73 miles

Longest Run: 5 miles

Terrain: 10% beginner; 65% intermediate; 25% advanced/expert

Lifts: 57

Snowmaking: Yes

Central Reservations: 49–88–21–180–700

Snow Report: www.garmisch.de

Accommodations: A wide range of hotels, inns, guest houses, and private homes.

Getting There: Innsbruck is 45 minutes away; Munich is 90 minutes. Train station at Garmisch.

Keep in Mind: Sharp-elbowed Munich skiers swarm here on weekends.

BEST BETS

Beginners: Alpspitz.

Intermediates: The 2-mile run from Schneefernerkopf on Zugspitze.

Advanced: The Kandahar World Cup downhill course at Hausberg/Alpspitz.

Experts: Horn run.

Lunch: Summit Restaurant on Zugspitze.

Off the Slopes: Explore the old Ludwigstrasse section of Partenkirchen and the Werdenfelser Museum.

Best Hotel: The Zugspitze.

BORMIO
Bormio, Italy

Bormio, with its cobbled streets backed by a magnificent circle of mountain peaks, is no upstart purpose-built resort from the 1960s. It has the rich patina of age, from its eighteenth-century De Simoni Palace, to its seventeenth-century town hall, to the fifteenth- and sixteenth-century frescoes on the Crocifisso Church. The town's thermal baths are mentioned in Roman documents dating back to the first century.

But it wasn't until 1985 that Bormio, population 4,200, took off as an international ski destination. That was the year the northern Italian resort hosted the World Alpine Ski Championships and Bormio spruced up the town and improved the ski area. Ski-racing fans discovered what a lovely place it is, and word quickly spread about the friendly, unpretentious village. Bormio was the venue for the world championships again in 2005.

Located at a crossroads in the Valtellina Valley in the mountains of Lombardy, with extraordinary views over Stelvio National Park, Bormio was the site of an early town at the foot of Stelvio Pass. The area, near the Swiss and Austrian borders, prospered during the Middle Ages as a major trade route from Venice.

Skiing at Bormio plays out at two main areas—Oga and Vallecetta—both easily handled by intermediate-level skiers and boarders. There is no linked ski circus like the Sella Ronda that is shared by Val Gardena and Cortina d'Ampezzo. The slopes directly above Bormio on Vallecetta, reached via cable car and gondola, offer the most challenge, particularly from the 9,880-foot summit of Cima Bianca (White Peak), where the vertical drop is a whopping 5,860 feet. Pista Stelvio, Bormio's World Cup downhill course, runs for 2 miles without a flat spot anywhere. The tops of the runs are wide open while the lower halves of the slopes are tree lined, offering a nice New England touch. Still, the snow is usually far better up top, and skiers and snowboarders often ride back up from two different midmountain stations called Ciuk and Bormio 2000 (as in 2,000 meters, or 6,500 feet). Bormio 2000 is actually a midmountain resort with two hotels. Children are treated royally at Bormio 2000, which has a roped-off learning and play area in the snow with a moving-carpet lift.

A ten-minute shuttle bus links Oga across the valley to Bormio. Oga's slopes rise out of the mountain hamlets of Oga, Le Motte, and Isolaccia. They are reminiscent of Aspen's Buttermilk resort with gentle, wide-open terrain for beginners and low-level intermediates. The east-facing slopes catch the morning sun, and there are long green runs stretching from the Masucco peak to the valley floor at Le Motte. There also are gentler, wide-open runs above Masucco.

 Authentically Italian and ideal for families and couples, this medieval mountain village in northern Italy near the Swiss border offers some of the longest runs in the Italian Alps. Day trips to the Italian duty-free resort of Livigno and the Swiss resort of St. Moritz are popular.

During the summer, when the Stelvio Pass is open to traffic, there's summer skiing on its glacier alongside the Italian national ski team training camp.

Bormio's lift pass includes access to neighboring Valdidentro and Santa Caterina. Both are a short bus ride from Bormio and offer high-altitude snow. But experts find the slopes at Santa Caterina more to their liking. The lift pass also includes Livigno, just an

hour's drive over a pass to the west. A seven-day lift pass includes a day at St. Moritz, across the Swiss border three hours away.

The Bernina Express, one of the most beautiful trains in Europe, stops in Tirano, a town about 20 miles from Bormio.

The dining in Bormio's cozy restaurants is worthy of an Italian grandmother. The same is true for the mountain *rifugios* (restaurants). The local specialty not to be missed is *pizzocheri,* a mixture of noodles made from buckwheat flour and vegetables, served with butter and Alpine cheeses.

Off the slopes, the thermal baths are a must-do experience. There's also a sports center with an ice rink and indoor swimming pool. Also popular are excursions in nearby Stelvio National Park, Western Europe's largest protected wilderness.

Bormio Tourist Office
Via Roma 131/B
23032 Bormio
Italy

Phone: 39–0342–90–33–00

Web Site: www.valtellinaonline.com

E-mail: infobormio@provincia.so.it

Elevation: Top—9,880 feet; base—4,020 feet

Vertical Drop: 5,860 feet

Total Trails: 75 miles

Longest Run: 9 miles

Terrain: 48% beginner; 43% intermediate; 9% advanced/expert

Lifts: 24

Snowmaking: 30 miles

Central Reservations: www.valtellina online.com

Snow Report: www.valtellinaonline.com

Accommodations: Forty-plus hotels, mostly 2- and 3-star; also many apartments.

Getting There: Milan (125 miles) is 3 hours.

Keep in Mind: Not much challenging terrain.

BEST BETS

Beginners: At Oga, from Masucco peak to Forte to Le Motte.

Intermediates: Bimbi al Sole from Cima Bianca.

Advanced: The men's downhill—Pista Stelvio.

Experts: A couple of black runs on Cima Bianca.

Lunch: La Rocca, above Ciuk.

Off the Slopes: The Bagni Vecchi (ancient baths).

Best Hotel: The 4-star Palace.

CERVINIA
Breuil-Cervinia, Italy

The old mountain hamlet was called Breuil until the 1930s, when Mussolini and his Fascists selected the site for a high-altitude ski resort and changed the name to Cervinia. It sounded more Italian and acknowledged the hamlet's storybook location at the foot of the Matterhorn, which Italians call Monte Cervino. Today the official name is Breuil-Cervino, and it is very much Italian. And it is very good.

From its cobbled streets to its cozy cafes and sun-splashed slopes, Cervinia delivers everything a North American skier hopes to find in Europe. And it all plays out beneath Europe's, and perhaps the world's, most recognizable mountain. Even the clang-clang of weathered church bells adds to the scene.

Located at 6,500 feet in the Aosta Valley, within two hours of Turin and three hours from Milan, Cervinia offers Italy's highest slopes and some of the longest runs in the Alps. Most of the skiing and snowboarding happens in a large west-facing bowl next to the shoulder of the 14,692-foot-high Matterhorn. The snow conditions near the top of the resort are almost always good. The lower slopes above the village are equipped with enough snowmaking artillery to outgun Mussolini.

Intermediate-level skiers and snowboarders have the run of the place. The trails are well groomed. If you hate moguls but love skiing, this is your mountain. Even beginners get wide-open, consistently gentle runs high on the mountain with extraordinary views overlooking Italy and Switzerland. At most resorts, beginners wedge their way down machine-made snow low on the mountain with views of hotels.

At Cervinia, novice skiers make rapid progress. An important aspect of learning to ski is choosing the right terrain, and Cervinia probably has more long, ideally suited learning slopes than anyplace else.

But you also can test your mettle on Cervinia's "Kilometro Lanciato," the venue for

 Plenty of sunshine, long cruising runs, and Italy's best snow makes Cervinia popular with skiers from Turin and Milan. Part of the appeal also is Cervinia's proximity to the Matterhorn and the opportunity to schuss across the Swiss border to storied Zermatt. Of all the ski links in the Alps, Cervinia and Zermatt might be Europe's best one-two punch.

the World Cup of speed skiing. Every Saturday, regular skiers get to tuck the track and have their speed recorded. Snowboarders enjoy a terrain park, halfpipe, and bordercross. Cervinia's slopes and lifts also connect with Valtournenche, another Italian resort 5 miles down the Aosta Valley. Heliskiing also is popular from Cervinia.

One of the biggest draws here is the thrill of dropping down into Switzerland and scooting around the slopes of storied Zermatt, perhaps dining in one of the more than thirty mountain restaurants that have become almost as well known as the skiing. The border is a mere yellow line painted on a piece of rough concrete—no passports, border guards, or import duties. You will need to buy a supplement to your Cervinia lift pass. Purchase it in Cervinia; in Zermatt it costs much more. So does everything else.

The views from the high slopes are out of this world. The panorama includes more than thirty-six mountains higher than 13,000 feet, which is taller than any peak in the Canadian Rockies. Spectacular glaciers rimmed by steel-blue seracs glisten in all directions. On clear days, which are most days in this southern corner of the Alps, the sky is the intense blue of high altitude, tracked by streamers of high clouds.

In the compact village, some of Cervinia's original buildings remain from the 1930s. But there also are concrete edifices from the purpose-built era of the 1960s. More recent times have been kinder, with wood-and-stone structures built in more traditional Alpine style. The traffic-free main street, dominated by a lovely old steepled church, is vibrant and bustling. It sports a nice hodgepodge of hotels, shops, and restaurants. Add 800 friendly residents to the setting, and you can't help falling in love with the place.

Off-slope activities are limited but include snowmobile tours, ice skating, and indoor swimming. There also are well-maintained cross-country tracks sweeping across the narrow valley next to the village.

Cervinia might lack the chocolate-and-cowbell charm of Zermatt, but there's something about this village and its friendly inhabitants that gives the place its own special charm. It's like putting on a comfortable pair of faded old blue jeans and just having a good time.

Breuil-Cervinia Tourist Office
Via Carrel, 29
11021 Breuil-Cervinia
Italy

Phone: 39–0166–94–91–361

Web Site: www.cervinia.it

E-mail: info@sportepromozione.it

Elevation: Top—11,420 feet; base—5,000 feet

Vertical Drop: 6,420 feet

Total Trails: 125 miles (including Valtournenche)

Longest Run: 8 miles

Terrain: 28% beginner; 60% intermediate; 12% advanced/expert

Lifts: 30

Snowmaking: 11 miles

Central Reservations: 39–0166–94–01–34

Snow Report: www.cervinia.it

Accommodations: A wide range of hotels and apartments, including a family-oriented Club Med.

Getting There: The nearest international airport is Turin, 1½ hours away. The nearest railway station is Châtillon (about 45 minutes away by bus).

Keep in Mind: Weekends are busy. Bad weather closes many of the high lifts.

Beginners: The Cretaz lift.

Intermediates: Follow the sunshine; the mountain is yours.

Advanced: The 8-mile cruiser from Plateau Rosa to Valtournenche.

Experts: A couple of short pitches beneath Plateau Rosa.

Lunch: Chalet Etoile, beneath the Rocce Nerre chair.

Off the Slopes: The town's bars, restaurants, and fitness center are about it.

Best Hotel: The 4-star Hotel Hermitage.

CORTINA D'AMPEZZO
Cortina d'Ampezzo, Italy

Viewed from a distance, the Dolomites, fourteen separate massifs stretching over northeastern Italy hard on the border with Austria and Switzerland, emerge as jagged walls of rock and snow. In the geopolitics of Europe, the Dolomites have effectively separated the northern Germanics from the southern Mediterraneans for most of human history. The 1919 Treaty of Versailles gave Italy control of the formerly Austrian-held Dolomites.

There's nothing like these Dolomites. They rise sun kissed in brilliant grays and pinks, and at times even lavender—the colors forged by the residues of coral and sponges from an ancient tropical sea that once existed here.

The spectacular Dolomites play host to Italy's premier ski resort, Cortina d'Ampezzo,

 It's La Dolce Vita on the slopes or off in this legendary Alpine valley, site of the 1956 Winter Olympic Games. Tucked into the vaunted Dolomite Mountains, Cortina offers seemingly endless skiing, breathtaking scenery, and Italian cuisine—a skier's perfect 10.

which is also one of the world's glitziest. In the village, fur coats outnumber ski suits along the Corso, the resort's car-free main street. It is an old mountain town, elegant yet warmly human, full of comfortable old hotels built in a blocky chalet style.

As with most areas of the European Alps, skiing in the Dolomites is mostly above tree line, with the odd piste extending lower down the valley through the larch forest. The range of runs in the five ski areas above the valley is extensive. But for the most part, they are intermediate pitches made for linking swooping giant-slalom turns. You'll also find endless novice runs, a handful of in-your-face steep pitches, and, at the end of the day, sheer fatigue.

Cortina interconnects with 750 miles of downhill trails in twelve valleys utilizing some 464 lifts in forty-five ski areas. It is the largest lift-serviced ski network on the planet, and it takes an endless silken string of see-forever days to ski it all.

Yet half the winter guests who come here don't ski.

Welcome to splendid Cortina, whose outstanding skiing and snowboarding and temperate weather combine with cosmopolitan ambience and artistic and cultural excesses to create a spot unique even among European resorts. The dining in the Cortina area has little competition in the rest of the Alpine world. Dolomiti cuisine is an exquisite mélange of Mediterranean and Germanic flavors. For Italians, life is too short for fast food.

The storybook town of Cortina d'Ampezzo consists of the village center and about thirty surrounding hamlets. Cortina is the name of the central hamlet; Ampezzo indicates the valley. Narrow, winding roads weave drunkenly from village to village. Steep slate roofs and age-darkened pine-and-stucco walls dominate the architectural landscape. It is an antique and appealing setting.

Cortina hosted the 1956 Winter Olympic Games in which Austrian Toni Sailor's flawless performance won him three gold medals. Years later Alberto Tomba, winner of fifty World Cup races plus medals in three different Winter Olympics, began his ski-racing career in Cortina, where he now lives.

Four mountain faces shelter Cortina in a large amphitheater-like setting. Two cable-car lengths above the village, the open bowls of Faloria provide the perfect warm-up and a terrain park for boarders. Novices should head to Socrepes, Cortina's largest ski area, with its carpetlike novice slopes. Elsewhere in the valley, the overwhelming expanses of Cristallo and Tofana offer challenges for every level. The Ra Valles chairs service miles of rolling intermediate bowls, where you ski in the shadow of towering dolomite rock walls. The pickings are much slimmer for expert skiers and snowboarders, but you'll find daring runs at the top of the Tofana cable lift at Ra Valles and at the summit of the Cristallo area. The flow between areas works well for snowboarders, but there are a few surface lifts to negotiate.

Lift lines are rare. It takes sunshine to get Italian skiers on the mountain. And even then, they rise late, lunch long, and stop well before the lifts do to enjoy an afternoon vertical of Merlot del Trentino.

Cortina is a great place to learn to ski. The ski school is the largest in Italy, and you'll always find an English-speaking instructor. First-time visitors are wise to hire a guide from the ski school to get their bearings.

"Americans don't know how to ski here," says Mansueto Siorpaes, a veteran Cortina instructor. "They don't move from area to area during the day as the sun and snow change." He suggests a minimum three-day tour: Day One, ski Cristallo in the morning and Faloria in the afternoon. Day Two, ski Ra Valles in the morning and the area below Ra Valles in the afternoon. Day Three, explore the Lagazuoi and Cinque Torri areas.

The best skiing is from the end of January to the end of March for long, sunny days and a good chance of excellent snow cover. In January the World Cup with its races and legions of fans takes over Cortina.

One of the joys of skiing the Dolomites is the network of *rifugios,* rustic stone-and-pine mountain huts that serve an extensive menu ranging from espresso to exquisite risotto and pastas. There are five *rifugios* above Cortina. It's wise to make lunch reservations when skiing past one in the morning. Many also offer dormitory-style accommodations with brilliant sunsets and sunrises, and first tracks in the morning.

Cortina Turismo
Corso Italia, 83
1-32043 Cortina d'Ampezzo
Italy

Phone: 39–0436–86–62–52

Web Site: www.cortina.dolomiti.org

E-mail: cortina@infodolomiti.it

Elevation: Top—10,640 feet; base—4,015 feet

Vertical Drop: 6,624 feet

Total Trails: 72 miles

Longest Run: 6 miles

Terrain: 33% beginner; 62% intermediate; 5% advanced/expert

Lifts: 39

Snowmaking: 83 miles

Central Reservations: 39–0436–86–62–52

Accommodations: There are about 60 hotels in Cortina.

Getting There: The closest gateway airport is Venice (100 miles); ground transportation available.

Keep in Mind: Get advice on where to ski if you don't know the area.

BEST BETS

Beginners: Socrepes area.

Intermediates: Cinque Torri for fast cruising among splendid Dolomite scenery.

Advanced: Top half of the cable car at Ra Valles.

Experts: Forcella Rosa in the upper Ra Valles ski bowl.

Lunch: Rifugio Averau, perched at 7,850 feet near Cinque Torri.

Off the Slopes: Stroll the Corso in the center of Cortina.

Best Hotel: Hotel de la Poste, which has been run by the Manaigo family since it opened in 1835.

COURMAYEUR
Courmayeur, Italy

Skiers from stylish Milan and Turin crowd the resort on weekends in anticipation of sunny, snow-sure slopes and outstanding mountain cuisine. For Italians, the physical act of skiing is never an end in itself, which is why Courmayeur is so popular.

Located at the intersection of Switzerland, France, and Italy, on the sunny side of Mont Blanc, Courmayeur is a small, picturesque village with a car-free center, fabulous restaurants, and serious shopping. Most of the hotels reflect the mountain character of the town. Cable cars stretch across the valley. The slopes are dotted with twenty-one traditional wooden mountain huts transformed into cozy mountain restaurants known as *rifugios* in the Italian Alps.

Courmayeur's cultural history goes back two millennia. Its natural springwaters have attracted visitors since the seventeenth century; by 1850 the village was a center for mountaineering in the Mont Blanc region. It

became a popular international ski resort when the 8-mile-long Mont Blanc tunnel opened in 1965, linking it with the Chamonix Valley.

There are two main ski areas—Checrouit and Val Veny. The slopes are mostly intermediate fare above the tree line and offer outstanding views of Mont Blanc, or Monte Bianco (as the Italians say). Beginners have a modest selection of runs to choose from without a natural progression to slightly more difficult runs. Experts find exciting terrain off-piste, but these are serious mountains. Only a fool would venture into the backcountry of the Mont Blanc Massif without a guide or a close group of friends experienced in avalanche-hazard evaluation and crevasse-rescue training. Guides are highly recommended and readily available from the guides' office in the village. They also carry insurance in case a helicopter rescue is required.

The main slopes are centered on Checrouit at the opposite side of the valley from Mont Blanc and accessed by a tram from the village. The slopes start at the top of the tram. You can ski or snowboard back down to the village, or catch the tram back down and then ride a shuttle bus to the village. Most skiers and boarders enjoy the morning sun on the slopes of Colle Checrouit, which offers a nice variety of intermediate runs and a few lengthy beginner trails. A tram stretches to the 8,700-foot level of Cresta Youla. From there, a small tram carries adventurous snowriders to the 9,000-foot Cresta d'Arp summit and the start of two exciting back-country runs that are neither patrolled nor maintained and drop 7 miles down to Dolonne, where you can catch a shuttle back to the village.

Until a couple of seasons ago, skiers and boarders had to be accompanied by a ski guide just to ride the Cresta d'Arp tram. That restriction has since been lifted, but the routes down are no place for the inexperienced or lone rider. This is big-mountain skiing with variable snow conditions on steep and narrow terrain.

The Val Veny side of the resort, which is separated from Checrouit by a steep ridge, faces northwest and catches the afternoon sun. The slopes offer mostly intermediate runs through the trees, where nature's dumps of snow are supplemented by heavy snowmaking.

Another cable car whisks skiers, snowboarders, and their local guides to 11,000-foot Helbronner Point and the start of the Vallée Blanche guided ski trip, following the glacier leading to Chamonix in France. Another option from Helbronner Point is to descend 6,500 vertical feet down the Toula Glacier to La Palud.

Doable day trips include Cervinia in Italy, Chamonix in France, and Verbier in Switzerland. A Mont Blanc ski region pass covers lifts in thirteen resorts around Mont Blanc.

 With a combination of Alpine charm, mountaineering tradition, and great skiing at the base of Mont Blanc, Courmayeur is the foremost ski resort in Italy's stunningly beautiful Aosta Valley. The skiing and boarding suit intermediate cruisers, and the storied 12-mile run down Vallée Blanche to Chamonix in France is an option.

Heli-skiing, which is not permitted in France, is popular from Courmayeur. Day trips via helicopter fly to slopes on the Italian side of Mont Blanc and its surrounding peaks.

Off-slope activities at Courmayeur include ice skating, dogsledding, and a large sports center that features indoor tennis and squash, workout facilities, a climbing wall, and Italy's only indoor curling rink. There's also a fun snow park for children. The Duke of Abruzzi's Alpine Museum is well worth a visit, and the nearby town of St. Vincent offers a swanky casino.

There also are more than 20 miles of maintained cross-country ski trails offering extraordinary views of Mont Blanc and the surrounding Alps.

Courmayeur Tourist Office
Apt Monte Bianco
P. le Monte Bianco 13
1-11013 Courmayeur (AO)
Italy

Phone: 39–0165–84–20–60

Web Site: www.courmayeur.net

E-mail: info@courmayeur.net

Elevation: Top—9,127 feet; base—4,029 feet

Vertical Drop: 5,039 feet

Total Trails: 62 miles

Longest Run: 7 miles

Terrain: 20% beginner; 70% intermediate; 10% advanced/expert

Lifts: 23

Snowmaking: 11 miles

Central Reservations: 39–0165–84–20–60

Snow Report: www.courmayeur.net

Accommodations: About 65 hotels in all categories. Also apartments and rooms in private homes.

Getting There: Courmayeur is 2 hours (65 miles) from the Geneva airport. The nearest train station is Pre St. Didier, 8 minutes by taxi or bus.

Keep in Mind: Expect lift lines on weekends.

BEST BETS

Beginners: The Tzaly area above the Entréves tram.

Intermediates: The Checrouit area.

Advanced: The red runs on Val Veny.

Experts: The 7-mile-long Arp trail at the top of the Youla cable car.

Lunch: Maison Vieille.

Off the Slopes: Explore the ancient castles, churches, and monuments of the surrounding Aosta Valley.

Best Hotel: The 4-star Gallia Gran Baita.

MADONNA DI CAMPIGLIO
Madonna di Campiglio, Italy

Try to say it like an Italian. Ma-DOONA di Camp-IG-lio. Imagine skiing at a place with such a beautiful name!

When North Americans think about Alpine Europe, it's usually Switzerland or Austria that comes to mind. But only Italy embraces the entire 900-mile-long crescent-shaped Alps. It's easy to forget that half of Mont Blanc is in Italy, where it is known as Monte Bianco. So is part of the Matterhorn, or Monte Cervino, as the Italians call it. (It was the great Italian climber Walter Bonatti who alone did the improbable first winter ascent of the Matterhorn's spectacular north face.)

Indeed, the Alps are deeply rooted in Italy. But the extraordinary people and artistic influences so often overshadow the peaks. It brings to mind Orson Welles's line in *The Third Man:* In Italy for thirty years under Borgias, they had warfare, terror, murder, bloodshed—but they produced

Michelangelo, Leonardo da Vinci, and the Renaissance. In Switzerland they have brotherly love, 500 years of democracy and peace, and what did they produce? The cuckoo clock.

You don't have to ski to enjoy Madonna, making it a good place to be when someone you're with doesn't want to ski. The crowd

 With more runs and lifts than any other Italian ski resort, this sexy mile-high town tucked into the Trentino region of the extraordinary Dolomites offers miles and miles of groomed cruisers set above a beautiful old village. The sunshine and off-slopes attractions appeal to nonskiers. It's also Italy's premier destination for snowboarders.

is mostly stylish Italians who split their time between the village's beauty and diversions and three mountains, each offering a different experience with a variety of mixed terrain. The legendary World Cup downhill course extends to the village. So does the slalom course, which is floodlit for evening races.

The slopes surround the town. You can follow the sun on mostly gentle, well-groomed terrain perfect for beginners and intermediates who want to ski as well as they believe they can. Beginners enjoy both isolated nursery slopes and top-to-bottom blue runs. (Italy's beginner runs are color-coded blue, not green; intermediate runs are red; expert trails are black.) There are plenty of tree-lined runs, as well as wide-open cruisers above the forest. The Dolomite scenery is spectacular, and the resort is popular with posers.

But Madonna di Campiglio also is the heartland of Italy's snowboarding scene and the venue for many of the sport's international competitions. There is a wide world of terrain park features in the Grosté area of the resort. Two specially groomed runs for snowboarders start at the top of Passo Grosté. The links between the lifts near the village are all ridable.

One of Italy's most efficient lift systems fans out from the old village with the slopes coming right down to town. The almost 100 miles of runs roll across three separate areas, offering top-to-bottom beginner and intermediate skiing. A lift pass covers the neighboring resorts of Pinzola, Pejo, Monte Bondone, and Passo Tonale (which offers year-round glacier skiing). Madonna also is linked by lifts with the resorts of Folgarida and Marilleva.

At Madonna, and elsewhere in Italy, the ski school for children is excellent. The trend is to transform learning slopes to playgrounds under the tutelage of obliging instructors. Kids don't want lessons. They want to have fun and interact with their instructor.

But the pleasure of an Italian ski vacation doesn't just come from time spent on the mountain. Charming, rustic, and often idiosyncratic family-run hotels thrive in a cosmopolitan atmosphere that boasts outstanding cuisine and Old World architecture. Moreover, the weather is usually fine. The Alps seldom dip into the freezing extremes of winter that are common in the northern Rocky Mountains, and Italy is the sunniest region of the Alps.

Madonna sits a mile high in a narrow valley of the Brenta Dolomites, site of a mountain hospice 800 years ago. To reach it, you climb a 50-mile-long road through tunnels and past precarious drop-offs beyond the valley town of Trento. Before the 1919 Treaty of Versailles, the Dolomites belonged to Austria, and Madonna was a popular getaway for the Austrian Emperor Franz Joseph and his family. The first cable car took to the air in 1935. Compared to Cortina d'Ampezzo, the other popular Italian resort located in the majestic Dolomites, Madonna is small. But the name carries as much prestige, and the guests are almost exclusively Italian.

The town maintains a busy social calendar. One of the highlights is the Habsburg Carnival, held every February when a contemporary version of the Austrian imperial couple arrives by carriage, setting off a week of celebrations with fireworks and all-night Vienna-style balls.

Other outdoor activities include cross-country skiing on trails that wind through the nearby villages, as well as ice skating, dogsledding, tobogganing, and snowshoeing.

Everything is set against the extraordinary pink-tinged Dolomites, ancient-seabeds-turned-mountains that rise between the more familiar Alps. Imagine skiing in such a beautiful place.

Madonna di Campiglio Tourist Office
Centro Rainalter
38084 Madonna di Campiglio (TN)
Italy

Phone: 39–0465–44–20–00

Web Site: www.campiglio.net

E-mail: info@campiglio.to

Elevation: Top—8,038 feet; base—5,085 feet

Vertical Drop: 2,953 feet

Total Trails: 93 miles

Longest Run: 4 miles

Terrain: 44% beginner; 30% intermediate; 26% advanced/expert

Lifts: 20

Snowmaking: Yes

Central Reservations: 39–0465–44–20–00

Snow Report: www.campiglio.net

Accommodations: There's a wide range of hotels and apartments.

Getting There: The resort is 100 miles from Verona, 130 miles from Milan. The nearest rail station is Trento, 48 miles by shuttle bus.

Keep in Mind: Not much expert terrain.

BEST BETS

Beginners: Graffer run at the top of Passo Grosté.

Intermediates: Pradalago gondola.

Advanced: 3-Tr, the World Cup run.

Experts: Spinale Direttissima.

Lunch: Malga Montagnoli.

Off the Slopes: Boutique shopping and a high-watt après-ski scene.

Best Hotel: Relais Club Des Alpes.

VAL GARDENA
Selva Gardena, Italy

Located in the heavenlike heart of the Sella mountain range of the Italian Dolomites, Val Gardena resort consists of three villages—Ortisei, Santa Cristina, Selva Gardena—and a vast skiing circus that includes eighty-one lifts and 109 miles of trails particularly well suited to intermediate skiers and boarders.

It is as scenic a winter destination as a skier or boarder could hope to find. As an added bonus, the weather is mild and temperate in the southern Alps.

In recent years Val Gardena has upgraded its lifts and invested heavily in snowmaking, which blankets 87 miles of trails. The slope grooming rivals any resort in the Alps.

Val Gardena is part of the Dolomite SuperSki Pass, one of the largest lift-serviced ski networks in the world, which interconnects with 750 miles of prepared downhill trails in twelve valleys utilizing some 464 lifts in forty-five ski areas.

From the expansive, sun-drenched valley, the splendid mountains around Val Gardena thrust elegantly skyward, tinged with a redness that hints at their genesis as a sea bottom. The cathedral-like rock faces are topped with varied pinnacles as fine as needles, as jagged as saws, or as blunt as hammers. Together, they create a stunning backdrop for thousand-year-old towns and skiers exploring the trails.

Situated in the heart of the stunning Dolomites with its legendary Sella Ronda ski route, seamlessly linking village to village all the way to Cortina d'Ampezzo, Val Gardena is a haven for intermediate skiers and families. The skies are usually blue, and the scenery, turns, and dolce vita are all you can hope for.

Visitors feel passionately about all three towns in the Val Gardena. Still, most agree that its jewel is Selva, a cozy village tucked beneath the pinnacles of the Sassolungo and the Gruppo Sella at an elevation of more than 5,100 feet. Narrow streets of gabled houses end in views of a soaring wall of rock. But all three villages are lively and interesting to stroll around, exploring hotels, shops, restaurants, and galleries.

From Selva, a gondola whisks skiers to the area called Ciampinoi and Val Gardena's famous World Cup men's downhill run. Across the valley from Ciampinoi is the Dantercëpies gondola and the women's downhill. Other lifts fan out across the extraordinary scenery and stretch as far away as the glacier on Marmolada, the highest peak in the Dolomites, which tops out at almost 11,000 feet. Many of the runs are fairly straightforward, and the terrain is ideally suited for intermediates. But there also are plenty of beginner runs on the gentle slopes beside Selva that are ideal for children or skiing newcomers. The Alpe di Siusi above the village of Ortisei also is perfect for novices and more often than not bathed in sunlight.

Expert skiers and adventurous boarders have slimmer pickings. The downhill racecourse runs are exciting, and there's some steep terrain near the area called Arabba. There are some steep, carving off-piste

routes; the best way to find to find them is to hire a guide.

But elsewhere things are mostly tame.

Val Gardena might lack the large vertical and challenging terrain of Chamonix or Verbier, but it offers other pleasures such as a high tree line and generous doses of sunshine. Clouds often brood over the Austrian Tyrol farther north, while the Italian Tyrol is bathed in sunlight.

Visiting skiers have the impression of gliding across cultural borders as well as the glittering snow. Like many parts of Europe, this area of northeastern Italy has changed hands over the years. The South Tyrol was part of Austria until the Versailles Treaty of 1919. As a result, you'll find both German efficiency and Italian effervescence. German is the primary language, and indeed, the place frequently feels more German than Italian. Selva Gardena is also known as Wolkenstein, its old German name.

Whatever the language, the cultural mix yields great food. The pleasures of pasta and polenta may be alternated with those of potatoes and wurst. The wine and beer are equally good, too.

When in the Val Gardena, don't miss the Sella Ronda's all-day tour, one of Europe's finest intermediate-level ski experiences. Towering above Selva is the Gruppo Sella, a massive circular formation of dolomite rock and limestone with villages scattered throughout. The Sella Ronda, which literally means "around the Sella," is a 14-mile circuit (side excursions can double the distance) of lifts and runs that wind through the villages of four different valleys. Each village has its own ski area, and collectively they make up the Sella Ronda. You can ski the route clockwise or counterclockwise. Clockwise, the lifts are more efficient and the runs perhaps more interesting. There are many *rifugios* (mountain huts with restaurants) en route offering warm drinks and excellent food.

There are resorts in the Alps with more difficult and extraordinary runs. But the weather at Val Gardena is pleasant, the skiing varied, the mountains glorious, and the food delicious. What more do most skiers want?

Val Gardena Tourist Office
Selva Gardena
39048 Selva "1" (BZ)
Italy

Phone: 39–071–79–51–22

Web Site: www.val-gardena.com

E-mail: info@val-gardena.com

Elevation: Top—8,796 feet; base—3,937 feet

Vertical Drop: 4,859 feet

Total Trails: 109 miles (more than 750 miles in Dolomiti Superski)

Longest Run: 5 miles

Terrain: 30% beginner; 60% intermediate; 10% advanced/expert

Lifts: 81 (464 in Dolomiti Superski)

Snowmaking: 87 miles

Central Reservations: 39–071–79–51–22

Snow Report: www.val-gardena.com

Accommodations: Dozens of 4- and 3-star hotels.

Getting There: Gateway airports include Milan and Munich. Verona's airport is 114 miles. The train from Bolzano or Bressanone to the resort is 20 miles.

Keep in Mind: Few expert runs.

BEST BETS

Beginners: The gentle runs near Selva.

Intermediates: The Sella Ronda circuit.

Advanced: The men's World Cup downhill.

Experts: The slopes above Arabba.

Lunch: Rifugio Dantercëpies.

Off the Slopes: Stroll the villages and visit the hot springs in Ortisei.

Best Hotel: Alpenroyal.

SIERRA NEVADA
Sierra Nevada, Spain

If Spain's favorite fictional character, Don Quixote, the man from La Mancha, had been a skier, Sierra Nevada is where he would have skied. It's the perfect place to dream the impossible.

After all, this is not northern Spain, where the rocky Pyrenees border France and there are a handful of quite good ski areas anchored by Baqueira-Beret in the Valle de A'ran. Sierra Nevada is in the sunny south, just beyond the old Moorish city of Granada, and less than an hour from the sand-swept beaches of the Mediterranean. It seems impossible.

Skiing, and especially snowboarding, are extremely popular with Spaniards, and their elite international competitors have won their share of medals on the snow. In 1996 the resort hosted the World Alpine Ski Championships.

Sierra Nevada rises in the rarified air at 10,000 feet in the mountains of the same name. The humidity is low, ensuring light, dry powder when it snows. For the most part, the area is unaffected by the weather patterns hitting the Alps. When it doesn't snow, the sun blazes overhead like a kite, yielding more hours of sunshine than any other resort in Europe. To compensate for all the blue skies, Sierra Nevada has one of Europe's most powerful snowmaking systems.

The purpose-built village at the base of the ski area is called Pradollano. Lively restaurants, bars, and shops are clustered around a main square, but the resort lacks traditional Alpine charm. It consists mostly of hotels and apartments built in the 1960s and 1970s. Still, there is plenty of nightlife with a Spanish flair. The resort mainly attracts Spaniards, and the late-night hours they keep can make New York City seem provincial.

Like Italians, Spaniards hit the slopes at the crack of midmorning, break for a lengthy lunch, and then make a run or two before heading for the tapas bars. About the time most North Americans are ready for dinner, the locals take a nap to rest up for the evening. The restaurant crowds peak at 11:00 P.M. Dancing starts after midnight. If you want to get into the swing of things, you'll have to adopt the siesta.

 Sierra Nevada in sunny Spain is Europe's southern-most resort. Even better, this is the only European resort with an ocean view. On a clear day—and there are many clear days— you can see across the Mediterranean to the Atlas Mountains in Morocco.

The slopes are as varied as the ingredients that make up paella, Spain's national dish. The resort's highest area is snow-sure, consisting mostly of wide-open cruisers above the tree line, which can be easily handled by intermediate-level skiers and boarders. Plenty of tamer areas cater to beginners. The vertical drop is an impressive 3,772 feet, which stacks up well against most Colorado resorts. Overall, the ski area is small compared to most European resorts. Many of the nineteen lifts are modern high-speed detachable chairs, however, and you can cover a lot of miles in a day. You'll also find several good restaurants on the mountain.

Most of the slopes face northeast, which helps protect them from the sun. But if it hasn't snowed for weeks, expect to find ice in the morning and slush in the afternoon, especially in the large, high bowl that is the heart of the ski area. The terrain park compares favorably with other European parks, and there's some good off-piste freeriding. There's also night skiing.

The nearby ancient Moorish city of Granada has national monument status in Spain. It's home to the Alhambra Palace and is the capital of the Andalusia region, the last surviving bastion of Islam when Spanish rulers Ferdinand and Isabella took control of the region in 1491. The new rulers enriched the area with Renaissance and baroque buildings, but many of the Moorish treasures remain.

Off the slopes, there's a sports center with a swimming pool and indoor tennis. There are also cross-country ski trails, dogsledding, and winter walking trails. Paragliding is popular, and the resort hosts many of the sport's major international competitions. The sunny Costa del Sol, with its beach resorts, sailing, and golf, is only 60 miles away.

High-mountain views, friendly locals, and the region's cultural heritage combine to make Sierra Nevada a great resort. Especially if you love skiing but hate winter.

Sierra Nevada Tourist Office
Plaza Marina Pineda 10-2
18196 Sierra Nevada (Granada)
Spain
Phone: 34–958–24–91–00
Web Site: www.sierranevadaski.com

E-mail: cetursa@sierranevadaski.com

Elevation: Top—10,808 feet; base—6,890 feet

Vertical Drop: 3,772 feet

Total Trails: 60 miles

Longest Run: 4 miles

Terrain: 15% beginner; 50% intermediate; 25% advanced; 10% expert

Lifts: 19

Snowmaking: 14 miles

Central Reservations: 34–958–24–91–11

Snow Report: www.sierranevadaski.com

Accommodations: A wide range of hotels and apartments in the village.

Getting There: It's 1 hour from Granada's airport; 2 hours from Malaga.

Keep in Mind: Crowded on weekends and holidays.

BEST BETS

Beginners: El Zorro.

Intermediates: El Rio.

Advanced: Loma de Dilar.

Experts: El Puente.

Lunch: Genil, halfway down River Run.

Off the Slopes: Explore ancient Granada.

Best Hotel: Sol Melia Sierra Nevada.

ÅRE
Åre, Sweden

The Alps don't stretch all the way to Sweden, so you won't find large interconnected ski areas offering milelong vertical drops down rock-ribbed glacier peaks. Nonetheless, the resort of Åre (pronounced *or-ee*) is perfectly enjoyable for skiers and boarders of all abilities, although experts will have to search for challenges off-piste. And for aficionados who keep a tick list of far-flung mountains they want to ski or ride, Åre is Sweden's leading alpine ski area.

The resort is bordered on one side by great whaleback mountains rising from rolling, forest-covered hills that climb above 4,000 feet. On the other side of the resort is a long, frozen lake. The ski mountains, with their trails winding through the forest, would be at home in New England, except that the top half of the mountain is above the timberline.

Åre's season starts in November and runs until mid-May. The snow is reliable; average

winter temperatures are between fifteen and twenty degrees. The far-north setting is marked by short winter days. In January the sun doesn't rise until 9:45 A.M., and it sets at 2:30 P.M. By April, though, the daylight hours increase dramatically.

Four linked ski areas—Åre, Duved, Tegefjäll, and Åre Björnen—rise side by side from the Åre Valley, in west-central Sweden, near the Norwegian border. A popular way to arrive is via the night train from Stockholm, which leaves the capital at 11:00 P.M. and pulls into Åre at 8:30 A.M.

Each of the four areas has a village at its base. A funicular railway and Sweden's only cable car rise from the Alps-like main village of Åre to the high slopes of Åreskutan, the principal ski mountain. Swedes have been skiing here since the funicular was built in 1910, and there's a nice collection of brightly colored historic buildings centered around the train station.

Many of the resort's fifty-plus restaurants are located here, and so is the raucous nightlife.

Next to Åre is the Tegefjäll area, rising into the forest and linking with the high slopes above Åre. At its base is a collection of slopeside accommodations consisting primarily of chalets and condos that offer quick access to the ski lifts. The Duved area is next to Tegefjäll, with its six-pack chairlift serving a variety of ski trails that are sheltered in the forest. It's a popular area with families. The base area offers a wide range of accommodations, including a number of self-contained apartments.

On the other side of Åre is Åre Björnen. It's the area for kids and sits apart from the main skier traffic, offering lifts adjusted to fit children. In the middle of the base village is a children's center offering supervised games and activities.

All totaled, the skiing and boarding play out on a network of mostly intermediate and beginner trails that stretch for 6 miles across the mountains. Most of the runs wind through the forest following the contour of the mountain. A few of them are floodlit for night skiing. Above the tree line are wide-open bowls. There are only a couple of posted expert runs, although many exciting off-piste options exist that are best explored with a local guide. One popular route for experts involves a snowcat shuttle from the top lift station to the summit of Åreskutan and a 5-mile backcountry trip down the mountain's back side.

Snowboarding is popular in Sweden, and at Åre boarders chase the freeriding and off-piste routes high up on the mountain. There's also a terrain park with a World Cup halfpipe. Heli-skiing in the untracked snow of the surrounding mountains is popular with both riders and skiers.

Åre's ski and snowboarding school has a good reputation, especially for its children's program. And you don't have to struggle trying to speak Swedish; practically everyone

 Scandinavia's largest ski resort offers plenty of long intermediate runs, a dedicated beginner area, and a World Cup downhill course. But there are many other reasons to visit Åre. The valley buzzes with all sorts of outdoor winter activities enjoyed by Swedes. The ambience feels almost Swiss—except for all the saunas.

throughout Scandinavia speaks English as a second language.

Beyond the alpine slopes, there's another world of winter activities playing out in the valley. Horseback riding, dog- and reindeer-sledding, tobogganing, snowmobiling, and horse-drawn sleigh rides are popular. On the lake, skaters and boardsurfers glide across the ice. And of course, cross-country skiing is big in Sweden. Two hundred miles of trails sprawl across the Åre Valley; some are lit for night skiing.

Åre Tourist Information
Årevägen 93
S-83013
Åre, Sweden

Phone: 46–647–17700

Web Site: www.areresort.se

E-mail: infomaster@areresort.se

Elevation: Top—4,180 feet; base—1,312 feet

Vertical Drop: 2,919 feet

Total Trails: 55 miles

Longest Run: 4 miles

Terrain: 11% beginner; 43% intermediate; 36% advanced; 10% expert

Lifts: 44

Snowmaking: Yes

Central Reservations: 46–771–84000

Snow Report: www.areresort.se

Accommodations: A wide range of hotels, chalets, apartments, and bed-and-breakfast inns at the base.

Getting There: The nearest airport is in Östersund, 53 miles from Åre. There's also 6-hour train service from Stockholm, 400 miles away.

Keep in Mind: Unpredictable weather patterns. Daylight hours are short in December and January.

BEST BETS

Beginners: Susarbacken.

Intermediates: Lundsrappet.

Advanced: World Cup downhill.

Experts: Off-piste with a guide.

Lunch: Buustamons.

Off the Slopes: Plenty of nightlife and other winter activities.

Best Hotel: Hotel Åregarden.

AROSA
Arosa, Switzerland

Sir Arthur Conan Doyle put Arosa on the winter-recreation map when he famously skied across the pass from Davos in 1894. By the turn of the century, Arosa was a well-known high-altitude health resort for patients recuperating from tuberculosis.

Just getting to Arosa is an adventure. The dramatic, stand-alone resort sits at the head of the steep, wooded Schanfigg Valley at an altitude of 6,000 feet. By rail or road it takes about one hour to grind up the winding route from the medieval city of Chur, the capital of southeastern Switzerland's wild Graubünden canton. The train is one of those bright red, narrow-gauge models that make Switzerland such a pleasing and relaxing place to travel. The road is a lulu, though, looping around 250 curves.

Linger in Chur before making your way up to Arosa. The compact old section of town is a museum of sixteenth-century buildings, decorative fountains, and warrens of Old World streets rebuilt after a devastating fire in 1492.

Arosa is divided into two sections: an older inner village, surrounded by an outer village, which is next to a forest-rimmed lake. Snow-covered-mountain backdrops complete the picture-postcard scene. Arosa's pleasing ambience attracts as many non-skiers as skiers and boarders, even though the resort lacks charming chalet-style architecture. Après-ski is relatively low voltage, centered at restaurants and hotel bars. Given Arosa's location at the end of the road, there's no noisy through-town traffic. Motorized vehicles are even banned altogether from late in the evening until morning.

Arosa serves as the base for an army of lifts that stretch across three mountains to the region's two major summits—8,241-foot Hörnli and 8,704-foot Weisshorn. The annual snowfalls are dependable. But the skiing is relatively contained, especially for Europe. The resort has just fifteen lifts, and the vertical drop is less than 3,000 feet. It links with no other ski area, although several of the largest ski circuses in the Alps are within day-trip distance. If your idea of skiing or snowboarding is nothing but black runs, then Arosa is not your mountain of dreams. Expert terrain consists of a couple of overrated black runs and any off-piste lines you can find.

Not surprisingly, families love Arosa. The wide-open, tilted-to-the-sun slopes are right next to town. They ramble on and on above the tree line, ideally pitched for beginners and intermediates. And even though there are many resorts in the Alps with twice the vertical drop, Arosa's efficient lifts make it easy to rack up mileage. At a convenient spot halfway up the Weisshorn, you'll find a terrain park, a halfpipe, and bordercross. The top of Hörnli is the starting point for some interesting off-piste terrain.

Arosa also sports the cachet of attracting a well-heeled clientele, without the swagger of Davos or St. Moritz. It celebrates an ongoing calendar of events that includes horse racing on snow over the frozen lake. Many of the families vacationing in Arosa aren't just here for the skiing. They come for the wide range of winter sports experiences available: ice skating on the lake, tobogganing down a mountainside, tossing curling stones, and wrapping themselves in furs on a horse-drawn sleigh. Arosa also offers miles of winter walking paths that meander through the woods, sometimes leading to mountain restaurants. The ski lifts permit rides by nonskiers who want to meet friends or family on the mountain. Down in the valley there are scenic cross-country trails. And if the kids are holding you back, several hotels offer day care.

Arosa Tourist Office
CH-7050 Arosa
Switzerland

Phone: 41–81–378–7020

Web Site: www.arosa.ch

E-mail: info@arosabergbahnen.ch

Elevation: Top—8,702 feet; base—5,904 feet

Vertical Drop: 2,798 feet

Total Trails: 45 miles

Longest Run: 5 miles

Terrain: 31% beginner; 57% intermediate; 12% advanced/expert

Lifts: 15

Snowmaking: Yes

Central Reservations: 41–81–378–7020

Snow Report: www.arosa.ch

Accommodations: A wide range of hotels, lodges, and apartments near the slopes.

Getting There: Zurich Airport is 3 hours away. A narrow-gauge rail departs hourly from Chur for Arosa.

Keep in Mind: Few expert runs and no linked ski circus.

BEST BETS

Beginners: The blues on Tschuggen.

Intermediates: Almost everywhere.

Advanced: The "Runtour" to Lenzerheide.

Experts: Weisshorn to Carmennahütte.

Lunch: Carmennahütte.

Off the Slopes: Explore the medieval city of Chur.

Best Hotel: Tschuggen Grand Hotel.

 It's not the biggest or the most challenging ski area, but Arosa is still popular. Swiss families are thrilled with its sunny location in the high Schanfigg Valley and the range of memory-making winter activities enjoyed there. The gentle slopes encourage novice and intermediate skiers and snowboarders to explore the entire Alpine region.

CHAMPÉRY

Champéry, Switzerland

The idyllic Swiss village of Champéry, with its streets of high chalets and overhanging roofs, is part of the wildly extensive Portes du Soleil (Gates of the Sun) ski and snowboarding region that sprawls across the Swiss and French Alps, encompassing fourteen resorts. The Portes du Soleil includes more than 200 ski lifts, 400 miles of trails, seven terrain parks, and three halfpipes, all covered by one lift ticket.

The resorts on the Swiss side include Champéry, Les Crosets, Morgins, Champoussin, Torgon, and Val d'Illiez. The French resorts of the Portes du Soleil are Avoriaz, Morzine, Châtel, Les Gets, Abondance, La Chapelle d'Abondance, Montriond, and La Grande Terche.

 Dominated by the majestic Dents du Midi, the vast Portes du Soleil ski region of the Swiss and French Alps encompasses a dozen ski areas and is one of the largest interconnected ski regions in the world. From the rustic Swiss village of Champéry, an aerial tramway leads to more than 400 miles of ski and snowboarding trails.

To help navigate the vast terrain, there are twelve "discovery circuits" signed according to difficulty level. Each circuit is named for an animal and grouped according to ability level and time required to complete it. The routes include the best viewpoints, summits, and mountain restaurants, while ensuring you don't lose your way. Confident intermediate skiers can go almost anywhere. So can intermediate snowboarders if they can negotiate surface lifts. But the famous sunshine of the Portes du Soleil region also has a downside: Snow can be scarce at lower elevations.

During World War II, these slopes were smuggling routes linking Switzerland and France. Today customs officers discreetly patrol on skis while visitors freely slide between the two countries.

Located below Lake Geneva and next to the French border, Champéry is easily accessed from Geneva in two hours via rail or car. It is a world away from the diplomatic and financial scene of Geneva, which juts into France at the southwest corner of Switzerland, and is an ideal home base for exploring more than a dozen of the region's major ski resorts. Everywhere there are stunning vistas of glaciers, domes, deep valleys, and dazzling white-ridged crests.

Rustic Champéry is the prototypical Swiss village. Chocolate-colored chalets house cows in their ground floors, and the smell of manure wafts from side streets. There are a few cozy hotels, a good selection of chalets and apartments, and many fine restaurants. It is not a glitzy, jet-set resort town. A modern tram rises up a steep mountain ridge to a ski and snowboarding world of alpine bowls, sprawling meadows, and steep chutes. The farmers who own the land individually own many of the lifts as well as more than fifty mountain restaurants, where the rural cuisine is rich, delicious, and filling.

The craggy Dents du Midi (Teeth of Noon) mountain range dominates the landscape above the village like an island of granite rising out of a sea of summits along the French-Swiss border. From the top of Champéry, ski runs and lifts fan out in almost every direction. The majority of the terrain is for intermediates. Beginner terrain is sadly lacking. Experts find their own choice lines off-piste. There's also a steep and moguled run called the Swiss Wall on Chavanette that looks as jagged as porcelain hurled against a wall.

There is no run back to Champéry. You must download on the tram or ski down elsewhere and ride a shuttle bus back to the village.

Champéry has 6 miles of cross-country ski trails. Off the slopes, a sports center offers ice skating, curling, swimming, and fitness equipment. A nightclub called La Crevasse offers infectious rhythms until the wee hours of the morning. The lakeside resort cities of Montreux and Lausanne are a short train ride away, making Champéry an ideal base for visitors who want to ski part of the time and explore cultural attractions the rest, all the while staying in a beautiful village that rivals the idyllic winter scenes pictured on the wrappers of Swiss chocolate bars.

Champéry is so pretty that sometimes you might just want to sit back and enjoy the movement of resort life. It offers fantastic skiing, friendly villagers who lack pretension, and a setting that resembles a toy-store window at Christmas.

Champéry Tourist Office
CH-1874 Champéry
Switzerland
Phone: 41–24–479–2020
Web Site: www.champery.ch

E-mail: info@champery.ch

Elevation: Top—7,544 feet; base—3,460 feet

Vertical Drop: 4,084 feet

Total Trails: 400 miles

Longest Run: 4.5 miles

Terrain: 51% beginner; 40% intermediate; 9% advanced/expert

Lifts: 206

Snowmaking: 522 acres

Snow Report: www.champery.ch

Accommodations: There are plenty of slopeside accommodations in chalets and hotels.

Getting There: It's 2 hours from Geneva. By rail or car, head for Aigle, then follow the road or ride the narrow-gauge rail to the village.

Keep in Mind: Not a lot of beginner or expert terrain. The sunny slopes can suffer from lack of snow.

BEST BETS

Beginners: Planachaux runs.

Intermediates: Grand Paradis.

Advanced: The Swiss Wall on Chavanette.

Experts: Off-piste on Chavanette.

Lunch: Chez Coquoz at Planachaux above Champéry.

Off the Slopes: Narrow-gauge railway to Montreux, Lausanne, and Scion.

Best Hotel: The Champéry.

CRANS-MONTANA
Crans-Montana, Switzerland

The shopping may be more varied and high-end than the skiing at this glitzy resort located in Switzerland's Valais canton above the city of Sierre. The two main centers—Crans (pronounced *crawh*) and Montana—are a mile apart and joined by their sprawling suburbs (population 7,000). Soaring mountains and acres and acres of slopes surround the resort, which is touted as the sunniest in the country.

The scenic skiing and snowboarding include 100 miles of trails across three areas that are well linked by lifts. Five gondolas whisk skiers from valley to the slopes. Most of the runs are consistently pitched intermediate fare—wide, white boulevards offering ballroom skiing with few surprises. Nonetheless, the 4,920-foot vertical drop tops anything in the United States.

The largest ski and snowboarding area is Cry d'Er, directly above Montana. Here you'll find forested slopes leading to a large open bowl above the tree line. The second area, Violettes, includes the year-round snow of the Plaine Morte Glacier. Petit Bonvin, the third area, is reached by gondola from Aminona, a small community at the eastern end of the resort.

For beginners, Crans-Montana offers lots of variety in three beginner areas of ascending difficulty. Rank novices start out on the gentle slopes of the golf course. After they acquire a little technique, they comfortably ride the Violettes gondola to just under 10,000 feet and the mellow blue slopes at the top of the Plaine Morte Glacier. That's right: Beginners enjoy the very top of the mountain. And if they want more, Cry d'Er has a host of lifts serving several choice blue trails that wind through the woods back down to the village.

The forest also is crisscrossed by intermediate runs winding between the trees. And from the summit of Plaine Morte Glacier, there's a long, scenic intermediate run that meanders back to the village. Most days it glitters in the sunshine and is as fine and transcendent as a trip down a mountain can be.

But the pickings are much slimmer if you want steep, expert terrain. There are a few steep bump runs at La Toula, and there's plenty of off-piste potential when the snow is right, especially above Aminona. In the past Crans-Montana has hosted the World Alpine Ski Championships and is the site of a number of ski and snowboard competitions. Advanced skiers and boarders enjoy the Piste Nationale Men's World Cup downhill course. Day trips to the challenging slopes of nearby Verbier are easily doable.

 The view of the Alps stretches from the craggy Matterhorn all the way to white-domed Mont Blanc. The mostly gentle slopes face south. The two French-speaking towns of Crans and Montana sit on a high, sun-drenched plateau overlooking the vineyards of the Rhône Valley and have been a popular resort for more than one hundred years.

Snowboarding is popular at Crans-Montana. Veteran boarders enjoy the slopes of Petit Bonvin above Aminona, where there's also a terrain park. You'll find a halfpipe at Cry d'Er. The slopes of Crans-Montana can get quite slushy when the spring sun beats down—conditions much more appealing to boarders than skiers.

There are 25 miles of cross-country ski trails that wind through the forest and the award-winning golf course. There's another 6 miles of cross-country trails at the top of the resort on the guaranteed snow of Plaine Morte. There also are miles of maintained winter walking trails and several nearby lakes to visit.

Off the slopes, there's plenty of action. The twin towns offer a high-watt social scene as well as quiet restaurants and bars in which to enjoy Dôle, the delicious regional red wine. But don't expect the quaint Alpine charm of Zermatt or Saas-Fee. Much of the accommodations and dining are housed in unimaginative, blocky buildings.

Crans is the more upscale of the two resorts, and many in the fur-coat scene don't ski. Other activities include ice skating, curling, dogsledding, and a 4-mile toboggan run.

Crans-Montana Tourism
P.O. Box 372
Crans-Montana CH-3963
Switzerland

Phone: 41–27–485–0404

Web Site: www.crans-montana.ch

E-mail: information@crans-montana.ch

Elevation: Top—9,840 feet; base—4,920 feet

Vertical Drop: 4,920 feet

Total Trails: 100 miles

Longest Run: 8 miles

Terrain: 38% beginner; 50% intermediate; 12% advanced

Lifts: 35

Snowmaking: 11 miles

Central Reservations: 41–27–485–0444

Snow Report: www.crans-montana.ch

Accommodations: There are more than 40,000 beds in hotels, chalets, and apartments.

Getting There: Geneva is 2½ hours away. Good road and rail connections to Sierre, where a funicular railway climbs to Montana.

Keep in Mind: The sunny slopes often have poor snow, and the sprawling towns lack a Swiss-village atmosphere.

BEST BETS

Beginners: Complete novices have ski lifts on the gentle golf course.

Intermediates: Plaine Morte to Les Barzettes (7 miles).

Advanced: La Tza to Plumachit above Aminona.

Experts: La Toula.

Lunch: The Merbé at the Crans–Cry d'Er gondola midstation.

Off the Slopes: Visit the snowshoe-accessed Colombire Alpine Museum.

Best Hotel: Pas de l'Ours.

DAVOS
Davos, Switzerland

The high, serrated mountains line up in rows on either side of chic Davos. The steep slopes are sprinkled with chocolate-box chalets with gingerbread detailing. Along the town's main shopping streets, fur-coat-clad women and men gaze at their reflections in the glistening windows of jewelry and pastry shops. High above it all, ski lifts climb the slopes of the famously large and largely famous Parsenn ski area.

It is a scene that makes winter appear the gentlest season of them all. And in Davos, maybe it is.

The heady, centuries-old town serves as an international catwalk for the rich and famous and brilliant, especially during the end of January when the annual World Economic Forum draws the world's elite from almost every field of human endeavor. Compared to its neighbor, Klosters, Davos is larger, with many more hotels, restaurants, après-ski bars, and nightclubs.

International visitors started coming to Davos in the 1860s, seeking health in the natural spa waters of a high, sunny, and dry climate. By the turn of the century when the mountain railway opened, Davos was flush with grand sanatoriums where victims of tuberculosis recuperated in the

mountain air. The life is well documented in Thomas Mann's *The Magic Mountain*.

After medicine developed more effective cures for tuberculosis in the 1930s, the sanatoriums wisely converted to hotels. About the same time, ski trains and ski lifts started operating, and Davos quickly grew to be one of the leading recreation centers in the Alps. Today it's the largest ski resort in Switzerland.

Located in southeastern canton of Graubünden, Davos's 14,000 permanent residents share the wide, flat-bottomed Landwasser Valley with high-altitude farmers gifted in the making of Davos cheese. The 5,118-foot elevation makes Davos the highest town in Europe. (In the Alps a village has fewer than 10,000 people; a town has more.) The altitude often ensures better early- and late-season snow than other resorts in the Alps. The huge snow cannons installed on the village-bound runs ensure you can ski to the bottom of every mountain.

Like St. Moritz, Davos is divided into two sections—Davos Platz and Davos Dorf. They are about a mile apart, and each has its own train station. On the high side of town, next to Dorf, is Davos Lake. But for those who come to Davos to be seen, Platz is what matters most. That's where you find Promenade, the aptly named main shopping, entertainment, and walking street.

Skiers and snowboarders have a wealth of mountains to explore. A single ski pass covers six nearby ski areas—Parsenn, Pischa, Jakobshorn, Rinerhorn, Schatzalp, and Madrisa above Klosters—connected by lifts, shuttle buses, or rail. Included in the ski pass are the trains and buses between the ski areas.

The slopes of the Schatzalp/Strela area rise from Davos Platz. A cogwheel train

This sophisticated, citylike Alpine playground and think tank, with its chalets, snowfields, and forests, is one of the oldest and largest resorts in the Alps. The Davos ski region includes seven areas offering 200 miles of trails that range from passive to outrageous. Bring your furs and your thinking caps.

covers the first part of the journey to Schatzalp, where a number of ski lifts take over and serve mostly intermediate terrain. A cable car spans an enormous chasm linking the area to the 9,330-foot summit of Parsenn and its wraparound views that reach into Austria. Parsenn offers some steep pitches and miles and miles of long and interesting intermediate slopes.

From Parsenn, 4,000-foot-vertical runs ramble across the Gotschna slopes on a 6-mile journey to fairy-tale Klosters. From the summit of Weissfluh to Klosters, the runs drop more than a vertical mile. The advanced 8-mile run from Weissfluh to Kublis, a village down a side valley from Klosters, drops 6,660 vertical feet. These two runs are among the longest continuous runs in the Alps.

Across from Klosters there are family slopes at the Madrisa area. There's also a popular, daylong ski-touring trip to the resort of Arosa. Sir Arthur Conan Doyle, who came to Davos in 1894, made the route to Arosa famous in his literature.

In 1924 Parsenn was the site of the first downhill race in skiing. There were no lifts yet, but competitors climbed to the Weissfluh start and raced all the way to Kublis. When the funicular opened in 1932, there were more than 600 competitors. The race is still run annually.

Across from Parsenn, the Jakobshorn area offers shorter but more challenging slopes. The area is particularly popular with snowboarders and is a venue for international freeriding competitions. Down the road, served by shuttle buses, are the Rinerhorn and Pischa ski areas, both offering miles of easy, intermediate terrain popular with families.

Off the slopes, some of the attractions include ice skating, snowshoeing, sledding, and miles of maintained winter walking trails. In Davos the Kirchner Museum is a star attraction. The expressionist painter Ernst Ludwig Kirchner lived in Davos for twenty-one years until his death in 1917; the museum is home to the world's largest collection of his paintings.

Davos Tourism
Promenade 67
CH-7270 Davos Platz
Switzerland

Phone: 41–81–415–2121

Web Site: www.davos.ch

E-mail: info@davos.ch

Elevation: Top—9,330 feet; base—3,907 feet

Vertical Drop: 5,423 feet

Total Trails: 200 miles

Longest Run: 8 miles

Terrain: 30% beginner; 50% intermediate; 20% advanced/expert

Lifts: 50

Snowmaking: 11 miles

Central Reservations: 41–81–415–2121

Snow Report: www.davos.ch

Accommodations: A wide range of hotels, lodges, and apartments.

Getting There: It's 3 hours from Zurich (130 miles). Rail service direct to town.

Keep in Mind: Lacks Alpine-village charm.

BEST BETS

Beginners: The Bolgen area.

Intermediates: The Parsenn area.

Advanced: Long runs from Weissfluh to Klosters.

Experts: Meierhofer Tälli run to Wolfgang.

Lunch: Conterser Schwendi.

Off the Slopes: Kirchner Museum.

Best Hotel: Fluela.

ENGELBERG

Engelberg, Switzerland

Like Coloradoans who are loyal to their precious Winter Park Resort, Swiss skiers are smitten with centrally located Engelberg. Let the tourists go to St. Moritz, Davos, and Gstaad.

Founded as a Benedictine monastery in 1120, Engelberg is Switzerland's oldest holiday resort. The first cable cars were constructed in 1912. Mention Engelberg to a Swiss skier and it's likely to elicit some heartfelt memory from childhood. Families flock here—for good reason.

Nestled beneath towering 10,624-foot Titlis Mountain, Engelberg yearns to be all things to all skiers. And it comes very close to succeeding. The fairy-tale town straddles two mountain ranges offering contrasting ski terrain. The Brunni area has sunny, south-facing slopes that appear as a field of dreams for novice and intermediate cruisers. On the other side of town, advanced riders can carve till the summer cows come home on the steep slopes of Titlis. There's also a terrain park and halfpipe.

The Brunni side, which is easily accessible from town, offers wide-open slopes perfect for beginners and low intermediates. Every run is a pat on the back and a compliment to your fine technique. And then there's broad-shouldered Mount Titlis—the yang of the yin. Here you find all you couldn't get at Brunni.

Titlis offers more than 6,000 vertical feet of snow-covered glacier and twisting, forested runs with spectacular views of the village at the end of the corduroy snow. But in the final analysis, the resort is heaven for intermediate-level riders and skiers. Even after the cows resume life on their summer pastures, snowriders are carried to the glacier for some of the best summer skiing in Europe.

The scenery is so striking that Engelberg built the world's first revolving gondola. All the better to see you with, dear Switzerland. Passengers gawk as though they were in an IMAX theater while the lofty summits scroll by. The panorama includes St. Gotthard Pass, Lake Lucerne, and even the Bernese Oberland beyond Interlaken.

Engelberg's appeal even extends to a loyal following of graceful, swanlike telemark skiers. The resort boasts the largest telemark ski club in Switzerland, a strong vote of confidence for the quality of the snow on the vast slopes and wide-open glacier.

Even the ski school has an excellent reputation, especially for teaching children. Not surprisingly, many of the instructors are homegrown.

 Close to Zurich and Lucerne, Engelberg is central Switzerland's largest ski resort and one of the oldest villages in the country. It's perfect for a family ski holiday. But it's no bunny hill. Engelberg offers one of the largest verticals in the Alps, the guaranteed snow of a glacier, and a revolving gondola from which to take in the extraordinary mountain scenery.

But lovers of the slopes would be remiss not to explore the centuries-old village. The main cruising street is Dorfstrasse, with many fine restaurants and congenial bars. You also find the usual array of glitzy shops selling fine watches and Swiss army knives, located next to mouthwatering pastry shops.

A few blocks away is the Benedictine monastery, which has been rebuilt over the centuries and is one of only five in the country. Its baroque-style church houses the largest pipe organ in Switzerland (8,838 pipes)—there are regular organ concerts. The monastery also has cheese-making demonstrations from which you can sample and buy. Nearby is the Valley Museum, located in a 1786 farmhouse. There's even a casino in town.

Along the valley floor are plenty of cross-country trails and 25 miles of winter hiking trails that skirt Engelberg's snow- and ice-covered summits. You'll also find dogsledding, horse-drawn sleigh rides, and a 2-mile toboggan run. And back up on the slopes there's lift-served tubing.

Accommodations run the gamut from four-star hotels to small pensions. Tourists have come to Engelberg for a long time, and the place is congenial and efficient. English is widely spoken.

Tourist Center Engelberg
Klosterstrasse 3
CH-6390, Engelberg
Switzerland

Phone: 41–41–639–7777

Web Site: www.engelberg.ch

E-mail: welcome@engelberg.ch

Elevation: Top—9,906 feet; base—3,444 feet

Vertical Drop: 6,462 feet

Total Trails: 51 miles

Longest Run: 8 miles

Terrain: 30% beginner; 60% intermediate; 10% advanced/expert

Lifts: 25

Snowmaking: Yes

Central Reservations: 41–41–639–7777

Snow Report: www.engelberg.ch

Accommodations: There's a wide range of hotels and vacation homes.

Getting There: Lucerne is 22 miles away; Zurich, 60 miles. From Lucerne, there are hourly departures from the train station.

Keep in Mind: Crowds on weekends. Swiss school holidays fill the place in February.

BEST BETS

Beginners: The lower slopes of Titlis.

Intermediates: Upper Titlis.

Advanced: Upper Titlis.

Experts: Kannonenroh on Titlis.

Lunch: Panorama restaurant atop Titlis.

Off the Slopes: Tour the 900-year-old Benedictine monastery.

Best Hotel: The 4-star Ramada Treff Hotel.

GRINDELWALD
Grindelwald, Switzerland

It's always an adventure. With skis in hand you board the cogwheel train at Grindelwald, bound for the ski area of Kleine Scheidegg, directly beneath the Eiger's infamous North Wall in the heart of the Jungfrau region. The brown-toned train winds its way across the valley and then,

like a dog on a hunt, catches the scent of the Eiger's North Wall; under the cover of several avalanche tunnels, it delivers you straight to Kleine Scheidegg.

It takes about half an hour to get to the handful of hotels, restaurants, train station, and ski lifts that make up Kleine Scheidegg.

This uniquely Swiss story-book village is dramatically set in a valley dwarfed by glacier-covered summits and visited by toylike electric trains that climb the mountains. Toss in the vast ski terrain and Grindelwald is about as good as the Swiss experience gets. It even links to the historic and car-free resorts of Wengen and Mürren.

From there, ski runs lead back to Grindelwald or down the Lauterbrunnen Valley to Wengen and, by riding another cogwheel train, Mürren. Most of the runs are long, undulating intermediate terrain, where skiers and riders look like heroes on forgiving snow.

The Jungfrau region sits at the top of Switzerland's Bernese Oberland, surrounded by many of Europe's largest glaciers and most famous mountains, including the granite Jungfrau, the Mönch, as well as the Eiger. The skiing plays out in three interconnected areas offering more than 125 miles of maintained slopes sprawling across four mountains.

Another ski area, First (pronounced *feerst* and meaning "peak"), is located directly above Grindelwald and has had an international following for more than fifty years. The 3-mile-long access gondola climbs the slopes of 9,607-foot Schwarzhorn. From there, other ski lifts fan out across the south-facing mountain, serving a snowy playground for intermediate-level skiers and snowboarders that offers more than 25 miles of groomed trails and vast backcountry opportunities. For boarders, there's a terrain park with kicks and rails and a halfpipe. The vertical drop back to Grindelwald covers a whopping 4,705 feet.

On the other side of Grindelwald, in a small settlement called Grund, a gondola

rises more than 4,000 vertical feet to open up vast intermediate terrain in the Männlichen ski area, which drops down the back side of the mountain into the Lauberhorn Valley. This is your chance to ski the infamous Lauberhorn World Cup downhill course, the longest race on the demanding international circuit. The ride back up the mountain is via the longest gondola cableway in the world.

The cogwheel train for Kleine Scheidegg also departs from Grund. But directly above Grund you'll also find another twenty-one ski lifts and more than 60 miles of far-flung prepared trails, mostly above the tree line and seemingly spitting distance to the Eiger.

The Eiger, which pierces the sky at 13,026 feet, remains an indelible achievement for climbers. Watching their attempts to scale the treacherous North Wall has been a spectator sport on the sun-drenched decks of Kleine Scheidegg ever since the first ascent in 1938. Every year, 200 climbers attempt the North Wall.

Back at Grindelwald, the 1,000-year-old village of 4,000 inhabitants is as appealing as the skiing at the surrounding areas. Glaciers slide to the edge of the village, and more than 150 farms are still active in the area. In winter you can only imagine the clang of cowbells that ring all summer long.

The romantic painters of the late 1700s and early 1800s first popularized the area. By 1811, climbers reached the Jungfrau summit, which is much less intimidating than the Eiger. By 1906, one of the first cable cars in the Alps was built near Grindelwald, and mass tourism arrived.

Don't miss a ride aboard the cogwheel train at Kleine Scheidegg bound for the Jungfraujoch, the highest rail station in Europe. The narrow-gauge train winds its way through a paper-clip tunnel into the mass of the Eiger and the Mönch, climbing to 11,333 feet and the airy platform known as the Top of Europe. Two stops en route allow passengers to get out and walk across the tunnel to peer through observation windows. One stop, the Eiger Wall station, is popular as an escape route for Eiger North Wall climbers in trouble, and a departure point for mountain rescues.

Summit views take in the 14-mile Aletsch Glacier, the longest in the Alps. Neighboring Germany and France are visible, too. And while you're on the Top of Europe, don't miss the Ice Palace. Created in 1934 by two local mountain guides, it is located deep inside the glacier and exhibits ice-carved sculptures. Numerous scientific facilities also are stationed near the Top of Europe.

Off the slopes, more than 50 miles of winter walking paths are maintained, as well as 30 miles of sledding hills and the world's longest toboggan run—9 miles from First to Grindelwald. Also in the Grindelwald Valley are 20 miles of cross-country ski trails.

Grindelwald Tourismus
Postfach 124
CH-3818 Grindelwald
Switzerland

Phone: 41–33–854–1212

Web Site: www.grindelwald.ch

E-mail: touristcenter@grindelwald.ch

Elevation: Top—9,740 feet; base—3,100 feet

Vertical Drop: 6,640 feet

Total Trails: 125 miles

Longest Run: 9 miles

Terrain: 30% beginner; 50% intermediate; 20% advanced/expert

Lifts: 45

Snowmaking: 20 miles

Central Reservations: 41–33–854–1212

Snow Report: www.grindelwald.ch

Accommodations: Many 3- and 4-story chalet-style hotels in the village and near the lift at Grund.

Getting There: By car, 2 hours from Zurich's airport. By rail, there are international trains to Interlaken; it's a 35-minute ride on the Bernese Oberland Railways to Grindelwald.

Keep in Mind: Not a lot of expert terrain. Getting to Kleine Scheidegg takes time, and there can be long lines on weekends.

BEST BETS

Beginners: The lengthy Mettlen-Grund run.

Intermediates: The First area directly above Grindelwald.

Advanced: The Wixi area of Kleine Scheidegg.

Experts: The black run down the Schilthorn.

Lunch: Jagerstubli in Grund.

Off the Slopes: Ride the train to the Jungfraujoch.

Best Hotel: Chateau-style, 5-star Hotel Regina.

GSTAAD
Gstaad, Switzerland

Like Aspen, Gstaad's following of the rich and famous has helped put the place on the map. Unlike Zermatt, where everybody actually seems to ski, many visitors to Gstaad come just to be part of the wholesome, ruddy-cheeked winter scene.

But Gstaad, a centuries-old Alpine village in Switzerland's German-speaking Bernese Oberland, also harbors traditions. Generations of European families come for winter holidays and to enjoy the slopes year after year. They are drawn by the sheer drama of picturesque dairy farms surrounded by chiseled white peaks.

Skiers and snowboarders are also drawn by the vastness of the slopes, by the quality of service in the family-run hotels and restaurants, and by the historic architecture and charming atmosphere—the very reasons North Americans should make a ski trip to Europe.

Gstaad is also the centerpiece of a collection of ten mostly tame ski villages: Chateau d'Oex, Glacier 3000, Gsteig, Lauenen, Rougemont, Saanen, Saanenmöser, Schönried, St. Stephan, and Zweisimmen. You won't find all of them in an atlas. It's not unlike Chamonix with its quiverful of nearby ski areas all sharing the geographical name. In the Gstaad area, ski lift ownership changes with the hill, and unfortunately only a few of the resorts are lift-linked. Still, trains, buses, and a ski pass do tie them all together. Each is a drop-dead-gorgeous Swiss village, with some lifts climbing into the forest.

Some say the slow pace of Gstaad is part of its charm. "Come Up—Slow Down," reads the tourist office's slogan. There is surprisingly little pretension at Gstaad. No one flaunts their wealth. People come for a superb winter holiday—nothing more, noth-

ing less. Riding a polished electric train to the ski lifts reflects the slower pace and lends a festive feeling to getting there.

From high on the slopes, the train looks like a toy. The vertical drop is often more than 6,000 feet, far exceeding any lift-serviced resort in North America. But even with a string of mountains and sixty-two lifts, Gstaad lacks expert terrain. Instead you get spacious novice and intermediate pistes along with twenty-five mountain restaurants. As they used to say about Utah's Deer Valley: Steep skiing might rattle the jewelry of the rich folks.

The ski and snowboarding terrain rolls across four loosely connected main areas. At Chateau d'Oex and Rougemont, you even cross the boundaries into French-speaking Switzerland. Most of the action occurs below tree line, which is unusual in the Bernese Oberland.

The Wasserngrat ski area east of the village and the Wispile area to the south are not much to write home about. Wispile offers several good beginner trails near the foot of the mountain and a few expert pitches up high in the trees.

The jumping-off points for the largest ski area are the villages of Saanenmöser and Schönried. The lifts lead to intermediate skier and boarder heaven, with nothing but long, rolling undulating terrain that stretches into next summer's dreams. Here the lifts link with those above the village of St. Stephan, as well as the interesting terrain above Zweisimmen, where there is a half-pipe. A terrain park is located at the Eggli area, the largest of the area's ten resorts.

But if snow is scarce—and it can be, because Gstaad's 3,120-foot elevation is relatively low for the Alps—the main ski and boarding area is Glacier 3000. The snow is

There is much more to Gstaad than fur coats and sparkling jewelry shops. The ski pass for the Gstaad region includes sixty-two lifts, 150 miles of maintained runs, and a precious string of mountain villages all worthy of the extraordinary surroundings. The high-altitude glacier guarantees snow.

guaranteed, even in summer. During a snow-bound winter, the runs below the glacier offer some of the best fall-line skiing in the region.

Off the slopes, there are 30 outstanding miles of prepared walking trails, three maintained toboggan runs, skating and bal-looning, and just about everything else you'd expect at one of the world's most famous winter addresses.

Gstaad Saanenland Tourismus
Haus des Gastes
CH-3780 Gstaad
Switzerland

Phone: 41–33–748–8181

Web Site: www.gstaad.ch

E-mail: info@gstaad.ch

Elevation: Top—9,840 feet; base—3,444 feet

Vertical Drop: 6,396 feet

Total Trails: 150 miles

Longest Run: 9 miles

Terrain: 45% beginner; 35% intermediate; 20% advanced

Lifts: 62

Snowmaking: 7 miles

Central Reservations: 41–33–748–8181

Snow Report: www.gstaad.ch

Accommodations: Many 3- and 4-star hotels. Also, private chalets are popular.

Getting There: Located 2½ hours from Geneva.

Keep in Mind: Not much expert terrain. Resorts are linked by ground transportation.

BEST BETS

Beginners: Eggli, the Skilift Schopfen trail.

Intermediates: Wasserngrat area.

Advanced: Combe d'Audon on the Dia-blerets Glacier.

Experts: Off-piste and in the trees at Eggli and Wispile.

Lunch: Rellerli Mountain Restaurant.

Off the Slopes: Gstaad offers a wealth of restaurants and nightlife.

Best Hotel: The Gstaad Palace.

KLOSTERS
Klosters, Switzerland

Prince Charles was a winter regular long before William and Harry tagged along. Like his sons, the prince learned to ski on the south-facing slopes of the Madrisa area directly above Klosters (pronounced *close-tears*). In 1988 an avalanche almost swept him to his death and killed one of his com-panions as they skied off-piste on the nearby Gotschna slopes. They were enjoying the massive ski circus that surrounds Klosters and stretches all the way to the famed Parsenn ski area above Davos.

But citylike Davos with its bright lights and bustle is a world apart. Well-preserved Klosters is a cluster of chocolate-colored chalets enveloped in Swiss-village charm. Klosters's best hotel, the Chesa Grischuna, exemplifies that charm. A local mountain guide named Hans Guler and his buddies built the hotel in 1938. Since then, its ten rooms have attracted the likes of Audrey Hepburn, Winston Churchill, and assorted European royalty. Mr. Guler passed away in 1991, but the hotel remains in the family and is, quite simply, one of the best hotels in all the world of skiing.

Once you find Klosters, it's hard to let go. The quaintness and elegance of the former twelfth-century monastery town combined with vast beginner and intermediate slopes keep mountain lovers coming back winter after winter.

Located in southeastern Switzerland's large but sparsely populated Graubünden canton, which borders on Austria to the north and Italy to the east and south, Klosters is tucked into a folded landscape of deep, isolated valleys, sheer rocky summits, and thick pine forests. Nearby glaciers launch two of Europe's great rivers—the Rhine and the Inn—on their journeys to the North Sea and Black Sea, respectively.

Like Davos, Klosters is divided into two distinct areas about a mile apart. Klosters Platz is the main center of activity, home to many of the small, chalet-style upscale hotels and specialty shops. Klosters Dorf is the quieter, residential side of the village. Klosters is 1,500 feet lower than Davos's 5,118 feet, which might provide a little relief for those who don't react well to mile-high altitudes.

For skiers and snowboarders, Klosters is linked to Davos and its famous Parsenn ski slopes. The two resorts share a pass covering six different ski areas—Parsenn, Klosters, Jakobshorn, Madrisa, Pischa, and Rinerhorn—all connected by lifts, shuttle buses, or rail. The sprawling ski region includes fifty-five lifts, 200 miles of trails, and 5,000-foot vertical drops. Intermediate skiers and snowboarders can handle 80 percent of the terrain. There is a nice progression of runs for those on the learning curve ranging from windshield-wiper beginner to carving intermediate.

 One of the most rustic of the Swiss resorts, Klosters links with the sprawling pistes of Davos, which includes six ski areas across 200 miles of trails. But Klosters stands alone on charm. It is a favorite haunt of the rich and famous who want excellent skiing in an elegant but relaxed ambience.

An aerial tram from the center of Klosters Platz climbs the long, breathless fall lines of the Gotschna slopes that eventually link to the Parsenn ski area. An extraordinary gondola ride makes the leap across to the high shoulder of Weissfluh, one of the highest peaks in the region, in one stretch, with views of miniature villages below and massive snowy ridges above. Most runs are above tree line. Experts can perfect wide carving turns while heading off-piste for powder. Intermediates can build up confidence chasing speed, and novices can progress to tame intermediate slopes. All this makes it perfect for mixed-ability groups.

Beneath Weissfluh's summit lift is some of the most famous intermediate terrain in Europe. The best-known Parsenn run snakes across the top of the mountain, drops into the woods of Gotschna, and tumbles all the way to the village of Kublis on the other side of Klosters, a total descent of 8 miles. The route is the course of a mass-participation ski race that has been an annual tradition at Klosters since the resort's earliest days. Almost all the runs from Weissfluh to Klosters are European classics, dropping more than a vertical mile. Even when matched to ability, they keep skiers on their toes.

A cable car from Klosters Dorf climbs the sun-splashed southern slopes of the Madrisa area. The mostly intermediate and beginner terrain served by seven lifts here appeals to families. There's a terrain park and a bordercross to help keep everyone interested.

Across from Parsenn, the Jakobshorn area has several short but challenging runs for expert skiers. There's also some steep stuff off-piste areas on Gotschna, but that's about it for true expert terrain. Snowboarders are Jakobshorn's most loyal fans. Along with the sweet fall lines, boarders enjoy a terrain park and halfpipe. The family ski areas of Rinerhorn and Pischa are just a shuttle bus ride away.

Off-slope activities around Klosters include ice skating, tobogganing, snow-shoeing, horse-drawn sleigh rides, and miles of maintained walking trails in the valley. There are also 66 miles of cross-country ski trails.

Klosters is like a fine, tailor-made suit. It discreetly radiates style, sophistication, and a relaxed elegance. The après-ski scene is understated. There are no DJs playing loud Euro-rock and American golden oldies. Town billboards tout Vivaldi and Mozart recitals.

Klosters Tourismus
CH-7250 Klosters
Switzerland

Phone: 41–81–410–2020

Web Site: www.klosters.ch

E-mail: info@klosters.ch

Elevation: Top—9,330 feet; base—3,907 feet

Vertical Drop: 5,423 feet

Total Trails: 194 miles

Longest Run: 8 miles

Terrain: 20% beginner; 42% intermediate; 38% advanced/expert

Lifts: 55

Snowmaking: 11 miles

Central Reservations: 41–81–410–2020

Snow Report: www.klosters.ch

Accommodations: Klosters offers many top-end, privately owned, chalet-style hotels.

Getting There: It's 3 hours from Zurich (125 miles). Direct rail service.

Keep in Mind: This is a quiet village with little beginner terrain.

BEST BETS

Beginners: Bolgen.

Intermediates: Parsenn run from Weissfluh to Kublis.

Advanced: Drostobel to Klosters.

Experts: Off-piste on Gotschna.

Lunch: Conterser Schwendi.

Off the Slopes: Ride the train to the spa at Scuol.

Best Hotel: Chesa Grischuna.

SAAS-FEE
Saas-Fee, Switzerland

It is a Swiss winter scene that would sell a million calendars. And maybe it has. It's a world too bright for unshielded eyes. You can almost reach out and touch the jumbled seracs and crevasses that rim the upper ski runs. But resist the temptation and stay on the marked trails. Crevasses are deadly.

The high-altitude resort of Saas-Fee is downright lovely. This centuries-old mountain village is a ski town that actually supports residents rather than just visitors looking for a place to sleep, drink, and catch a chairlift. There's also plenty of nightlife, but a town ordinance prevents carousing on the streets outside the clubs after 10:00 P.M.

 Switzerland's highest mountain, Dufourspitz, and more than a dozen other peaks exceeding 13,000 feet all rim the beautiful village of Saas-Fee. No wonder it's called the Pearl of the Alps. Skiers and boarders feast on 60 miles of trails, many of them set on active glaciers, guaranteeing good sliding even in summer. Snowboarders rule the slopes.

Saas-Fee is located at the head of the extraordinary Saas Valley in southern Switzerland, just one mountain range away from Zermatt. As with its glitzy neighbor, the streets are car-free, there's a fine range of hotels and restaurants, and the snow is guaranteed, thanks to the 10,000-year-old glaciers.

Set in the Wallis region, where crevasse-ridden glaciers tumble down to the edge of town, Saas-Fee's glacial backdrops rival the famed Vallée Blanche at Chamonix in France.

From town, which lies at almost 6,000 feet, an aerial tram rises to the nearby glaciers at Felskinn. From there, the Alps' highest funicular railway climbs under the glacier to emerge among the summits at 11,375 feet. Above the rail terminus is the world's highest revolving restaurant. During its one-hour revolution, diners rub shoulders with Switzerland's highest mountains. In the distance you see the Eiger, the Mönch, and the Jungfrau above Grindelwald. The views even extend to the plains of the River Po in Italy.

But for expert skiers, the skiing is hardly as dramatic as the scenery. For the most part, Saas-Fee offers outstanding snow to carve swooping parabolas down intermediate slopes. The lower runs are supplemented with snowmaking machines, and most of the runs face north. Beginners are in the same fix as the experts—too little variety. Adventurous novices will find some terrain to their liking up high on the mountain, but for the most part, they're stuck on the short lifts directly above the village, looking like strollers on an evening paseo.

Saas-Fee is extremely snowboarder friendly, however. There's a nicely planned terrain park, including three 260-foot half-pipes. In summer, snowboarding is popular on the glacier slopes, even though riders face the ordeal of surface lifts.

For a little more variety you can ski the nearby slopes of Saas Grund and Saas-Almagell with your Saas-Fee lift ticket, which includes the bus ride. Day trips to Zermatt and Crans-Montana are also doable.

Seventeen hundred inhabitants occupy Saas-Fee. Amid the nightclubs and modern chalets, you'll see plenty of century-old larch-timber granaries sitting on raised pillars and resting on broad discs of stone to keep the rodents out. And you can still buy a pail of fresh milk, if you have the desire.

For nonskiers, there are cross-country trails, hiking paths, a 3-mile-long toboggan run, ice skating, curling, and a sports center with swimming and spa facilities.

For intermediate skiers and boarders who want a taste of some of the best Europe has to offer—stunning views, an opportunity to experience a glacier from the surface (there are no glaciers in the contiguous United States), and an ancient mountain village that exudes Swiss charm and hospitality—you could hardly do better than Saas-Fee.

Saas-Fee Tourist Office
Saas-Fee, 3906
Switzerland

Phone: 41–27–958–1858

Web Site: www.saas-fee.ch

E-mail: to@saas-fee.ch

Elevation: Top—11,808 feet; base—5,904 feet

Vertical Drop: 5,904 feet

Total Trails: 62 miles

Longest Run: 5.5 miles

Terrain: 25% beginner; 50% intermediate; 25% advanced/expert

Lifts: 26

Snowmaking: 6 miles

Central Reservations: 41–27–958–1858

Snow Report: www.saas-fee.ch

Accommodations: Plenty of charming 3-star hotels.

Getting There: Swiss postal bus service from Brig and Wisp, with regular train connections from Geneva and Zurich.

Keep in Mind: There isn't much for either beginners or hard-core. The glacier restricts off-piste skiing.

BEST BETS

Beginners: Lower slopes directly above the village.

Intermediates: Längfluh chairlift.

Advanced: Mittelallalin T-bars next to the restaurant.

Experts: Felsental off the Felskinn tram and steep drops from the Hinterallalin lift.

Lunch: Mittelallalin, the world's highest revolving restaurant.

Off the Slopes: Stroll the village and visit the museum.

Best Hotel: The 4-star Hotel Walliserhof.

ST. MORITZ
St. Moritz, Switzerland

The inspiration for the world's first winter resort began at a small hotel in the village of St. Moritz in 1864 when a group of British summer tourists stayed with innkeeper Johannes Badrutt at the Kulm Hotel. When summer ended, he invited them back to spend the winter, assuring them they would not be disappointed. He offered a money-back guarantee if they weren't satisfied. They fell in love with the place.

Alpine skiing was not yet part of the scene, but by 1890 the resort had built its famous Cresta skeleton run and a bobsled track. In 1892 Switzerland's first electric tramway rose out of the blue-skied Engadin Valley. By 1928, St. Moritz was a well-established winter resort and hosted the second Winter Olympic Games. In 1948 it hosted the Games again. Of course, the village's history goes back much further. Traveling south to St. Moritz from Zurich, you cross over the Julier Pass—where there are two stone pillars left by Julius Caesar in the first century B.C. Its mineral springs have been popular since the Middle Ages. And a village church near St. Moritz is etched with frescoes from the thirteenth and fifteenth centuries.

Set within the spectacular mountains of the heart-shaped Upper Engadin above a string of lakes beneath 13,000-foot Piz Bernina in southeastern Switzerland, St. Moritz is arguably the most famous winter address in the world. It attracts a chic clientele drawn by the thrilling slopes, the dramatic setting, and the après-ski scene of fireside fondue and *glühwein*. The town is split into two villages—St. Moritz Dorf (village) and St. Moritz Bad (bath, as in mineral springs). The Upper Engadin Valley stretches across 30 miles at an elevation of 6,000 feet. Along with St. Moritz, population 5,800, there are twelve neighboring villages. They're traditionally Swiss, from the cows, to the cheese, to the chairlifts. For visitors, the ambience of daily life is as appealing as the skiing.

But the mountain beckons. The Ski Engadin lift pass covers nine different ski areas that stretch from Maloja via St. Moritz to Zuos and include fifty-seven lifts and 217 miles of trails. You'll fine everything from bunny slopes to Daytona-style cruisers to off-piste elevator shafts. Nonetheless, the majority of the slopes are ego-building intermediate runs. The sun shines most of the time, but the high altitude usually ensures snow when storm clouds move in.

The main ski areas are Corviglia-Marguns and Corvatsch-Furtschellas, both close to the village. Diavolezza-Lagalb and Zuoz-Albanas are a little farther down the valley. South of St. Moritz, near the village of Pontresina, are the dual ski areas of Lagalb and Diavolezza.

A free bus connects all the resorts.

The well-groomed, south-facing slopes of Corviglia are accessed via a monorail from Dorf. From Bad, a cable car climbs to the slopes of Piz Nair. Both top stations are above 10,000 feet. Most of the main runs are fortified by snowmaking. There's also a halfpipe here.

Across the valley are the north-facing slopes of Corvatsch/Furtschellas, which top out at 10,837 feet, offering a spectacular wraparound view into Italy, Austria, and Germany. The runs are a little more challenging than at Corviglia, dropping 5,000 vertical feet with many off-piste possibilities. There's also a terrain park.

The Diavolezza-Lagalb combination faces each other near the summit of the Bernina Pass. Here you'll find skiing on the Morteratsch Glacier and a spectacular 5.5-mile run down to the train station at Morteratsch.

Sprinkled around the slopes are some of the most glamorous mountain restaurants anywhere.

Perhaps feeling its age like much of its clientele, St. Moritz underwent a major face-lift to ready itself as the venue for the 2003 World Alpine Ski Championships. The area is also well known for its more than 90 miles of superbly maintained cross-country trails. The Engadin cross-country ski race, with more than 13,000 participants—the biggest sporting event in the country—is held here every second Sunday in March.

From polo played on snow to the world-famous skeleton Cresta Run, this chic, elegant, and sporty town offers everything imaginable to occupy the idle rich and assorted nobility who winter here. (Alfred Hitchcock reportedly visited St. Moritz for thirty winters but never skied. They say he conceived some of his best films while staying in his suite at the Palace Hotel.)

The resort is on the route of Switzerland's famed Glacier Express train, which traverses the Alps from Zermatt to St. Moritz.

St. Moritz Tourist Office
CH-7500 St. Moritz
Switzerland

Phone: 41–81–837–3333

Web Site: www.stmoritz.ch

E-mail: information@stmoritz.ch

Elevation: Top—10,830 feet; base—5,807 feet

Vertical Drop: 5,023 feet

Total Trails: 217 miles

Longest Run: 6 miles

Terrain: 35% beginner; 25% intermediate; 40% advanced/expert

Lifts: 56

Snowmaking: 28 miles

Central Reservations: 41–81–837–3333

Snow Report: www.skiengadin.ch

Accommodations: www.skiengadin.ch

Getting There: Rail service to the village with connections to the rest of Europe. It's 3 hours from Zurich.

Keep in Mind: St. Moritz is no small Swiss village. Bring your no-limit credit card.

BEST BETS

Beginners: Celerina area.

Intermediates: Diavolezza offers lots of variety.

Advanced: The 4-mile-long Hahnensee run on Corvatsch.

Experts: The Il Muro run from the top of Lagalp.

Lunch: La Marmite on Corviglia.

Off the Slopes: The Segantini Museum.

Best Hotel: The Palace in St. Moritz-Dorf.

 The world's most famous winter address, where the sun shines an average of 322 days a year, has just about every imaginable winter activity. Geographical features shape life in St. Moritz, even the rich life. It is the only Olympic site in Switzerland, host of the Winter Games in 1928 and again in 1948.

VERBIER
Verbier, Switzerland

At the 10,925-foot summit of Mont Fort, the high point on the expansive slopes of Verbier, the wind can blow in from Italy or France. In the distance are some of the highest and grandest peaks of the Alps. To the southeast is the Matterhorn; to the west is the broad massif of Mont Blanc.

Beneath you, the fall lines drop 6,000 vertical feet through a pillowy snowpack. Nothing in North America can match the vertical. It's the equivalent of stacking Telluride on top of Stowe. Most of it is too steep for novices.

Verbier links to the resorts of Nendaz, Thyon, Veysonnaz, and a few other jewels in a strung-out ski region south of the Rhône River that is marketed as 4 Valleys. The entire area is massive. It takes a full day just to ski or ride around the perimeter— and you've got to hustle to pull that off.

Perched on a sun-drenched plateau above the exquisite vineyards of Switzerland's Rhône Valley, Verbier's reputation for vast slopes and challenging terrain is well earned. The shapely mountains that dominate the area offer some of the longest stretches of lift-serviced vertical in the world, attracting a young crowd that rocks both on and off the slopes.

Given good snow conditions, you can ride anywhere within the boundary and, with a guide, almost everywhere beyond. Like Chamonix, most of Verbier's epic, Horatio-at-the-bridge skiing happens off-piste.

The 4 Valleys region sprawls with ninety-four ski lifts and 250-plus miles of groomed runs looping across six mountains. The terrain folds into itself, exposing gnarly ridges and wide-open bowls. There are never-see-the-light-of-day chutes and sun-crusted, steeply pitched faces. The challenges attract professional big-mountain skiers like American Chris Davenport, who can put together an on-piste run of more than 8,000 vertical feet. If you see a line you like, you ski it. The in-your-face stuff is easily accessible, without having to cross glaciers bridged by snow that would require you to pack crampons, an ice ax, and a rescue harness. (Avalanche transceivers are widely used at Verbier.)

The mammoth peaks surrounding the sprawling town, Mont Gelé and Attelas, provide 360 degrees of skiable exposures. There are wooded slopes directly above the resort, but the real skiing is above the tree line in the wide-open bowls and tough bump runs that resemble a violent white sea frozen in plaster and pasted on a wall.

Intermediates have endless days of carving terrain to explore. Most of the local slopes face south or west and are below 8,000 feet. Good places to start are the bowls around Lac des Vaux. And you can always find good snow on the Mont Fort glacier. Novice skiers can ski down to the village of La Tzoumaz and its gentle slopes.

But Verbier's trademark image is that of a dazzling skier defying gravity on a snow-covered, waterfall-like drop. These adventures are mostly played out off-piste, where taking a guide is the smart thing to do. Seldom does a winter pass without a deadly avalanche. (The extreme couloirs between Mont Gelé and Les Attelas are infamous.)

Experts can find both bumps and couloirs below the Gentianes tram. When the snow extends all the way down the valley, there's a 7-mile run to the villages of Fionnay and La Châble below Verbier. And beneath the popular L'Olympique mountain restaurant are the 3,000-vertical-foot chutes of Vallon d'Arbi. After that, you can head off-piste—with your guide.

If you need even more options, Chamonix, Champéry, and Crans-Montana are all doable day trips.

Verbier itself is no quaint village, even though the cuckoo-clock style of architecture dominates, and a popular excursion is to a nearby seventeenth-century chapel. The first ski lift was built in 1946. It's a trendy, well-schooled resort offering everything off the slopes from sophisticated shopping to spa treatments. The place sprawls across a sunny plateau; second homes dot the lower slopes. It draws a fairly young crowd of international snowriders and, on weekends, hip Geneva professionals. Most shops and hotels are centrally located near a traffic circle in the center of town. The nightlife is as wild as the skiing. A host of fine restaurants serve excellent Valais wine, and bars and clubs for night owls abound. The Pub Mont Fort sells more beer than any other bar in Switzerland.

With its never-ending skiing and easygoing resort life, all dripping with French-Swiss charm, Verbier is among the top of the batting order of European resorts.

Verbier Tourist Office
CH-Verbier 1936
Switzerland

Phone: 41–27–775–38–88

Web Site: www.verbier.ch

E-mail: info@verbier.ch

Elevation: Top—10,930 feet; base—4,920 feet

Vertical Drop: 6,010 feet

Total Trails: 255 miles

Longest Run: 8 miles

Terrain: 32% beginner; 42% intermediate; 26% advanced/expert

Lifts: 94

Snowmaking: 31 miles

Central Reservations: 41–27–775–38–88

Snow Report: www.verbier.ch

Accommodations: A wide range of hotels, chalets, apartments, and private residences.

Getting There: A 2-hour drive or train ride from Geneva. A bus runs from the rail station at Le Châble.

Keep in Mind: Beginners are better off at nearby Crans-Montana.

BEST BETS

Beginners: Gentle runs close to the village and at the top of Les Esserts.

Intermediates: The Savoleyres area.

Advanced: Front face of Mont Fort.

Experts: Chutes at Vallon d'Arbi.

Lunch: Chez Dany at Clambin (intermediate skier access only). Otherwise, try L'Olympique at Les Attelas.

Off the Slopes: Explore the towns of the Rhône Valley.

Best Hotel: Hotel Rosalp.

WENGEN AND MÜRREN
Wengen, Switzerland

Perched across from each other, both a mile high and separated by the spectacular Lauterbrunnen Valley, Wengen and Mürren nestle beneath the glacier-ridden 13,642-foot Jungfrau, next to two other spectacular peaks, the Mönch and the Eiger. Both villages are centuries old, but they hold a commanding grip on today's skiers who flock to Switzerland's Bernese Oberland to explore its remarkable mountains and graceful, long intermediate ski and snowboarding runs.

Along with St. Anton in Austria, Mürren lays claim to being the birthplace of modern skiing. It was here in 1922 that British ski

aficionado Sir Arnold Lunn organized the first-ever timed slalom race. And the tradition continues. Every January since 1928, the Inferno citizens' ski race has been held in lofty Mürren. Competitors start high above the village near the almost 10,000-foot-high pyramidal summit of Schilthorn. More than 18,000 skiers race the 10-mile-long course, starting down in fifteen-second intervals over a six-hour period. It's one of the oldest and largest downhill ski races in the world. In 1936 one of the world's first T-bars was erected near the town.

The longest cogwheel rail route in Switzerland leads to the town, whose two main streets are lined with welcoming chalets and shops along with the century-old cowsheds.

Mürren, which sits on a 5,361-foot-high shelf of a mountainside, has its own 33 miles of ski and boarding terrain that falls away from the summit of Schilthorn. At the top cable-car terminus there is a revolving restaurant made famous in the James Bond film *On Her Majesty's Secret Service.* In the novel Ian Fleming called the place Piz Gloria, and the name has stuck. The restaurant's one-hour revolution reveals 200 peaks and forty glaciers. A jumble of rock outcrops, ski trails, and lifts crisscrosses the runs that lead down from the restaurant.

 Two historic, car-free picture-postcard villages lie across from each other along Switzerland's deep Lauterbrunnen Valley, which rises to meet the Grindelwald Valley at the Kleine Scheidegg–Männlichen ski areas beneath the Eiger's North Wall. Wengen and Mürren are quintessential Swiss ski destinations in the extraordinary Bernese Oberland.

The skiing and boarding are far more limited than across the valley at Wengen, but both resorts link with the other forty-nine ski lifts of the Jungfrau region, including the slopes above nearby Grindelwald. Most of the terrain is wide open and suitable for intermediate carving that flows on over rolls and down short, steep pitches into transitions.

Wengen lies on a sheltered terrace above 4,000 feet facing southwest. Along with Mürren it is one of the few Swiss villages not accessible by road. Cars are left at a multistory parking garage in Lauterbrunnen, fifteen minutes away on the Wengernalp Railway.

The two must-ski runs above Wengen are the men's and women's World Cup downhill courses. On Thursdays a former World Cup racer from the Swiss National Ski Team leads recreational skiers down the Lauberhorn, the longest course on the men's international racing circuit. The women's course, Tschuggen, allows wide sweeping turns all the way down from the Honegg lift to Grindelwald.

But some of the best, wide-open intermediate skiing is directly above Wengen on the spacious pistes of the Männlichen area, which also leads down to Grund and Grindelwald. Wengen has a terrain park and a halfpipe as well.

Nightlife is limited in both Wengen and Mürren, although there are plenty of bars and outdoor decks for après-ski. Most hotel stays include breakfast and dinner, so entertainment usually revolves around the hotels.

Other activities at Wengen and Mürren include numerous walking trails, curling, paragliding, sledding, and ice skating. There are cross-country ski trails up and down the Lauterbrunnen Valley. Heli-skiing takes place on nearby glaciers.

Wengen Tourism
CH-3825, Wengen
Switzerland

Phone: 41–33–855–1414

Web Site: www.wengen-muerren.ch

E-mail: info@wengen-muerren.ch

Elevation: Top—9,741 feet; base—4,198 feet

Vertical Drop: 5,543 feet

Total Trails: 61 miles

Longest Run: 10 miles

Terrain: 30% beginner; 50% intermediate; 20% advanced/expert

Lifts: 49 in the Jungfrau region

Snowmaking: 19 miles

Central Reservations: 41–33–855–1414

Snow Report: www.wengen-muerren.ch

Accommodations: Three- and 4-star hotels close to the lifts, and many chalets.

Getting There: Trains bound for Wengen and Mürren depart the Interlaken East station, which connects via rail with the rest of Europe.

Keep in Mind: Not much nightlife.

BEST BETS

Beginners: Wengen has a beginner area in town.

Intermediates: Most of the runs from Wengen to Grindelwald.

Advanced: Piz Gloria to the bottom of the Muttleren lift.

Experts: Eigergletscher to Wixi has a black run and several off-piste options.

Lunch: Gimmelm Restaurant in Mürren.

Off the Slopes: Don't miss a trip on the cog railway inside the Eiger to the Jungfraujoch.

Best Hotel: Wengen's 4-star Silberhorn. In Mürren, the Eiger Hotel.

ZERMATT
Zermatt, Switzerland

The symbol of Zermatt is the Matterhorn, probably the most photographed mountain in the world. But the village itself is a jewel, one of only a handful of ski towns in the world worthy of such proximity to the Matterhorn's pyramidal perfection.

Tucked into southwestern Switzerland's tradition-steeped Valais canton—which is German speaking, and enjoys a lifestyle that has French and Italian influences—Zermatt is an old, old village. Some of the timber structures go back 500 years. This is one of the most beautiful of ski towns, and it has been a magnet for adventurers since the 1880s.

The extraordinary snowbound slopes range and roam across two countries. The vertical drop is more than 7,000 feet, the longest in Switzerland and the equivalent of stacking Aspen Mountain on top of Steamboat Resort. The skiing and snowboarding includes three interconnected areas—Rothorn, Stockhorn, and Klein Matterhorn. You also can take a thigh-burning, 6-mile cruise down to the happening resort of Cervinia on the Italian side of the Matterhorn. It is a must-do lunch spot.

The scenery is out of this world. Thirty-six mountains higher than 13,000 feet circle the resort like a white-domed color guard. Brilliant white glaciers walled by cobalt-blue seracs rise in all directions.

And unlike some of Europe's top-tier resorts, Zermatt has visitors who actually ski. They are swept up the mountain by seventy-one lifts as varied as the blades of a Swiss army knife, including a train and an underground funicular. The downhill options cover 150-plus miles of far-flung runs that fall away from the Alpine Swiss-Italian border, covering more than 8,800 acres. But if the snow is right, you can ski everywhere. It's like squeezing a lemon, as the Swiss expression goes. Most of the slopes are wind protected and south facing. The high altitude allows the normal ski season to extend to May. And the high glaciers provide Zermatt with guaranteed snow.

The slopes are inclined to favor intermediate and advanced skiers. For the most part, they tumble down scenic ridges and sparkling glacial valleys above the tree line. But you'll also ski through centuries-old summer farming villages like Rothorn and Gornergrat. Over on the ski runs of Klein Matterhorn, served by the highest cable car in the Alps, you ski right next to the Matterhorn's elegantly sculpted face. Still, the skiing is good everywhere, and the meticulous slope maintenance sets a high standard for Europe. Many of the lift stations feature screens from Web cams showing real-time conditions at various spots on the mountain.

Expert skiers and snowboarders find challenging terrain off the Rothorn tram and the Stockhorn tram above Gornergrat, where the train ends. Intermediate skiers are comfortable just about anywhere and pretty much have the run of the place.

For boarders, Gravity Park on the Theodul Glacier boasts a 650-foot-long halfpipe, as well as kickers and rails. There's also a halfpipe, tables, quarters, bumps, slides, and a kids' corner at Rotenboden. The freeriding is good everywhere on the mountain. In summer six surface lifts and a cable car access the highest summer ski area in the Alps.

Zermatt is a gourmand's delight. Nearly forty mountain restaurants have earned Zermatt a reputation as the best mountain dining in Europe. You'll find a collection of these fine family-run eateries on the mountain at Fluhalp, where live music, great *glühwein,* and chocolate with rum are all elements of dining, along with the excellent regional dishes.

And always in the backdrop is the 14,691-foot Matterhorn, the mountain that sparked Switzerland's tourism industry after two Zermatt guides led the first ascent, which was made by their client, British climber Edward Whymper, in 1865. The successful ascent opened the icy gates to the golden age of alpinism.

The setting had attracted visitors before that, however, with the first guest house opening in 1838. The first ski lift didn't rise above the village until 1942. Today the town accommodates 13,000 guests in more than 115 hotels and 1,500 apartments. The village has more than one hundred restaurants.

But Zermatt, which sits at 5,315 feet, is an exclusive enclave. You can't drive there. You must park your car 3 miles away in the town of Tasch and take a cogwheel train, and then be shuttled to your hotel in electric carts or horse-drawn sleighs. It's wonderful.

Along with alpine skiing, Zermatt offers prepared winter hiking paths, cross-country skiing, and sledding paths. Also popular are curling, ice skating, and tandem paragliding. The luxurious Riffelalp Resort, midway up the mountain, is a world unto itself. It even has its own curling area on a perfectly laid-out sheet of ice next to a ski run. Every January, the annual International Zermatt Symposium brings big-name artists for lectures and concerts in town.

There's a world of adventure beyond Zermatt. Heli-skiing, mountain touring, and weeklong excursions along the legendary Haute Route to Chamonix can all be arranged at the Alpin Center (www.zermatt.ch/alpin center).

Zermatt Tourism
Bahnhofplatz, P.O. Box 247
3920 Zermatt
Switzerland

Phone: 41–27–966–8100

Web Site: www.zermatt.ch

E-mail: info@zermatt.ch

Elevation: Top—12,530 feet; base—5,314 feet

Vertical Drop: 7,216 feet

Total Trails: 153 miles

Longest Run: 9 miles

Terrain: 29% beginner; 38% intermediate; 33% advanced/expert

You can almost reach out and touch the Matterhorn in this carless village, whose ambience is as rich as a Swiss chocolate bar. It's the kind of place that would stop a thousand tour buses a day, if they were allowed up this extraordinary valley. The skiing is all you could ask for—even offering summer skiing.

Lifts: 62, plus 30 on the Italian side

Snowmaking: 27 miles

Central Reservations: 41–27–966–8111

Snow Report: www.zermatt.ch

Accommodations: A wide range of 3- and 4-star hotels.

Getting There: Easily reached by train—4 hours from Geneva, 5 hours from Zurich.

Keep in Mind: Bring your no-limit credit card.

BEST BETS

Beginners: Blauherd to Findeln areas.

Intermediates: The top of the Klein Matterhorn area.

Advanced: Breitboden.

Experts: Stockhorn, or the bumps on the Garten Buckelpiste.

Lunch: A collection of great restaurants midmountain at the Findeln area.

Off the Slopes: Take a historic walking tour of Zermatt.

Best Hotel: Riffelalp Resort (located midway up the mountain). The best hotel centrally located in Zermatt is the Grand Hotel Zermatterhof.

SOUTH OF THE EQUATOR

New Zealand presents a dramatic setting in a quirky country that North Americans quickly fall in love with. The mountains on the South Island, where most of the ski resorts lie, are both rugged and beautifully sculpted, particularly in the vicinity of 12,316-foot-high Mount Cook, the highest peak in the antipodes. The skiing, however, is quite limited compared to Europe and North America.

The most famous ski run is the Tasman Glacier, an 18-mile descent along an ice-covered valley that scrapes against ethereal Mount Cook. A ski-equipped aircraft serves as the only chairlift.

New Zealand's ski areas do not have slopeside accommodations. Nearby towns, which are below the snow line, serve as the headquarters for a whole range of outdoor adventures in the winter, including river rafting and the original bungee-jumping bridge. For the most part, the ski season tenders springlike weather in the valleys.

In South America the 5,000-mile-long Andes stretch along the Pacific coast from Venezuela to Tierra del Fuego and rise at many points to more than 22,000 feet. The major resorts are in Chile and Argentina, far removed from the areas of crime and turmoil that so often make the news.

The skiing is mostly above tree line and varied enough to offer terrain for all skill levels. The resorts are exceedingly friendly, well run, and offer plenty of comforts. Evenings yield the kind of exciting nightlife enjoyed in Southern Europe.

But what sets the skiing and snowboarding apart is the seemingly endless high-altitude backcountry terrain that is easily reached from the lift-serviced main runs. Skiing and snowboarding in the Andes are always an adventure.

In both New Zealand and South America, the season runs from June through October. Both destinations boast outstanding ski schools because so many professional skiers from the Northern Hemisphere are attracted by winter below the equator when it's summer back home. The best time to visit is July, August, and early September.

BARILOCHE
Bariloche, Argentina

Bariloche is Argentina's oldest and most famous ski area. It takes its name from the nearby city of San Carlos de Bariloche, which may be the only town in South America with a real ski culture and enough Alpine architecture to call itself the "Little Switzerland of South America."

The city was founded in 1902 by immigrants from Austria, Switzerland, and Germany, who must have been homesick. It's loaded with chocolate shops, fondue pots, and photo opportunities of buskers in lederhosen tethered to St. Bernards with brandy casks. Lacquered logs are the dominant building material. And you'll see plenty of brightly colored wood-carved gnomes standing guard, reminding you that some traditions need to die. But it's a great town for dining, and the nightlife is as wild as the surrounding Patagonia region is rugged. Argentinean students consider a jaunt to Bariloche a rite of passage after graduation.

Bariloche's ski area consists of three side-by-side mountains located 8 miles from Bariloche. (Free shuttles run between the city and the resort.) The ski area also is known by the name Cerro Catedral, and competing lift companies and ski schools have united under the name Alta Patagonia.

 Argentina's oldest ski center rises on three mountains with slopes above and below the tree line. The high bowls and off-piste terrain offer exciting possibilities. But most of the runs were made for cruising—as is the nightlife. The Swiss-like city of Bariloche is just 8 miles away and yields a wonderful social experience.

The smart-looking village at the base is known as Villa Catedral. It offers slopeside accommodations and a wide range of shops and restaurants.

The slopes tower above lovely Lake Nahuel Haupi. Forty-two miles of trails are served by thirty-three lifts, including a cable car. More than fifty runs and countless high-octane off-piste options are scattered across the resort's 1,600 acres. The vertical drop is a respectable 3,400 feet, which compares favorably to many Rocky Mountain ski areas. The view from the summit reveals Lake Nahuel Haupi—a tranquil island in a wide sea of rolling peaks.

The best skiing and snowboarding are found on the treeless upper bowls, which have reliable snow and the most challenging terrain. The lower slopes meander through trees and gentle meadows, where adequate snow is a perennial problem early and late in the five-month season, which runs from June through October. The average annual snowfall at the base is 16 inches; at the summit it's 16 feet. To overcome nature's lower-elevation shortfalls, the resort has invested in powerful snowmaking equipment in recent years.

For the most part, the slopes face east and are wide open and perfect for intermediate skiers and boarders who like to make high-speed swooping turns. But there also are long gullies that tumble down the mountain's ridges where skiers and snowboarders get a rush of adrenaline while banking like bobsledders. Near the top of the mountain there's a pleasant beginner area served by the Plaza poma lift, affording novices a sweeping panorama of the soaring mountains. The summit is also the site of a terrain park and halfpipe. If you're lucky enough to visit during a full moon, sign up for the mountaintop dinner followed by a nighttime descent of the mountain.

A six-passenger chair with a bubble cover rises from the base to the bowls. From there, a high-speed lift continues to the summit. Also spread throughout the resort are nine double chairlifts and twenty-two surface lifts. A master plan calls for many of the lifts to be upgraded over the next couple of years.

Bariloche, like most Southern Hemisphere ski resorts, attracts a lot of professional North American skiers waiting out the north's warm-weather months on southern slopes. Ski schools and equipment rentals are top-shelf.

The summit elevation is a relatively low 6,800 feet and presents few problems for skiers susceptible to altitude sickness. (In comparison, Portillo in nearby Chile tops out at 10,800 feet.) Jet lag also is minimized because Argentina is south of North America, and few time zones are crossed getting there.

Other resort activities include cross-country skiing, snowmobiling, and paragliding.

Alta Patagonia S.A.
Suipacha 967, Piso 1A
1001 Buenos Aires
Argentina

Phone: 54–4315–1750

Web Site: www.catedralaltapatagonia.com

E-mail: info@catedralaltapatagonia.com

Elevation: Top—6,725 feet; base—3,445 feet

Vertical Drop: 3,400 feet

Total Trails: 42 miles

Longest Run: 3 miles

Terrain: 15% beginner; 60% intermediate; 25% advanced/expert

Lifts: 32

Snowmaking: Yes

Central Reservations: www.catedralalta patagonia.com

Snow Report: www.catedralaltapatagonia.com

Accommodations: Hotels and apartments are at the base area. The city of Bariloche offers a wide range of accommodations. There are a few good hotels along the lake between the city and the ski area.

Getting There: Buenos Aires, 600 miles away, is the closest international airport. Domestic flights continue to Bariloche.

Keep in Mind: Snowfall is inconsistent.

BEST BETS

Beginners: The slopes directly above the village.

Intermediates: Beneath the Condor III chairlift.

Advanced: Largo T-bar.

Experts: The chutes and bowls of Punta Nevada.

Lunch: Protocolo.

Off the Slopes: Stop over in Buenos Aires, a pleasant European-style city reminiscent of Madrid.

Best Hotel: Hotel Catedral in Villa Catedral; Hotel Panamericano in Bariloche.

LAS LEÑAS

Las Leñas, Argentina

In 1983 Argentina's first purpose-built resort was constructed after owners consulted with the planners of Les Arcs in France. And like France's string of purpose-built ski areas, the prime consideration was finding spectacular terrain offering enormous skiing possibilities. That's why the developers settled on the Valle de Las Leñas, where there's nothing but majestic mountains stretching to all four compass points under winter skies as blue as the Argentine flag. The name relates to a bushy shrub that grows in the treeless valley. The resort is lost in a sea of white peaks among the world's second largest mountain range. It is more than 600 miles west of Buenos Aires and 125 miles from Malargue, the nearest airport. They had to be extremely confident about the terrain before building in such an out-of-the-way location.

A stark testimony to the area's remoteness is visible in summer from the summit of Las Leñas: the wrecked aircraft that in 1972 crashed with the Uruguayan national soccer team on board. Their ordeal was recounted in the book, and later the movie, *Alive.*

The decision to build a resort here proved to be insightful. This is the area in South America that attracts extreme skiers during the North American summer. Many veterans consider its off-piste potential to be the finest of any resort in the Southern Hemisphere. They also praise the quantity and quality of the snow, although its above-tree-line location exposes it to severe winds and a high potential for avalanches. In 1987 a midnight avalanche destroyed the Marte chairlift, which accesses the most extreme terrain high on the mountain.

But the resort also attracts skiers of every ability level who appreciate comfortable slopeside digs and vigorous nightlife, including casino gaming. In many respects the resort resembles the vastness of Whistler-Blackcomb, except the village at Las Leñas is much smaller and the 10,000 skiable acres are above tree line.

 This Euro-style purpose-built Argentinean resort offers almost 4,000 vertical feet of some of the most challenging ski and boarding terrain in the Southern Hemisphere. Think Chamonix, France, or Verbier, Switzerland. Factoring in all the accessible backcountry, the resort boasts more lift-accessed skiable terrain than any other resort in the Western Hemisphere.

Three lifts rise from the base to connect to a higher web of lifts. The 40 miles of marked trails range from gentle runs to groomed cruisers and steep bumps. The season lasts from early June to mid-October, with the best snow in August.

The ski area neatly divides into two areas: the lower mountain and the upper mountain. Nine lifts serve the lower area, which includes the mountain's face and consists mostly of beginner and intermediate-to-advanced terrain. Although the area's statistics list a mere 5 percent of the slopes as beginner terrain, bear in mind that this represents a lot of terrain on a big mountain. Novice skiers won't be shortchanged.

The upper mountain with its three lifts offers almost limitless terrain for expert skiers and boarders on vast, wide-open bowls and elevator shaft–like chutes. The Marte chairlift alone accesses more than forty avalanche chutes for adventurers who have the right stuff. Newcomers should consider hiring a local guide to find the best routes. Lines that are visible from the base can be tough to find when you're traversing the top of the mountain. Many skiers and boarders have shredded down a perfectly sane-looking couloir, only to have to hike back up after meeting a rock cliff halfway down. That's no easy feat in one-skier-narrow terrain. Wear a helmet and an avalanche transceiver, and never ski alone.

Another twist of nature is the local population, who, for the most part, avoid powder and off-piste terrain. You're not going to be elbowing anybody up on the high slopes.

The base area consists of thirteen hotels, ten restaurants, a handful of bars, and a small shopping center. Most of the hotels are all-inclusive. English is widely spoken. Day skiers are almost nonexistent, and the resort's infrastructure limits it to about 3,500 guests at any one time. Like most of South America, Argentineans dine late and then dance the night away. And although it's small, the village rocks until the wee hours.

Las Leñas Ski Resort
Route 222—Mendoza
Las Leñas
Argentina

Phone: 54–2627–471100

Web Site: www.laslenas.com

E-mail: informes@laslenas.com

Elevation: Top—11,253 feet; base—7,349 feet

Vertical Drop: 3,904 feet

Total Trails: 35

Longest Run: 4 miles

Terrain: 5% beginner; 35% intermediate; 25% advanced; 35% expert

Lifts: 12

Snowmaking: Yes

Central Reservations: www.laslenas.com

Snow Report: www.laslenas.com

Accommodations: Thirteen ski-in/ski-out hotels at the base.

Getting There: From Buenos Aires, fly to Malargue, where a shuttle covers the remaining 46 miles to the resort.

Keep in Mind: Potential for whiteout conditions.

BEST BETS

Beginners: Venus 2.

Intermediates: Jupiter.

Advanced: Vulcano.

Experts: Cenidor.

Lunch: La Cuato Estaciones at the Hotel Piscis.

Off the Slopes: Plan on spending at least a day in Buenos Aires en route.

Best Hotel: Hotel Piscis.

PORTILLO

Portillo, Chile

Like tall dogs that attack a bear just to remind themselves they are tall dogs, many of the national alpine teams of the world come to Portillo in August, barking and nipping at the high Andes before retreating home for more dry-land training.

The always challenging ski resort of Portillo was showcased to the alpine world at the 1966 world championships when French sensation Jean-Claude Killy won his first gold medals at international races. Following the competitions, the present-day World Cup format of international ski racing was conceived at the Hotel Portillo's bar.

 South America's premier destination offers boundless skiing and snowboarding. Portillo is mostly a one-hotel resort, known for great skiing, particularly off-piste, and an entertaining cosmopolitan atmosphere. It's surprisingly easy to get to.

In later years speed skiers set world records at Portillo's daring Kilometro Lanzado competitions. It was here, in 1978, that the late, great American Steve McKinney first broke the 200-kilometers-per-hour (120-miles-per-hour) barrier. And over the years, four Olympic gold medalists, including Stein Eriksen, have directed Portillo's ski school.

There is no town, and the resort has only one hotel. But if you haven't heard of Portillo, you also should know that skis are no longer made of hickory.

The boutique resort, with its all-inclusive hotel, lies in a huge treeless amphitheater on the edge of a glacial moraine and the picture-perfect Laguna del Inca (Lake of the Inca). Towering above the resort are serrated black mountains forming the spine of the central Andes, some reaching 19,000 feet.

Portillo's extraordinary ski and snowboard runs tumble down from the massive shoulders of surrounding mountains that funnel to the moraine. The off-piste skiing is out of this world. It is one of the oldest, most beautiful, and most famous of all South American ski resorts. And it deserves a priority posting on the hit list of every serious skier, adventurer, and lover of the pisco sour, Chile's national drink (it resembles lime tequila in a five-ounce shooter).

The resort dates back to the early 1900s when railway workers near 22,841-foot Mount Aconcagua, the highest peak in the Western Hemisphere, sought recreation on the snowy slopes of Uspallata Pass. After the railway was completed, skiers rode the train into the region, and the Trans-Andean Railway became the first ski lift in Chile. By 1949, the government opened Portillo (the name means "little pass") and built and managed the hotel while the national army boot-packed snow. Today the ski area is in private American hands.

Portillo is located just off the Trans-Andean Highway, 4 miles from the border with Argentina and a two-and-a-half-hour drive from both the Chilean capital of Santiago and Mendoza in Argentina. Santiago is the main gateway, and transportation is easily arranged from the city's international airport. But a visitor would be remiss not to spend a day or two in the splendid capital at the foot of the Andes.

Anchoring Portillo is the arc-shaped, 140-room Hotel Portillo, painted bright yellow like the sun with the resort orbiting around it. Guests are treated to Chilean hospitality and American efficiency. Some compare the hotel to a sun-drenched cruise ship amid the moonlike landscape of rock and snow. And like a cruise ship, the hotel is all-inclusive and offers wide-ranging options, including an outdoor heated swimming pool, fine dining, and a movie theater.

The ski-in/ski-out accommodations afford views into the valley of Juncal in one direction, over the indigo waters of the lake in the other, and up the soaring peaks of the Andes on all sides.

For most of us, travel begins by considering geography. But on returning home the memories are usually of the people we meet. At the Hotel Portillo, skiers from around the world get to know one another. The new friendships are often reinforced over pisco sours; many of the guests are repeat visitors.

But more than anything else, it's the remarkable skiing and snowboarding that set Portillo apart. And there are endless miles of these. The maritime climate delivers plenty of snow, and the high altitude (the base is at 9,350 feet) ensures dry powder.

You'll ski rugged chutes and long, treeless pitches. You'll giggle over the simple beginner area and take pleasure in snowboarders carving the wide-open bowls. Plus, there are plenty of gut-wrenching 1,200-foot-vertical double blacks. Lift lines are nonexistent.

The lifts, both chairs and surface, are reliable and, at times, strange. One of the surface lifts is the infamous five-person Va et Vient with its baffling rope and tackle whisking skiers uphill at 20 miles per hour like a slingshot. Hiking to earn-your-turns country is also part of the ski experience. And if you want more, helicopter skiing is available.

Portillo Ski Resort
Renato Sanchez 4270, Las Condes
Santiago
Chile

Phone: (800) 829–5325

Web Site: www.skiportillo.com

E-mail: info@skiportillo.com

Elevation: Top—10,800 feet; base—9,350 feet

Vertical Drop: 2,664 feet

Total Area: 1,250 acres

Number of Trails: 23

Longest Run: 2 miles

Terrain: 24% beginner; 33% intermediate; 43% advanced/expert

Average Annual Snowfall: 240 inches

Lifts: 12

Snowmaking: Yes

Season: Mid-June through early October

Central Reservations: (800) 829–5325

Snow Report: www.skiportillo.com

Accommodations: Hotel Portillo plus two hotel annexes and eight chalets. Less expensive off-mountain hotels are within a short driving distance.

Getting There: Portillo is 95 miles from Santiago on a well-maintained paved road. Transportation is available from commercial operators.

Keep in Mind: Snow and weather can be fickle.

BEST BETS

Beginners: El Correlito and La Princesa.

Intermediates: El Conejo, Las Lomas, Bajada del Tren, and the Plateau.

Advanced: Juncalillo, David's Run, and Descenso.

Experts: Roca Jack, the upper Plateau, and the Kilometro Lanzado.

Lunch: Tio Bobs, at midmountain.

Best Hotel: Hotel Portillo.

MOUNT COOK TASMAN GLACIER

Mount Cook National Park, New Zealand

It's not a ski resort in the traditional sense. But the quintessential New Zealand ski experience hasn't changed much since 1955, when an aviation landmark was achieved and ski-equipped planes landed on the Tasman Glacier in Mount Cook National Park.

The Tasman Glacier starts at the boxed end of a huge natural amphitheater surrounded by jagged 12,000-foot peaks. Its surface is serrated with crevasses and ice cliffs, like rough seas cast in plaster. The national park is a UNESCO World Heritage Site, mostly because of its heavy concentration of snow- and glacier-covered summits. It takes its name from Mount Cook, the highest peak in New Zealand, which rises next to the Tasman.

Glaciers have been the major force in shaping the topography of the park, and the Tasman is the largest remaining valley glacier in the world outside the polar caps. New Zealand has twenty-seven peaks over 10,000 feet—twenty-two of them in Mount Cook National Park. It is regarded as one of the best mountain climbing regions in the world.

The ski trip begins with a ten-minute flight over the glacier, offering a mountaineer's view of the massive ice-covered shoulder of 12,316-foot Mount Cook. In a thump of powder, the aircraft lands just below the saddle of Mount Tasman, which is the beginning of one of the world's most acclaimed ski descents. From there, skiers often hike to a nearby mountaineer's hut perched just below the saddle's dome. The refuge is maintained by the national park. It's a nice vantage point from which to admire the grandeur—and boil a billy—before skiing down.

The Tasman's storied reputation is not based on challenging terrain. The route down is all about the surrounding beauty, one of the prettiest high-alpine valleys imaginable. Even skiers barely past the steer-with-your-feet stage enjoy the Tasman. And experts are never bored. Depending upon snow conditions, you will probably have to skate some of the 6 miles before your aircraft picks you up near the glacier's toe.

The ski planes are either Cessna or Pilatus Porter aircraft. Most skiers make it a day trip by flying into tiny Mount Cook airport near the toe of the glacier and the village of Mount Cook. They board a flight up the Tasman, ski down, and fly back to wherever they came from, usually Christchurch or Queenstown. But there's a lovely, rustic national park lodge at Mount Cook Village called the Hermitage. It's similar to the three-star wood-and-stone lodgings found in American national parks. And a visitor to Mount Cook would be remiss not to overnight and arrange to ski the first run on the Tasman the morning after arrival, allowing time for the history and significance of the Mount Cook area to work their magic.

The park is a good place to stretch your legs. Sparsely populated and mostly rural, New Zealand is a land of snowcapped peaks, rain forests, trout-filled lakes, fjords,

 In a landscape and a tradition that mirror Switzerland's, small planes with retractable skis land near the headwall of a valley glacier near New Zealand's highest mountain, providing skiers with a breathtakingly beautiful 6-mile-long guided, glacier descent. It's one of the most famous ski runs in the world.

volcanoes, glaciers, and geysers. And Mount Cook National Park is one of the wildest regions on the nation's stunning South Island. Beneath the rugged mountain faces are networks of lovely, snow-free walking trails at easy-to-take elevations of around 2,500 feet. The scale is immense. The 10,000 vertical feet between valley and summit is the same vertical found between Mount Everest and its base camp.

For evening entertainment, the Mount Cook Lodge has a cozy lounge, but there's also a side-entrance pub where the local park rangers, ski guides, and pilots hang out and play darts. That's where you want to be. It hasn't changed much since the days when Sir Edmund Hillary was a regular prior to his 1953 Everest ascent.

After an evening with the ghost of Hillary, and perhaps even the man himself—he's not a stranger around Mount Cook—you're strapped into the canvas seat of a ski-equipped aircraft on an adventure worthy of the Southern Alps.

If you're traveling overland from Christchurch, Mount Hutt ski area is worth a stop. It's just two hours south of Christchurch. Nestled high inside the eastern rim of the Southern Alps, overlooking the Canterbury Plains and the blue Pacific in the far distance, Mount Hutt has the longest ski season in the Southern Hemisphere.

Alpine Guides (Aoraki) Ltd.
P.O. Box 20
Mount Cook 8770
New Zealand

Phone: 64–3–435–1834

Web Site: www.heliskiing.co.nz

E-mail: mtcook@heliskiing.co.nz

Number of Trails: 6

Longest run: 6 miles

Central Reservations: www.heliskiing.co.nz

Snow Report: www.heliskiing.co.nz/heliskiframes.html

Accommodations: If you wish to stay in the national park, there's only one lodge.

Getting There: You can drive from both Christchurch and Queenstown, but most fly into Mount Cook airport.

Keep in Mind: You need clear weather in a place known for its fickle climate. Keep your options open.

BEST BETS

Lunch: The Hermitage.

Off the Slopes: Hiking trails in the national park.

Best Hotel: The Hermitage.

QUEENSTOWN
Queenstown, New Zealand

Author James Michener wrote that "New Zealand is probably the most magnificent place on Earth," with "natural beauty difficult to believe." It was the last major landmass, apart from Antarctica, to be explored. And when the Maoris' Polynesian ancestors reached New Zealand 1,300 years ago, it

was unlike anything they had encountered elsewhere in the Pacific. Rudyard Kipling described it quite simply as "the eighth wonder of the world."

Most of New Zealand's geographical wonders are on the relatively unpopulated South Island. Ground Zero on the South

Island is Queenstown, serenely overlooking the pristine waters of Lake Wakatipu but home to a multitude of adventurous year-round sports. New Zealand winters are like a suspended spring, where life is lived below the snow line in a perpetually green, sheep-trodden farmscape. New Zealanders commute uphill to winter. The ski areas do not offer slopeside accommodations.

For snowboarders and skiers, Queenstown is high energy. Like many North American ski towns, Queenstown began as a bustling gold-rush outpost in the late 1880s with a boom-and-bust mentality. Now many of the best skiers in the world gather in Queenstown during the southern winter, following the snow, and then work south to north around the globe. National ski teams from the superpower ski nations come to train, and internationally renowned coaches teach regular ski school. You never know what champion might be riding the lift with you.

Located just twenty minutes from vibrant Queenstown, Coronet Peak, New Zealand's oldest and best-developed ski resort, offers a fairly sizable ski mountain with rolling intermediate and expert terrain. There's sensational bowl skiing, some of it quite steep, and outstanding views over Queenstown and Lake Wakatipu. The bowls make it seem as if you're skiing mountains within mountains. The slopes are well groomed, with top-to-bottom snowmaking capability. The mountainside is grassy in summer, so it requires little snow to open come winter.

The slopes lack deep snow to fill in the hollows, so the mountain skis like a natural terrain park with endless hits, undulating dips, and gullies. There also are two competitive-caliber halfpipes and a terrain park with jumps, tabletops, and banks. Night skiing or boarding under a full moon is extraordinary.

Across the valley from Coronet Peak, nestled in a craggy mountain range with the same name, is The Remarkables ski area. The mountains were named by settlers who thought the sight of the peaks in the evening light, snowcapped and mirrored in Lake Wakatipu, was simply remarkable. The ski area sports high-speed lifts, a modern base lodge, and plenty of groomed intermediate and beginner runs. Its higher base elevation means better snow than Coronet Peak.

 The Southern Alps run the entire length of New Zealand's South Island. The mountains rise to 12,000 feet, but the ocean is never far away. The ski season starts in mid-June and lasts to mid-November. The scenery is extraordinary.

The Remarkables has some truly formidable, but skiable, palisades and ridgelines along the top of the resort. And like Coronet Peak, it rewards the adventurous skier who explores off-piste. It also has plenty of beginner terrain, which is in short supply and high demand at Coronet Peak.

If skiing in New Zealand has its downside, it's the fickle weather. This is a maritime nation. If it's any consolation to skiers, when it's bad in the mountains, Queenstown shines as a resort destination. Many of summer's activities continue below the snow line in winter, including heart-stopping jet-boat rides on the Shotover River, white-water rafting, fly fishing, and scenic flights to New Zealand's west coast and storied Milford Sound, where the wild tropiclike landscape is a cross between Norway and Bali.

The Queenstown winter festival in early July lights up the season with fireworks, bands, and heaps of participatory events.

Coronet Peak/The Remarkables
P.O. Box 359
Queenstown
New Zealand

Phone: 64–3–442–4620,
64–3–442–4615

Web Site: www.nzski.com

E-mail: info@nzski.com

Elevation: Top—5,379 feet; base—4,002
feet

Vertical Drop: 1,365 feet

Total Area: 1,200 acres (Coronet Peak and
The Remarkables)

Longest Run: 1 mile

Terrain: 20% beginner; 45% intermediate;
35% advanced/expert

Average Annual Snowfall: 82 inches

Lifts: 11 (Coronet Peak and The Remarkables)

Snowmaking: 200 acres

Accommodations: A wide selection in
Queenstown, 20 minutes from the mountain.

Getting There: Queenstown is well served by
commercial airlines. Christchurch is South
Island's main international airport.

Keep in Mind: The skiing is not as vast as in
Europe or North America. The snow and
weather are fickle.

BEST BETS

Beginners: The Remarkables.

Intermediates: Almost everywhere at Coronet Peak.

Advanced: Exchange Drop, Coronet Peak.

Experts: Back bowls, Coronet Peak.

Lunch: Coronet Brasserie.

Off the Slopes: Plenty of nightlife in
Queenstown; also other adventure sports.

Best Hotel: The Heritage Hotel in Queenstown.

APPENDIX:
BEST OF THE BEST

What's the best ski resort in the world? That's the question I keep hearing since publication of the first edition of *100 Best Ski Resorts of the World*. But my answer remains the same: There is no best ski resort in the world, because no one resort can be all things to all adventurers.

Some skiers pine for elevator shaft–like slopes, while others seek gentle groomers with kids in tow. There are resorts rich in history and vibrating with nightlife; other resorts relax amid wild country and bucolic charm. And back up on the mountain, skiers and snowboarders get their kicks in different ways.

The real question is: What's the best ski resort in the world for you? Following are a few suggestions to point you downhill in the right direction.

Best Resorts for Snowboarding

Breckenridge Ski Resort, Colorado: In 1985 this was the first Colorado resort to allow snowboards on the ski lifts. Riders have been shredding the Continental Divide at the resort ever since.

Ischgl, Austria: Endless terrain, all-night partying, and duty-free liquor runs into Switzerland make this a must-ride in snowboard-crazy Austria.

Mammoth Mountain, California: High-voltage energy from the L.A. crowd, staircaselike steeps, wide bowls, and big-air terrain parks make this a mecca for riders.

Stratton Mountain Resort, Vermont: For snowboarders, this is Kitty Hawk. Local bartender Jake Burton Carpenter tested the first snowboard in the early 1980s. The resort remains at the cutting edge, as well as the place to learn.

Tignes, France: Wide glacier slopes, acres of powder, dynamite terrain parks, and few surface lifts attract snowboarders to the lofty Savoie region of France.

Best Resorts for Families

Madonna di Campiglio, Italy: You can follow the sun on slopes that wrap around town, riding one of Italy's most efficient lift systems. Life without children is no life for Italians.

Méribel, France: Schussing the massive Trois Vallées ski region is a rite of passage for young European skiers. And ski-in/ski-out Méribel is the place to base the family.

Solitude Mountain Resort, Utah: Salt Lake City airport is not even a restroom stop away. This is a tidy, car-free ski-in/ski-out village plunked down in Utah's snowbound Big Cottonwood Canyon.

Steamboat Springs, Colorado: This is the real American West, and those cowboy hats say something about a way of life. It's just a fun place to be, with plenty of off-slope diversions.

Sun Valley, Idaho: The resort's second ski area, Dollar Mountain, is a children's fairy-land of perfectly pitched runs and a base lodge built for pint-size skiers and boarders.

Best Resorts for Novices

Arosa, Switzerland: The tilted-to-the-sun slopes above a picture-postcard village and valley make this the quintessential Swiss ski experience. And novices can bask in it.

Aspen, Colorado: Yes, Aspen has it all. They've even got Buttermilk, one of the world's premier learning mountains.

Copper Mountain Resort, Colorado: Gentle but progressively steeper terrain defines the west side of the mountain. It's a perfect learning environment straddling the Continental Divide.

Cortina d'Ampezzo, Italy: Seemingly endless mellow slopes wind through the spectacular pink-tinged Dolomites and rustic mountain restaurants set above a glitzy Alpine town.

Killington Resort, Vermont: The ski school here has probably taught half the skiers in the East. The mountain offers a separate learning area, and novices can pick their way down from all seven summits.

Best Resorts for Advanced Skiers

Alta Ski Area, Utah: If it's a powder day—and it often is—you'll be in good company. On the best days, it just doesn't get any better than this.

Crested Butte, Colorado: This resort is home to some of the most radical in-bounds ski terrain in the country. Competitive extreme skiing was pretty much invented here.

Jackson Hole Mountain Resort, Wyoming: The aerial tram accesses chutes, moguls and, on the best days, powder on the leg-tiring continuous vertical of the Hobacks.

Portillo, Chile: South America's premier ski destination offers peerless skiing high above a lone hotel in the Andes. The surrounding skiing is out of this world.

Whistler-Blackcomb Resorts, British Columbia: With a whopping mile-high vertical drop and two bulging mountains, there are hundreds of challenging lines.

Help Us Keep This Guide Up to Date

Every effort has been made by the author and editors to make this guide as accurate and useful as possible. However, many things can change after a guide is published—establishments close, phone numbers change, facilities come under new management, and so on.

We would love to hear from you concerning your experiences with this guide and how you feel it could be made better and kept up to date. While we may not be able to respond to all comments and suggestions, we'll take them to heart and we'll also make certain to share them with the author. Please send your comments and suggestions to the following address:

The Globe Pequot Press
Reader Response/Editorial Department
P.O. Box 480
Guilford, CT 06437

Or you may e-mail us at:
editorial@GlobePequot.com

Thanks for your input, and happy travels!

ABOUT THE AUTHOR

GERRY WINGENBACH grew up in the Canadian Rockies. He is a former ski racer and Canadian ski coach. He likes to ski with kids and ride chairlifts with old folks who tell interesting stories. He lives in Washington, D.C.